Canada and International Affairs

Series Editors
David Carment, NPSIA, Carleton University, Ottawa, ON, Canada
Philippe Lagassé, NPSIA, Carleton University, Ottawa, ON, Canada
Yiagadeesen Samy, NPSIA, Carleton University, Ottawa, ON, Canada

Palgrave's Canada and International Affairs is a timely and rigorous series for showcasing scholarship by Canadian scholars of international affairs and foreign scholars who study Canada's place in the world. The series will be of interest to students and academics studying and teaching Canadian foreign, security, development and economic policy. By focusing on policy matters, the series will be of use to policy makers in the public and private sectors who want access to rigorous, timely, informed and independent analysis. As the anchor, Canada Among Nations is the series' most recognisable annual contribution. In addition, the series showcases work by scholars from Canadian universities featuring structured analyses of Canadian foreign policy and international affairs. The series also features work by international scholars and practitioners working in key thematic areas that provides an international context against which Canada's performance can be compared and understood.

Maxwell A. Cameron · David Gillies ·
David Carment
Editors

Democracy and Foreign Policy in an Era of Uncertainty

Canada Among Nations 2022

palgrave
macmillan

Editors
Maxwell A. Cameron
Department of Political Science
University of British Columbia
Vancouver, BC, Canada

David Gillies
Ottawa, ON, Canada

David Carment
School of Indigenous and Canadian Studies
Carleton University
Ottawa, ON, Canada

ISSN 2523-7187 ISSN 2523-7195 (electronic)
Canada and International Affairs
ISBN 978-3-031-35793-0   ISBN 978-3-031-35490-8 (eBook)
https://doi.org/10.1007/978-3-031-35490-8

© The Editor(s) (if applicable) and The Author(s), under exclusive license to Springer Nature Switzerland AG 2023

This work is subject to copyright. All rights are solely and exclusively licensed by the Publisher, whether the whole or part of the material is concerned, specifically the rights of translation, reprinting, reuse of illustrations, recitation, broadcasting, reproduction on microfilms or in any other physical way, and transmission or information storage and retrieval, electronic adaptation, computer software, or by similar or dissimilar methodology now known or hereafter developed.
The use of general descriptive names, registered names, trademarks, service marks, etc. in this publication does not imply, even in the absence of a specific statement, that such names are exempt from the relevant protective laws and regulations and therefore free for general use.
The publisher, the authors, and the editors are safe to assume that the advice and information in this book are believed to be true and accurate at the date of publication. Neither the publisher nor the authors or the editors give a warranty, expressed or implied, with respect to the material contained herein or for any errors or omissions that may have been made. The publisher remains neutral with regard to jurisdictional claims in published maps and institutional affiliations.

Cover credit: Emma Espejo/Getty Images

This Palgrave Macmillan imprint is published by the registered company Springer Nature Switzerland AG
The registered company address is: Gewerbestrasse 11, 6330 Cham, Switzerland

Dedicated to Professor Emeritus Maureen Appel Molot, former Distinguished Research Professor at the Norman Paterson School of International Affairs, Carleton University, and former editor of Canadian Foreign Policy Journal and several books in the Canada Among Nations series. We gratefully acknowledge her contributions as a brilliant researcher and teacher of several generations of Canadian scholars and practitioners.

Acknowledgments

The editors wish to acknowledge the excellent work of Racheal Wallace who once again has proven to be an indispensable editorial assistant communicating and working with authors on their chapters and in managing the collection. David Carment would like to thank Carleton University's Faculty of Public Affairs and the Social Sciences and Humanities Research Council for ongoing support to the Canada and International Series and the School of International Affairs for providing organizational support in hosting the authors workshops. We are grateful for Palgrave Macmillan's continuing support of the series and wish to especially acknowledge our editor Anca Pusca, who provided us with invaluable guidance and encouragement.

Ottawa and Vancouver   David Carment
2023   Maxwell A. Cameron
                                                                         David Gillies

Contents

Part I From Global Trends to Policy and Practice

1 Introduction 3
David Gillies, David Carment, and Maxwell A. Cameron

2 Canada's Support for Democracy: Some Wins
and Losses but Much Potential 21
Peter Boehm

3 In Search of Democratic Revival, at Home
and in the Lives of Others 37
Jeremy Kinsman

4 Democracy and Foreign Policy: A Retrospective 57
Maxwell A. Cameron

5 Policy and Practice in Canada's International
Democracy Support 77
David Gillies

6 The State of Democracy in the World—Problems,
Pitfalls, and Policy 101
Marshall Palmer and David Carment

Part II Challenges Ahead

7 Inclusive Approaches to Multilateral Democracy Cooperation: Challenges and Opportunities for Canada 133
Catherine Hecht

8 Toward Canadian Democracy Protection 2.0 in the Americas? 155
Kendra D. Carrión-Vivar and Thomas Legler

9 Feminism and International Democracy Assistance 179
Gabrielle Bardall

10 Quiet Helpful Fixer or Boisterous Norm Advocate? Canada as a Mediator 201
Peter Jones

11 Canada's Enduring Populism 219
David Moscrop

12 The Opportunities and Challenges of Courting India 241
Sanjay Ruparelia

Part III Conclusion

13 Conclusion 271
Maxwell A. Cameron, David Gillies, and David Carment

NOTES ON CONTRIBUTORS

Gabrielle Bardall Ph.D. is an educator, advisor, and activist. She has more than two decades of expertise in international democracy support in over 60 countries worldwide. Her work on feminist approaches to democratization has made landmark contributions to the field, including ground-breaking research and programs on gender-based political violence. She was affiliated with the Parliamentary Center and has advised and trained diplomats, legislators, and civil servants from Parliament Hill to Capitol Hill. Recognizing that "democracy" as we know it and support it around the world often replicates structures of male political control, she started her own company in 2019, Herizon Democracy (herizondemocracy.org) to bring feminist vision to international democracy assistance. She has advised the US National Security Council, State Department, NATO on feminist approaches to democracy support and offered testimony to Canada's Parliament. She previously served as Vice President of External Relations at Canada's Parliamentary Centre. She is a Visting Professor at the University of Ottawa.

Peter Boehm is a native of Kitchener, Ontario, and was appointed to the Senate of Canada in October 2018. He is currently the Chair of the Senate Standing Committee on Foreign Affairs and International Trade. A former career foreign service officer, he has served as Ambassador to Germany, Minister at the Embassy of Canada to the United States, as well as Ambassador to the Organization of American States, among other foreign postings. He is a former Deputy Minister of International

Development, Senior Associate Deputy Minister of Foreign Affairs, and Assistant Deputy Minister for the Americas, North America, and Consular Affairs. He served several Prime Ministers as their Personal Representative or "Sherpa" for the G8 and G7 Summits, as well as for the Summits of the Americas and Nuclear Security Summits. He was the Deputy Minister and Personal Representative of the Prime Minister for the G7 Summit, held in Québec in June 2018. He holds a Ph.D. in History from the University of Edinburgh, a Master of Arts in International Affairs from the Norman Paterson School of International Affairs, and an Honours Bachelor of Arts degree from Wilfrid Laurier University.

Maxwell A. Cameron is Professor in the Department of Political Science and the School of Public Policy and Global Affairs at the University of British Columbia (UBC). Before joining UBC he taught at Carleton University. He received his Ph.D. in political science from the University of California, Berkeley. He has held visiting professorships and research fellowships at Yale University, the Colegio de Mexico, the Centre for US-Mexican Studies at the University of California San Diego, the Kellogg Institute for International Studies at the University of Notre Dame, and the Peter Wall Institute for Advanced Studies. He co-founded the Institute for Future Legislators, a program that prepares aspiring legislators for service in public office. He is a frequent commentator on politics in the media and has provided advice to policymakers on topics, such as constitutional change, electoral reform, citizen engagement, proportional representation, participatory innovations, and the defense of democracy in the Americas. Among his publications are: *Democracy and Authoritarianism in Peru* (St. Martin's 1994), *Strong Constitutions* (Oxford University Press 2013), *Political Institutions and Practical Wisdom* (Oxford University Press, 2018), co-author of *The Making of NAFTA* (Cornell 2000), and co-editor of *Democracy and Foreign Policy* (Carleton University Press 1995), *The Peruvian Labyrinth* (Penn State University Press 1997), *Latin America's Left Turns* (Lynne Rienner 2010), *Democracia en la Region Andina* (Instituto de Estudios Peruanos 2010), *New Institutions for Participatory Democracy in Latin America* (Palgrave 2012), and *Challenges to Democracy in the Andes: Strongmen, Broken Constitutions, and Regimes in Crisis* (Lynne Rienner, forthcoming in 2022). In 2020, he was named Distinguished Fellow by the Canadian Association of Latin American and Caribbean Studies, and this year the Latin American Studies Association awarded him the Guillermo O'Donnell Prize and Lectureship for his work on democracy.

David Carment is Full Professor of International Affairs and Director of the School of Indigenous and Canadian Studies at Carleton University. He is series editor for Palgrave's Canada and International Affairs, Editor in Chief of Canadian Foreign Policy Journal, Fellow at the Canadian Global Affairs Institute, and Senior Fellow at the Institute for Peace and Diplomacy. His research focuses on Canadian foreign policy, mediation and negotiation, fragile states and diaspora politics. He is the author, editor, or co-editor of 21 books and has authored or co-authored over 90 peer-reviewed journal articles and book chapters. His most recent books focus on diaspora cooperation, corruption in Canada, branding Canadian foreign policy and state fragility. In 2017, he was a visiting Scholar at the World Institute for Development Economics Research, Finland and in 2015 a Fellow at the Center for Global Cooperation Research, Germany. He has held fellowships at the Hoover Institution, Stanford University, and the Belfer Center at Harvard University. His current SSHRC funded research examines Canadian diaspora and fragile and conflict affected states.

Kendra D. Carrión-Vivar holds a B.A. and M.A. in International Relations and is a Ph.D. candidate in Social and Political Sciences at the Universidad Iberoamericana. Her research focuses on international influences on domestic politics, including the contributions of the Organization of American States (OAS) to the national dialogues in Peru and Bolivia. Her doctoral dissertation focused on the role of the OAS in the autocratization process in Nicaragua. After working for the OAS' Mediation and Dialogue Unit, she served as International Analysis Coordinator at the National Secretariat of Communications of the Presidency of Ecuador. She collaborated with the 2021 OAS Electoral Observation Mission in Mexico. She has also consulted privately for electoral campaigns in Ecuador and Mexico.

David Gillies Ph.D. is an independent Researcher in democratic governance and a Research Fellow at the Centre for the Study of Democracy and Diversity, Queen's University. Retired from Global Affairs Canada, he was also a governance specialist at the former Canadian International Development Agency (CIDA). He was CIDA Head of Cooperation in

Zimbabwe and Counsellor, Development for Global Affairs Canada in Pakistan. Outside the public service, he has worked at Rights and Democracy, the Aga Khan Foundation, and the North-South Institute. His publications include *Elections in Dangerous Places* (editor) and *Between Principle and Practice: Human Rights in North-South Relations*. He was educated at Oxford and McGill.

Catherine Hecht is a sessional Lecturer at the School of Public Policy and Global Affairs at the University of British Columbia (UBC). In 2019–2020, she was a Senior Research Fellow at the Centre for Global Cooperation Research at the University of Duisburg-Essen in Germany. She previously held a Social Sciences and Humanities Research Council of Canada (SSHRC) post-doctoral fellowship and taught at the Vienna School of International Studies, Diplomatic Academy of Vienna in Austria. She has also taught at the Technische Universität Darmstadt in Germany and consulted at the United Nations Development Programme. She holds a Ph.D. in political science from UBC and a Master of International Affairs from Columbia University. Her research on international organizations, democratic norms, and multilateral diplomacy has appeared in *Cooperation and Conflict, Review of International Studies, Journal of International Organizations Studies, International Politics, and Canadian Foreign Policy.*

Peter Jones is a Full Professor in the Graduate School of Public and International Affairs at the University of Ottawa. Prior to joining the academy, he spent 14 years in the public service, including 7 years with the Department of Foreign Affairs (now GAC) and 7 years in the Privy Council Office. He is also Executive Director of the Ottawa Dialogue, a University-based organization which runs Track 1.5 and Track Two dialogues around the world. He is author of several articles on this subject and also of what is widely regarded as the standard text on the subject: *Track Two Diplomacy: In Theory and Practice*, published by the Stanford University Press. He holds a Ph.D. in War Studies from King's College, London and an M.A. in War Studies from the Royal Military College of Canada.

Jeremy Kinsman was a Foreign Service officer for 40 years, eventually as Minister both at the UN in New York and in Washington before concluding appointments as Ambassador in Moscow 1992–1996 and in Rome 1996–2000, High Commissioner in London 2000–2002, and

Ambassador to the EU in Brussels 2002–2006. He was earlier Chairman of Policy Planning in Foreign Affairs and later loaned to the Department of Communications as Assistant Deputy Minister for Broadcasting and Culture, 1985–1989. He returned to Foreign Affairs as Political Director from 1990 to 1992. Transferring his energies to civil society in 2006, he headed from 2007 to 2017 an international project on democracy support for the Community of Democracies, that produced "A Diplomat's Handbook on Democracy Development Support," while also holding university appointments at Princeton, Berkeley (Regent's Lecturer), and Ryerson. He is now a CIC Distinguished Fellow and since May 2021 has been leading a CIC and Konrad Adenauer Stiftung Canada joint project "Renewing Our Democratic Alliance." He writes and speaks regularly and widely on foreign affairs issues, notably for *Policy* magazine, and CTV News. He is currently writing a book for Simon and Schuster (The book's title is not settled.).

Thomas Legler (Ph.D. York University, 1999) is Research Professor of International Relations and former University Research Director at the Universidad Iberoamericana, Mexico City. He is a member of the Mexican National System of Researchers (SNI), level II. He has published extensively on multilateral democracy protection in the Americas, including Canada's role, the Inter-American Democratic Charter, Inter-American and African democracy promotion in cross-regional perspective, as well as regional responses to the political crises in Honduras, Peru, and Venezuela. He has served as an election observer for the Carter Center, the Organization of American States, and civil society organizations in seven Latin American countries, as well as consultant for the Honduran Truth and Reconciliation Commission.

David Moscrop is a contributing columnist for *the Washington Post* and the author of *Too Dumb for Democracy? Why We Make Bad Political Decisions and How We Can Make Better Ones*. He is a regular contributor to *the Globe and Mail, Jacobin*, and other publications. He is also a political commentator for radio, television, and print media. He holds a Ph.D. in political science from the University of British Columbia.

Marshall Palmer is an independent Scholar based in Ottawa, focusing on issues in Canadian national security and democratic decline. He obtained his Ph.D. in International Security at the Norman Paterson School of International Affairs. Before joining NPSIA, he worked as a Middle East and North Africa analyst for NATO and as a contributor to Oxford Analytica, a political risk firm. His research has appeared in *International Journal*, *Canada Among Nations*, *The Conversation*, the SSHRC Storytellers Competition, and elsewhere. He is the managing editor of the *Canadian Foreign Policy Journal*. He holds degrees in International Relations from the London School of Economics (B.Sc.) and the University of Oxford (M.Phil.).

Sanjay Ruparelia is an Associate Professor of Politics, and the Jarislowsky Democracy Chair, at Toronto Metropolitan University. His major publications include *Divided We Govern* (OUP 2015); *The Indian Ideology* (Permanent Black 2015); and *Understanding India's New Political Economy* (Routledge 2011). He regularly contributes op-eds and commentary to various international media. He is a co-chair of the Participedia network, which examines democratic innovations around the world; associate editor of *Pacific Affairs* and the *Oxford Encyclopedia of Asian Politics*; and co-hosts On the Frontlines of Democracy, a monthly public lecture series, with the Toronto Public Library. He previously taught at the New School for Social Research and Columbia University. He has held grants and fellowships at the American Council of Learned Societies, Notre Dame, Princeton, Social Sciences Research Council, Social Sciences and Humanities Research Council and Yale, and served as a consultant to the United Nations and the Asia Foundation. He holds a B.A. from McGill University, and a M.Phil. and Ph.D. from the University of Cambridge.

List of Figures

Fig. 6.1	Mean Global Democracy Scores According to Seven Surveys (*Note* All indices are rescaled to the 0–1 interval. Freedom House political-rights and civil-liberties scores are averaged and reversed)	104
Fig. 6.2	Canada and The United States are losing their status as least corrupt countries. Corruption Perception Index, 2012–2021	114
Fig. 6.3	The rise of private wealth and the decline of public wealth in rich countries, 1970–2021 (Data taken from World Inequality Database, https://wid.world/data/)	115
Fig. 9.1	Executing partners of democracy assistance pre- and post-FIAP	186
Fig. 9.2	FIAP core DG programs, by outcome theme	188

PART I

From Global Trends to Policy and Practice

CHAPTER 1

Introduction

David Gillies, David Carment, and Maxwell A. Cameron

In the mid-1990s, just a few years into the so-called third wave of global democratic expansion, Maxwell A. Cameron and Maureen Appel Molot curated a *Canada Among Nations* edition on democracy and foreign policy.[1] An organizing premise was that 'democracy matters as a principle and process in foreign policy; democracies make foreign policy differently

[1] *Canada Among Nations 1995: Democracy and Foreign Policy*. Ottawa: Carleton University Press.

D. Gillies
Research Fellow, Centre for the Study of Democracy and Diversity, Queen's University, Kingston, ON, Canada

D. Carment (✉)
School of Indigenous and Canadian Studies, Carleton University, Ottawa, ON, Canada
e-mail: david.carment@carleton.ca

M. A. Cameron
Department of Political Science and School of Public Policy and Global Affairs, University of British Columbia, Vancouver, BC, Canada
e-mail: Max.Cameron@ubc.ca

© The Author(s), under exclusive license to Springer Nature Switzerland AG 2023
M. A. Cameron et al. (eds.), *Democracy and Foreign Policy in an Era of Uncertainty*, Canada and International Affairs, https://doi.org/10.1007/978-3-031-35490-8_1

and they make different foreign policies.' In 1993, the Liberal Party of Canada released its Red Book which spoke of the democratization of foreign policy.

It has also been three decades since the Canadian International Development Agency (CIDA) commissioned the North–South Institute to consider whether and if so, how democracy should be supported in official development assistance.[2] Today, democracies around the world are in crisis, and this is reflected in global diplomacy. There have been three democracy summits: an initial meeting in December 2021, one in June 2022 in Denmark and a third in March 2023. It is important to understand what progress has been made at these summits and within that context evaluate Canada's specific contributions to democratic development in a multipolar and deeply divided world while facing political turmoil at home.

In an era of significant geopolitical shifts, with violent flashpoints around the world, and rising nationalism and identity politics, the institutions in which Canada and its allies have invested significant political capital, such as trade, political, and security organizations, are being tested and stretched to the limit. The European Union, a classic embodiment of democratic principles as the foundation for interstate cooperation, has been setback by Brexit. Closer to home, Canada has had to adjust to the erosion of democracy and the assertion of unilateralism in the United States. Canada's domestic constitutional bargain with the provinces is increasingly stressed as divisions on health, energy, and natural resources become more evident.

This edition of Canada Among Nations (CAN) is in two parts. It looks back on Canada's approach to encouraging, supporting, and protecting democracy abroad; it looks forward by examining the current state of

---

[2] Gerald J. Schmitz and David Gillies. *The Challenge of Democratic Development*. Ottawa: The North–South Institute, 1992. The authors focused on the developmental potential of democracy 'to expand the range of human possibilities and choices [and] to improve the human condition,' a vision that accords with Amartya Sen's 'capabilities' approach and with Canadian political theorist C.B. Macpherson's commitment to economic equality and social justice as integral to the project of a post-liberal democracy. Bilateral donors like CIDA were also prompted by World Bank interest in narrower, non-political aspects of 'governance,' notably support for public sector reforms, as 'enabling conditions' for long-term development. The World Bank saw governance as 'synonymous with sound development management.' *Governance and Development*. Washington, DC, 1992.

and trends in democracy around the world, and; it examines how effective middle power democracy statecraft can make a difference in an era of growing international and domestic insecurity, democratic backsliding and virulent populism. The first part of the volume draws on expert analysis of recurring themes in Canadian support for democracy including periods of relative activism. Authors draw on a comparative analysis of policy processes, linkages between democracy at home and abroad, and thematic issues, such as diplomatic initiatives, international cooperation programs, and summitry. In the second part, authors take a thematic, regional, or country-specific approach in order to evaluate variations in policies, conundrums, successes, and limitations of democratic development and policy initiatives that aim both to support democracy abroad and also prevent democratic backsliding and the breakdown of democratic regimes.

Global Trends

Beyond the cases examined in this volume several additional 'hard cases' underline policy choices among competing interests include situations where democracy and human rights are under threat and backsliding, or where Canadian domestic and foreign policy values must be reconciled with other interests. For example, in the greater Middle East, notwithstanding the short-lived Arab Spring, these include Canada's trade links with Saudi Arabia, a rights-restrictive absolute monarchy, and with Turkey, a NATO ally that has grown more illiberal. After a period where elections, term limits, and other innovations appeared to put Africa on the path to democratic governance, we are now seeing democratic reversals through the personalization of power and coup d'etats from Sudan and Chad to Mali and Burkina Faso. Some Latin American states (Colombia, Ecuador, Peru, and Chile, for instance) continue to struggle to reestablish their governmental legitimacy and rebuild social contracts that have been eroded by state violence and social explosions.

Conflict and poor governance driven by rent seeking is common in resource-rich economies in which Canada has a stake. For example, over several decades Canada's interests in Africa have put more focus on a few countries that are strategically important or have trade and resource extraction potential for Canada's powerful mining firms. These include South Africa, Nigeria, Ghana, Mali, Ethiopia, Tanzania, and Mozambique. IImmediately following the departure of Canada's peacekeeping forces from Mali, the government saw yet another coup; the second in eight years. Poverty reduction, protection for rights, and promotion of democracy appear to receive scant attention from countries like Canada that are the source of investment in these economies. Democracy promotion in sub-Sahara Africa has lacked a focus on building the kind of legitimacy that comes from addressing horizontal inequalities, inclusive policies, and equitable economic development.

In Europe, the protracted Ukraine crisis of governance and subsequent Russian invasion is a test both for collective security, defending rights, and democracy and, for some countries such as Canada and the United States, promoting regime change in Russia. The crisis has also galvanized action in defense of democracy against an aggressive autocratic government, perhaps leading to greater unity among democracies than we have seen in some time. In short order, Canada committed approximately $1.6 billion in economic support and $900 million in increasingly lethal military equipment and support. The ongoing crisis in the Ukraine has also underscored the importance of support for pluralism, minority rights, and controversial memory and language laws. At the same time we now see that parts of Europe, especially Central and Eastern, are not immune to democratic backsliding and reversals, while Western Europe has also experienced rising polarization, extremism, and voter alienation. Key questions regarding the causes and manifestations of such challenges must be considered. The passage of controversial asylum laws in the UK may well presage an increasing intolerance for open borders across all of Europe.

In Ukraine, Canada also supports a military training mission and, as a leading aid donor, provides support for Ukrainian legal and judicial reform, municipal governance, and electoral administration and observation. Canada's funding for Ukrainians fleeing war and seeking entry to Canada has been distinctly more enabling than its refugee policies toward Syrians, Afghans, and Yemenis; an unevenness in policy that invitescomparison about the privileging of Europeans over non-Europeans.

One region in which Canada has been deeply engaged in the defense and promotion of democracy is the Western Hemisphere. Canada joined the OAS in 1989, and one of its first initiatives was the establish the Unit for the Promotion of Democracy. As Foreign Minister, Lloyd Axworthy hosted a OAS General Assembly in 2000 in which the crisis in Peru dominated the agenda. Afterward, Canada, as host to the Summit of the Americas in Quebec City, worked with Peru and other nations to insert a democracy clause in the final declaration and issued a call for the creation of an Inter-American Democratic Charter, which was ultimately negotiated and signed in Lima, on September 11, 2001 (precisely the moment the Twin Towers were destroyed in NYC). Although the Democratic Charter was invoked on several occasions during democratic crises in Venezuela, Haiti, and Honduras, the general consensus leading up to the 9th Summit of the Americas, in Los Angeles in June 2022, was that the Democratic Charter had not been used effectively as an instrument of democracy defense and promotion due to the polarization and lack of unity in the hemisphere, especially after Latin America's left turns in 2000s and early 2010s.

Since the Democratic Charter was signed in 2001, several Latin American countries—perhaps most notably Venezuela, Nicaragua, Honduras, and Haiti—have experienced severe or protracted crises of backsliding leading to the breakdown of democracy. Haiti exemplifies poor governance in a fragile or failing state. The coup in Honduras in 2009 saw a vigorous effort by the OAS to apply the Democratic Charter that was undermined by divisions among member states. Canada's ambivalent role did not make the response more robust. The most disturbing developments in the region occurred in Venezuela under Maduro and Nicaragua under Ortega. Both have built authoritarian institutions (a process analytically distinct but empirically related to democratic backsliding, which is a more widespread phenomenon). In Venezuela, Canada has imposed sanctions, provided humanitarian assistance, and championed the Lima Group as a diplomatic forum of like-minded OAS partners. However, the Lima Group's focus on supporting Juan Guaido as leader of the opposition, perhaps appropriate at a time when he represented the highest official within the last remaining democratically elected institution, did not prevent the Maduro government from conducting flawed presidential elections in 2018 and legislative elections in 2020. The polarization within the Western Hemisphere, with countries like Mexico and Peru, drifting away from the Lima Group, has blunted the effectiveness of the initiative. By contrast, Norway avoided taking sides and has successfully facilitated mediations, albeit halting, between the principals.

Haiti is a country in which Canada has diplomatic influence that it has not used it to great effect in recent years. The large Haitian diaspora gives Canada both a stake in Haiti's future and opportunities to support people-to-people exchanges. But in the violent instability, regime changes, and dramatic twists of Haitian politics, Canada has tended to put alliance interests and regional security ahead of human rights and democracy. And it is not clear to what extent, if at all, Ottawa has responded to the concerns and preferences of the Haitian diaspora or Haitian civil society.

In all of these cases, democracy in poorly governed and highly inegalitarian contexts has provided fertile ground from which anti-democratic, populist, and nationalist policies often grow. Populism is often seen as a cause of democratic backsliding but it is also, typically, a political response to the ways in which oligarchic tendencies persist within liberal democracies where deep inequalities undermine mechanisms of representation (like robust, programmatic parties) and government responsiveness.

A core problem for liberal democracies is that, although they seek to protect individual dignity and rights, the cohesion of society often rests on foundations of identity that are threatened by neoliberal globalization. With its weak conceptions of the common good, liberalism does not foster the kind of civic culture and ethos of active citizenship that can balance the unrestrained individualism of our increasingly market-driven societies Further fragmentation and identity-based polarization will continue unless matched by a corresponding effort to strengthen the political engagement of citizens in the democratic process.

Domestically, Canada has made little use of participatory innovations that could build civic patriotism, except at the local and in some cases provincial level (the feeble and ultimately fruitless process of electoral reform in 2016 at the federal level is a case in point). Internationally, Canada has to balance its limited influence to promote and defend democratic values with other interests in its relations with both like-minded countries and illiberal regimes, particularly, as we shall see, in the pivotal but heterogeneous Indo-Pacific region.

Policy Trends and Problems

The end of the Cold War coincided with new Canadian policies and machinery to promote rights, democracy, and governance (RDG) abroad. Led by Canada's parliament, an arms-length International Centre for Human Rights and Democratic Development (later called Rights and Democracy) was established in the late 1980s. The former CIDA became more active in RDG programming, prompted by apparent democratic transitions, other bilateral aid agencies in the OECD Development Assistance Committee,[3] and by narrower interest in more effective public service delivery. There was also a modest outreach to widen input into policymaking, including an NGO-government Democracy Council and a Canada Corps to mobilize civil society governance expertise in transitional or unstable countries. Both entities were short lived. CIDA went on to establish an Office for Democratic Governance and the former DFAIT established its Democracy Unit. During PM Stephen Harper's first government, the House of Commons Foreign Affairs Committee undertook a major study on democracy assistance. Its report recommended establishing an arms-length Canada foundation for international democratic development. The government pledged to create such a body in its 2008 Throne Speech, but the commitment was never implemented. Instead, the Harper government shut down Rights and Democracy after bitter and very destructive struggles between Board members and the staff. Following some years of policy drift in this issue area, there is now renewed interest in democracy promotion from the Trudeau liberal government.[4] And while not reaching the proportions allocated by Sweden or Australia, RDG investments are now a significant part of Canada's overall ODA, accounting in FY 2018–2019 for approximately $404 million in aid spending from all government channels.[5]

Today, however, in contrast to the heady optimism at the end of the Cold War, democracy is on the backfoot across much of the globe, world order is in flux, and the rules-based system is being challenged both by those who were its chief architects and those who see such ideas

---

[3] The 1992 OECD/DAC Statement on the Importance of Political Reform as a Factor in International Economic Assistance noted that "It has become increasingly apparent that there is a vital connection between open, democratic and accountable systems of governance and respect for human rights, and the ability to achieve sustained economic and social development. Although these links are neither simple nor uniform, varying greatly from case to case and with respect to both time and place, DAC Members believe that sustainable development requires a positive interaction between economic and political progress. This connection is so fundamental that participatory development and good governance must be central concerns in the allocation and design of development assistance …".

[4] See, for example, commentary from David Gillies in *Open Canada*, March 16, 2022. "How Canada can help promote democracy abroad."

[5] Authors' calculation derived from Government of Canada Statistical Reports, various years. Canada uses sectoral coding systems consistent with the OECD/Development Assistance Committee.

as window dressing for geopolitical agendas. Moreover, the evidence to show that several decades of democracy support in a variety of political regimes has enhanced democratic values, institutions, and practices is thin on the ground. Alongside the waning influence of civil society in some countries in Eastern Europe, Africa, and Latin America is the failure of the Arab Spring to generate democratic transitions.[6]

In a rare moment of unity and collective action, NATO and other democracies of the Global North have worked more cohesively to defend an embattled Ukraine. As war grinds on, the mix of motives on the part of the rich nations becomes increasingly evident. On the one hand, lofty principles are invoked to secure a world in which democracies thrive; on the other, the desire has been expressed by some US officials, speaking in candid moments, to defeat Russia, impose regime change and permanently weaken its ability to challenge US hegemony. Whether NATO states are putting their full weight behind Ukraine in defense of democratic ideals or for geopolitical reasons remains open to debate. Instead of seeking to resolve this debate, we note that the use of democracy as justification for war has a long and troubled history.

Rhetorical references to the defense of democracy has been a primary diplomatic tool for galvanizing world opinion. In a March 23 speech to the European Parliament, Prime Minister Justin Trudeau called Putin's attack on Ukraine "an attack on the values that form the pillars of all democracies." The PM told European lawmakers that "We have a responsibility to make the case to people about why these values matter so much — not just to Ukrainians but to us all." He added that "We must recommit ourselves to the work of strengthening our democracies and demonstrate the principled leadership people are looking for." And the PM's Joint Statement with European Commission President Ursula von der Leyen noted that: "President Putin's attack on Ukraine amounts to an unprecedented attack on democratic principles and the rules-based international system. It has also underscored the need for democracies to strengthen international cooperation and coordination to stand up against authoritarianism and to develop new approaches to promote and

---

[6] See generally, Carothers, Thomas. 1999. *Aiding Democracy Abroad: The Learning Curve*. Washington, DC: Carnegie Endowment for International Peace. Carothers, Thomas. 2002a. "The End of the Transition Paradigm." *Journal of Democracy* 13, no. 1. And George Perlin, International Assistance to Democratic Development: A Review. Montreal: IRPP, 2004.

protect democracies around the world." One might find in these words a subtle subtext of frustration with the lack of global support for Ukraine's war effort and by extension support for America's desire to confront and hobble Russia.

Indeed, the rhetorical use of democracy in the service of a vision that divides the world into friendly democracies and autocratic enemies underpins President Joe Biden's Summit for Democracy, and like the war in the Ukraine, this diplomatic effort has produced decidedly mixed results. Calling the defense of democracy "the challenge of our time," President Biden hosted a December 2021 two-day virtual Summit "to renew democracy at home and *confront* autocracies abroad" (Italics added). Organized around the themes of defending against authoritarianism, combating corruption, and advancing human rights, the Summit brought together governments, multilateral institutions, and civil society and business leaders. The Summit invitation list was mired in politics, with debates over the inclusion of increasingly illiberal regimes like India, the Philippines, and Hungary and a sharp response from Russia and China. Nevertheless, the Summit also usefully convened like-minded countries, took stock of the global democratic landscape, and prompted commitments to action. It remains to be seen whether democracy is an effective glue for sustained collective action A follow-up Summit to address progress against commitments was held in March 2023. A comprehensive assessment of the achievements of these summits has yet to be written.

The Summit's defensive tone underscores the need for a shared approach at a time when America's credibility as a model democracy is tarnished and its ability to lead is still unclear and in the process of being reconfigured. There is, in short, a perceptible global leadership vacuum. This moment could provide opportunities for a middle power like Canada to play a more prominent role in defending and promoting democratic governance. To do so effectively, however, will take sustained and serious engagement, adequate financial resources and a whole-of-society approach that marshals Canadian expertise across government and civil society. At the December 2021 Summit PM Trudeau announced several commitments, including establishing a center to promote democracy and good governance abroad. The Prime Minister also committed to counter disinformation and repeated a promise to create by 2025 a beneficial ownership registry to expose corruption. These are good steps, but more is needed.

Recognizing that 'democratic renewal begins at home' Canada's domestic commitments announced at the Summit of 2021 include a Plan to Protect Canada's Democracy by safeguarding electoral integrity. These and other government initiatives are necessary but likely insufficient to address growing unease with our democratic institutions. Representative democracy faces challenges in Canada. Proposed electoral reforms have stalled in an era in which minority governments led by parties who do not win the popular vote is certainly not going to go away. . While the Pew Research Center survey found that most Canadians polled were satisfied with the state of their democracy, there are also clear and persistent democratic deficits linked to income inequality, inclusion, and reconciliation with indigenous nations. For too many ordinary Canadians, a deep and enduring disconnect with governing elites is growing more acute. We do not wish to overstate the importance of extremism, but protests like the Truckers Convoy appear to reveal a wider pool ofdiscontent within which disquietingly anti-democratic forces may recruit.

The Emergency Act, the Rouleau Commission Report, and the State of Canada's Democracy remind us that disagreement and the peaceful management of conflict are part and parcel of the real world of democracy. Public protest is a fundamental means to express dissent, grievances, and resistance. Freedoms of expression, assembly, and association are enshrined in the Canadian Charter of Rights and Freedoms, but they are not absolute and are subject to limitations.

Like any democracy, Canada has had its share of civil disobedience and public protest, some of it highly disruptive and occasionally violent (Moscrop, this volume). But our carefully honed global reputation— and indeed our sense of ourselves—as a well governed, stable, tolerant, and largely peaceable kingdom was rudely shaken by the February 2022 Trucker Convoy protests. It was ended after three weeks following the federal government's invocation of the never previously used 1988 Emergencies Act. The protest, the government's response, and the independent process that examined the circumstances leading to the determination of a "threat to the security of Canada" and the declaration of a national public order emergency are a barometer not only of the state of Canada's democracy but also of global democratic trends. In addition to providing valuable lessons for the management of future "emergency" situations, the Public Order Emergency Commission report may also be of relevance to Canada's approach to global democracy-support efforts.

In a highly anticipated report, Commissioner, Paul Rouleau, concluded "with reluctance" that "the very high threshold required for invocation of the Act was met." While a partial vindication for Prime Minister Trudeau, the report is hardly a ringing endorsement of the government's handling of the crisis. The thoroughness and transparency of a key oversight and review mechanism will be seen by many as evidence of a well-functioning system to "maintain accountability and confidence in our [democratic] institutions."[7] But critics will continue to regard the invocation of the Emergency Act as an egregious infringement of civil liberties and an unnecessary overreach by a fragile, less than well-coordinated, and possibly panicked federal government. Indeed, in a report that is a model of temperate language and a balanced weighing of the evidence, Justice Rouleau also underlines that "the state should generally be able to respond to circumstances of urgency without the use of emergency powers." And he takes virtually all the key players to task in highlighting a series of failures: of policing and intelligence, of government coordination, of the Prime Minister, of the protest organizers, and of federalism itself. While "some of the missteps may have been small" .... "others were significant, and taken together, they contributed to a situation that spun out of control. Lawful protest descended into lawlessness, culminating in a national emergency," the report reads.

In the context of the growing evidence of polarization in Canada, the Prime Minister's intemperate comments about the convoy as an "unacceptable" and "fringe minority" not only did not help social cohesion, but may also have been counter-productive by amplifying the emotional volume, and reinforcing the sense of alienation and grievance among a disaffected segment of the population.[8] At the very least, and while acknowledging the presence of more extreme elements, Justice Rouleau concludes that "more of an effort should have been made by government leaders at all levels during the protests to acknowledge that the majority of the protesters were exercising their fundamental democratic rights."

---

[7] *Report of the Public Inquiry into the Public Order Emergency.* Volume 1, p. 17. Ottawa.

[8] While most Canadians have supported the use of emergency powers to end the protest, a February 2022 Ipsos Reid poll found that nearly 46% of Canadians said that while they 'may not agree with everything' the convoy said and did, the 'frustration of protesters is legitimate and worthy' of sympathy. The poll found that sympathy with the protesters rose to 61% among the 18–34 age demographic.

Trust is indispensable, like an invisible currency, in a free and democratic society. But as the 2022 Edelman Trust Barometer underscores, trust in Canada's key public institutions is currently quite low.[9] Rebuilding trust is key to reinforcing social cohesion and avoiding polarization of the sort that can undermine democratic institutions. Notwithstanding a variety of public policy commitments to address the causes of polarization and low trust, notably by reinforcing open government and by combating disinformation, hate speech, and xenophobia, polarization in Canada remains an urgent and increasingly intractable problem. Canadians are increasingly polarized around attitudinal, values, and cultural issues. Pollster Frank Graves refers to these idealized but starkly different world views as "open and ordered." This values/opinion axis appears to be in some respects more potent than long-standing left–right configurations.

The paradox is that while much of Canadian society may be shifting toward more cosmopolitan values that embrace opennessand liberal or progressive values--for example on climate change and immigration--a significant number of Canadians embrace more traditional, socially conservative values and hold deep reservations about diversity and immigration, as well as a more pessimistic view of the future of their way of life. This segment of the population may include those who feel threatened by social change, which in Canada includes economic issues such as a declining middle class, wage stagnation, and the hyper-concentration of wealth at the top of the income distribution pyramid.

Since 2015, Canadians' trust in their public institutions and the credibility of governmental efforts to advance and protect democracy abroad has not been helped by the Liberal government's record on good governance and democratic reform at home. Political and ethics scandals have involved the PM, PMO, and Cabinet ministers, notably the WE charity sole-sourcing and the potential prosecution of SNC-Lavalin for corruption and fraud charges. Added to these very public controversies are a series of broken and unfulfilled promises ranging from an abrupt

---

[9] In its 2022 report, the Edelman Trust found that 'around two thirds of Canadians believe journalists and reporters (61%) and business leaders (60%) are purposely trying to mislead them, with government not far behind (58%). Further, less than half of Canadians view government leaders and CEOs as trustworthy (government leaders at 43% and CEOs at 36%).'

about face on electoral reform, to little or no uptake of Parliamentary Committee recommendations to address changes to the Access to Information Act and whistleblower protection.[10] Data from International IDEA, an intergovernmental democracy-support institution currently chaired by Canada, shows that Canada's 'checks on government' performance has been declining in recent years.[11] Sunny window dressing at the Summit for Democracy cannot easily remedy the disconnect between democratic practice at home and our professed commitment to advance and defend democracy abroad. Canada has not experienced the kind of mass demonstrations that have occurred in countries like France, with theGilet Jaune movement, much less the kind of threats to democracy that rocked the United states with the January 6th protests at the US Capitol. In comparison with those events,Canada's convoy protests were less disruptive and violent. The police might be faulted less for their brutality than their inaction and even complaisance toward the protesters. In Ottawa, at the center of nation-wide protests, there was no widespread rioting or looting and threats of serious violence by the protesters never materialized. For the future, it remains to be seen if more highly disruptive, combative, and complex-to -manage protests are likely to surface more frequently in Canada, or whether the discontent fueled by vaccine mandates and other perceived forms of heavy-handed government during the pandemic was *sui generis*. What lessons will the political right and particularly the 'alt right' in Canada draw from the convoy protests? For the federal level of government, the bruising experience of not quite getting the balance right in terms of executive discretion and public safety vis-a-visrespect for civil liberties and citizen political engagement seems likely to reinforce a sober, measured, and low-key approach to our international efforts to address conflict and protect and advance democracy abroad.

---

[10] For example, a 2021 International Bar Association study on the efficacy of national whistleblower laws placed Canada behind dozens of other surveyed countries. Describing Canada's whistleblower laws as 'nearly entirely dormant,' the IBA survey noted that between 2005 and 2021 only 8 cases were before the 2005 Public Servants Disclosure Protection Act. Of these only two received a decision on the merits with the adjudicating Tribunal ruling in both cases against the whistleblower. See also Centre for Free Expression 'What's Wrong with Canada's Whistleblower System?' Toronto, 2017.

[11] Global State of Democracy Indices.

Overview of the Book

The book is divided into two parts. The first begins with five chapters that offer alternative perspectives on the larger question of democracy and foreign policy. In "Canada's Support for Democracy: Some Wins and Losses but much Potential," Senator Peter Boehm looks at contemporary challenges to democracy and to the international rules-based order. He outlines newer forms of diplomacy and democratic engagement to address the converging impacts of growing authoritarianism, the COVID-19 pandemic, conflict-driven economic factors, disinformation, populism, and social media. Drawing the experiences Canada's role in high level Summitry and multilateral forums, Boehm examines Canadian efforts to promote and defend human rights and democracy. He contrasts Canada's focus on traditional forms of facilitation and outreach to all stakeholders during the 1992 Peru constitutional crisis, and the creative but more intrusive approach used to influence the current Venezuelan crisis. While reaffirming Canada's traditional modes of democracy support, Boehm provides ideas to advance and defend democracy abroad and a parliamentarian's perspective on trust in Canada's democratic institutions.

Another practitioner's perspective is offered by Jeremy Kinsman's "In Search of Democratic Revival, at Home and in the Lives of Others." A former senior diplomat and media commentator, Jeremy Kinsman, analyzes "what went wrong" with some of the transitions to democracy since the fall of the Berlin Wall, 1989. He charts the history of erosion of confidence in the inexorable spread of democracy, and the attractions of populism, illiberalism, and authoritarian nationalism. Kinsman argues that human rights, civil society, and human agency are key to inclusive democratic governance and sustainable development. While he recognizes that all human rights are indivisible, Kinsman's emphasis is on civil society and civil liberties. While democracies should now collectively recommit their support for more open societies everywhere, Kinsman recommends prudence and modesty in our approaches and ambitions. He argues that human rights are an essential precondition of democracy, and that, democracy cannot be exported but has to be built from the ground up. In practical terms, Kinsman calls for efforts through the formation of a democratic solidarity network to counter disinformation, polarization, and illiberal nationalism.

Maxwell A. Cameron's "Democracy and Foreign Policy: A Retrospective" returns to the moment of optimism in the mid-1990s when *Canada*

Among Nations 1995: Democracy and Foreign Policy was written and explores how, three decades later, this optimism has been replaced by pessimism about democratic backsliding, the spread of hybrid regimes, and the reassertion of authoritarianism. Outlining three alternative foreign policy frames (realist, neoliberal, and critical), Cameron offers an analysis of Chrystia Freeland's talk at the Brookings Institution as a point of departure for wider reflections on the ways in which the post-Cold War understanding of liberal democracy has been complicated by the effects of neoliberal globalization. Cameron concludes that present foreign policy thinking is inadequate to address the multiple, simultaneous, and intersecting crises facing contemporary liberal democracies, and calls for a rebuilding of the civic foundations of democratic government as a condition for contributing to the cause of democracy globally.

The fourth chapter in the initial set, "Policy and Practice in Canada's International Democracy Support," by David Gillies, examines Canadian policies and practice to support democracy abroad. It sets out key policy milestones and looks at Canada's current international engagement, including at the Summit for Democracy and plans to establish a Canadian Centre for Democracy. Observations are shared on the domestic environment for democratic policymaking and the demise of other publicly funded institutions, notably Rights and Democracy. The commitment of Canadian governments toward international democracy support has been episodic and inconsistent. But Parliament has been key in bringing forward issues, prompting new policy approaches, and in reinvigorating flagging support. The proposed democracy center provides another opportunity to galvanize a more coherent, networked, and whole-of-society approach to Canada's democracy support.

The final chapter in the first part of the book offers a broad overview of "The State of Democracy in the World." Written by Marshall Palmer and David Carment, this chapter examines trends in democratic processes since the end of the Cold War including backsliding and reversal as evidenced in large sample and related evidence-based research. The chapter evaluates and compares key findings in this body of research as well as primary root causes for democratic reversal and backsliding. The chapter includes an assessment of democracy promotion by Canada in the Ukraine context drawing on relevant data and policies in a Canadian context.

The second part of the book drills into specific aspects of the *problematique* of democracy solidarity or defense and examines challenges to democracy around the world. In "Inclusive Approaches to Multilateral Democracy Support: Challenges and Opportunities for Canada," Catherine Hecht begins with the issue of the inclusion and exclusion of countries that played out in media headlines around the 2021 Summit for Democracy and the 2022 Summit of the Americas. By limiting invitations to "democracies," the United States aimed to "build a shared foundation for global democratic renewal," yet its exclusive approach sparked criticism from democratic and non-democratic states alike. Considerably less academic and policy attention has been given to inclusive approaches to multilateral democracy support. This Hecht argues that the current context of a shrinking liberal international order, democratic erosion, and competing global priorities such as climate change, pandemic recovery, security, and achieving sustainable development requires expanding ideas about positive, non-coercive ways to support the deepening of democratic institutions. For common challenges -- such as such as fighting corruption, polarization, or improving the equitable delivery of social services -- Canada and other countries can gain from cross-regional policy platforms that support exchanges of good practices and developing partnerships.

Kendra Carrión-Vivar and Thomas Legler focus on the Western Hemisphere in their chapter "Toward Canadian Democracy Protection 2.0 in the Americas?" Consistent with a tradition of projecting its values through foreign policy, Canada has been an enthusiastic supporter of the multilateral promotion and defense of democracy in the Americas ever since it joined the Organization of American States (OAS) in 1990. However, in recent years, Canadian efforts to uphold democracy in the Western Hemisphere have been put to the test thanks to the emergence of an inhospitable environment across the Western Hemisphere for such actions. As evidenced by the recent Summit of the Americas held in Los Angeles in June 2022, both the Inter-American collective defense of democracy regime and the OAS itself confront an existential crisis. This chapter examines the challenges and dilemmas facing Canadian foreign policy in this unpropitious climate for defending democracy, as well its contradictions. The authors critically evaluate Canadian pro-democracy actions in the hemisphere with reference to a series of recent political crises, including Bolivia, El Salvador, Honduras, Nicaragua, and Venezuela.

One of the signature initiatives of the Trudeau government has been its feminist foreign policy. In "Feminism and International Democracy Assistance," Gabrielle Bardall reports the results of interviews with policymakers and programming evidence as she examines Canada's approach to feminism, gender, and democracy assistance. Since launching the 2017 Feminist International Assistance Policy (FIAP), Canada has transformed its development assistance by prioritizing women and marginalized groups. When it comes to democracy support, however, Bardall argues that these efforts have faltered. Canada's support for democracy abroad has failed to meaningfully integrate a feminist perspective. While the FIAP deepens and extends long-standing Canadian efforts to promote gender equality, combat gender-based human rights violations, and advance women's role in democratic decision-making, it provides only an aura of transformation by its limited focus on liberal and neoliberal assumptions and on the procedural aspects of democracy. To chart a roadmap for a more integrated feminist approach to democracy support, Bardall calls for Canada to move beyond a 'women first' approach by integrating more transformative approaches like explicit 'shifting power' criteria, intersectionality, and diversity.

Mediation has been another key theme in Canadian foreign policy. In "Quiet Helpful Fixer or Boisterous Norm Advocate? Canada as a Mediator" Peter Jones discusses the use of informal and semi-official dialogues to stimulate discussions between deeply divided adversaries. It has proven particularly effective in circumstances where such adversaries have publicly sworn that they will "never" talk to each other, and yet where at least some in their leaderships have come to the view that discussion is necessary. Under these circumstances, a trusted intermediary, known in the literature as a "third party," arranges and hosts these discussions, usually in conditions of secrecy and deniability. This is a role which so-called middle powers have played at critical moments. Canada would seem well-placed to make such efforts a part of its foreign policy tool box, but has rarely done so. The present Canadian Government, though it talks of an increased role in mediation, seems particularly reluctant. This chapter will examine why this is so, and comments on whether Canada might wish to more actively explore a role in this field.

For many observers, populism is one of the biggest challenges in the context of contemporary crises of democracy. In "Canada's Enduring Populism," David Moscrop concurs with the consensus that populism is on the rise around the world, including in Canada, but he cautions that populist politics are not inherently inconsistent with healthy democratic institutions. However, toxic and authoritarian right-wing populism, the likes of which we have seen in the United States, Hungary, and Poland are indeed corrosive to inclusive self-government that balances majoritarian and minoritarian interests, preferences, and rights. His chapter explores the history of populism in Canada and traces its recent return, with particular attention paid to the surge of toxic authoritarian populism in the United States and its effect north of the border. It also offers some reflections on how the country might resist the rising toxic populist tide and warnings about how, if it fails to, such a tide might shape—indeed, engulf—Canadian domestic and foreign policy in the years to come.

The penultimate chapter by Sanjay Ruparelia addresses the pivotal role that India plays in Canada's new Indo-Pacific strategy. New Delhi and Ottawa espouse a shared commitment to democracy, pluralism, and multilateralism. Moreover, there exist many opportunities to deepen economic ties, promote the transition to a net-zero economy, and counter security threats posed by China, highlighting convergent interests. Yet courting India poses dilemmas too. On the one hand, the erosion of the world's largest democracy, amid other instances of backsliding around the world, belies recent efforts to frame international cooperation through the prism of democracies versus autocracies. On the other hand, India's long-standing commitment to maintaining strategic autonomy and creating a multipolar order that no longer privileges the Global North challenges the Atlanticist worldview that has dominated Canada's foreign policy and national self-image.

The final chapter of the book by the editors concludes the volume. We evaluate the main findings from each chapter and assess their implications for Canada's place in the world. This chapter also identifies future areas of future research and policy implications.

CHAPTER 2

Canada's Support for Democracy: Some Wins and Losses but Much Potential

Peter Boehm

In this chapter, I would like to offer the perspective of a former diplomatic practitioner and now parliamentarian on Canadian efforts to promote democracy, whether through traditional international institutions or informal global organizations in the face of ongoing threats, both domestic and foreign to democratic rule. Attention will be given to developments and Canadian contributions in the western hemisphere, in international summitry, the challenges in Europe and the evolution of our own democratic institutions. Some of my observations will inevitably reflect personal experience.

"The problem with your proposed reference to '*the* rules-based international order' is that we don't know what it is". Those were the words directed to me by US National Security Adviser John Bolton on the morning of June 9, 2018, near the end of the Charlevoix G-7 Summit. This was the moment where leaders and their Sherpas found themselves

---

P. Boehm (✉)
Senate of Canada, Ottawa, CA, Canada
e-mail: Peter.Boehm@sen.parl.gc.ca

© The Author(s), under exclusive license to Springer Nature Switzerland AG 2023
M. A. Cameron et al. (eds.), *Democracy and Foreign Policy in an Era of Uncertainty*, Canada and International Affairs,
https://doi.org/10.1007/978-3-031-35490-8_2

at an American-induced impasse as to whether the indefinite or definite article should be applied to the definition in the summit's final communique. The now famous photograph of that instance, most versions of which have both Prime Minister Justin Trudeau's and my own head cropped out (despite the fact that we were guiding the discussion), shows a seated, bored-looking President Donald Trump facing Angela Merkel, Emmanuel Macron, Theresa May, and Shinzo Abe. Since the first of several Sherpa meetings of that year, as well as subsequent meetings of labour, development, finance, foreign, and interior ministers, it soon became clear that despite G7 support for most initiatives put forward and negotiated by the Canadian presidency, it was inevitable that there would be some sort of reckoning with the US at the end. The compromise was to refer to "**a**" rules-based international order in the first line. It remained "the" in the remainder of the document and was so released, despite an unrelated "Twitter" attempt by the US President to reject the entire communique and its related agreed initiatives, some of which dealt specifically with support for and threats to democracy. It was almost beyond irony that representatives of the country most closely associated with the establishment of the post-war rules-based international order would question its legitimacy. I will return to this theme later.

I mention this example to underscore the fact that disruption by international actors on the question of democracy has permeated not just the tradecraft in formal institutions such as the United Nations and its specialized agencies, but also those informal groupings such as the G7 and the G20 that were developed as a means to advance global leadership and initiatives outside the strictures that come with the formality of established institutions. Ironically, the departure from office of Donald Trump, the invasion of Ukraine by Russia, and to a degree the impact of the COVID pandemic, have given new strength to the informal organizations. With ongoing global economic concerns, the lingering pandemic and the war in Ukraine, there has been an unprecedented amount of G7 activity during the 2022 German Presidency, much of which has led to greater activity at the UN, NATO, and the Bretton Woods institutions. The pandemic spurred G20 action into injecting more liquidity and stimulus into the global economy. Whilst the problems of governance calcification, budgets and the challenges of secretariat and specialized agency leadership selection remain, there seems to be a greater sense of purpose to current and future work in the more established international institutions. Whether there is the requisite political will to make this work matter is open to question.

Democracy is a fundamental tenet of the rules-based international order. After all, the new multilateral system established after the war, enshrined in the UN Charter, was to deter authoritarian regimes and to ensure both peace and the proliferation of democratic values. The work of Canadian diplomats in post-hostilities planning in the 1940s, particularly in taking on a significant role in drafting the UN Charter and subsequently the North Atlantic Treaty, established a Canadian activist trend that extended through other formal global/regional institutions including the Commonwealth (apartheid in South Africa), l'Organisation Internationale de la Francophonie (establishment of political/social crisis response mechanism), the Organization of American States (strong support for the Unit for the Promotion of Democracy) and the International Criminal Court. Moreover, Canada's ongoing wish to pursue Article 2 of the North Atlantic Treaty, underscores the notion that even under a security pact, values-type relations can and should flourish. Whether consciously or not, Canada's reliance on the rules-based international order and indeed on multilateralism writ large, has traditionally served as an important counterweight to our deep and comprehensive bilateral relationship with the US.

Canada's commitment to promoting democracy internationally took several big steps at the end of the 1980s and into the 1990s. There were several international developments that provided an ideal backdrop for a middle power like Canada to seize the moment to engage and project its values. The collapse of the Soviet Union and its Warsaw Pact neighbours turned eastern European socialist governance on its head. The end of apartheid in South Africa—where the government of Brian Mulroney had played a significant role in the Commonwealth and other international bodies, signalled greater democratic change in Africa. Canada also joined the Organization of American States in 1990 after 28 years as an observer. There was a sense amongst civil society and in government that crisis in Central America and the Caribbean in particular could be assuaged by a more active Canadian multilateral presence in its own hemisphere. Both the governments of Brian Mulroney and Jean Chrétien used the benefit of their majority parliamentary status, as well as the personal networks and policy ideas cultivated by their long-serving foreign ministers Joe Clark and Lloyd Axworthy, to great effect.

In terms of higher level statecraft, the greatest theme in the early 1990s was how to assist the Russian Federation in following a democratic, free-market path. President Mikhail Gorbachev had a soft spot for Canada, from his visit here as Secretary for Agriculture in 1983 and through the then Soviet ambassador in Ottawa, Alexander Yakovlev, who had been influential in advising on the vaunted "glasnost" and "perestroika" themes. In preparing for hosting the 1995 G7 summit in Halifax and after discussing his idea with his peers, Chrétien invited Gorbachev's successor, Boris Yeltsin, to a dinner with leaders to discuss regional issues and democratization. The path had been cleared through a winter visit to Moscow by Foreign Affairs deputy minister and Sherpa Gordon Smith, whom I accompanied in my capacity as director of the G7 Summit Division at the Department of Foreign Affairs and International Trade. During that visit, we met with senior Russian politicians and officials, including Anatoly Chubais, deputy prime minister and the architect of economic privatization initiatives. In retrospect, we and our colleagues in other governments may have been too willing to dispel any doubts we may have had about the Russian path towards democratization, the aggressive push of free marketeers and our collective wish to bring the Russians into the club. Nonetheless, the Halifax summit set the stage for the establishment of the G8. Over the ensuing years, Canada did work reasonably well with Russia on a variety of themes in a G8 context, however, it became clearer by the last summit in Northern Ireland in 2013 that President Vladimir Putin was more intent on following his own path and promoting democracy either within Russia's borders or without was not to be a part of it. As then Sherpa for Prime Minister Stephen Harper, I attended a meeting in Moscow in early 2014 to plan for the Sochi Summit to take place later that year. But Russia took Crimea and the Donbas afterwards and, at Canada's recommendation, G7 leaders decided at the Nuclear Security Summit in The Hague in March to return to a G7 format and not attend the Russian summit. I was sanctioned by the Russian government then and more recently in the Russian sanctioning spree of 2022 when that fate befell all our senators. Our collective, perhaps even noble foray to help Russia towards democracy was over, felled by misconceptions, miscalculations (likely on both sides), a too strident commercial push by the West, nationalism and Putin's megalomania. On the other hand, the G7 has since established a greater solidarity and a more focused approach (despite the anarchic approach of the Trump administration), a harbinger for required concerted action in the face of pandemics, economic downturns, coordination difficulties in the G20, and of course, war.

In terms of promoting democracy, Canada seems to have found its niche in the establishment of democratic institutions as well as international electoral observation and reform. Continuing on the trans-Atlantic theme, Canada used its membership in the Organization for Security and Cooperation in Europe (OSCE), drawing a line from its earlier involvement in the CSCE/Helsinki Final Act (1975) to support democratic development in the mid-1990s in the shattered Balkan pieces of the former Yugoslavia. Since the OSCE basically falls under a UN Charter Chapter 8 mandate, this means that all 57 participating states are open to scrutiny. In practice, Canada has been a great supporter of the OSCE Office for Democratic Institutions and Human Rights (ODIHR), providing support for election observation missions in newly reconstituted countries of eastern Europe. Not surprisingly, a disproportionate amount of effort has been expended in supporting the growth of democratic institutions in Ukraine.

Since joining the OAS in 1990, various Canadian governments have pursued hemispheric democratic development through funding and high level personnel to the Unit for Promotion of Democracy which evolved into the Secretariat for Strengthening Democracy. There have been over 200 OAS electoral observation missions over the last few decades, many strongly funded by Canada and several with prominent Canadians at the helm. No doubt Canada's hemispheric history as a non-US middle power played a role in this emphasis, as did the interest of domestic civil society (particularly respecting Central America and Haiti). The work involved technical assistance to national electoral commissions, actual observation of voting conditions on election days, and dealing with both efforts and perceptions of interference on the part of ruling authorities. I recall from my assignment in Costa Rica (with multiple accreditations to other Central American countries in the late 1980s) that Elections Canada was seen as a fair and respected partner that was instrumental in providing technical assistance to the Nicaraguan election commission for the controversial election of 1990 which resulted in the Sandinistas losing power. Former Prime Minister and Foreign Minister Joe Clark was involved in election observation on both the policy end whilst in office and in the field afterwards. Whilst a great proponent of the value of such missions, he has reflected that the post-election period (i.e., once the observers and media have left) should merit the same priority and professionalism as the "before and during" phase, perhaps through the issuance of the equivalent of a public report card to exercise any necessary suasion of country leadership and a standardization of approach (Clark et al. 2006).

The combination of increasing calls for electoral observation in the hemisphere, a US policy push for greater hemispheric cohesion outside of the OAS, the rise of Hugo Chavez in Venezuela, and a wish to somehow codify democratic conduct led to the phenomena of the Summits of the Americas and the development of an Inter-American Democratic Charter. The late 1990s and early 2000s highlighted a "public sector democracy industry" amongst OECD donor countries where altruism and generous budgets ruled, and policy direction remained more elusive. In Canada's case, the line as to what could constitute Official Development Assistance in support for democracy between CIDA programming and the efforts of the Department of Foreign Affairs and International Trade (DFAIT) was at times blurred and there was sometimes inconsistency in the choice of on-the-ground partners (Lippert 2021). In addition, there was a confluence of hemispheric planning interests: foreign minister Axworthy had volunteered Windsor, Ontario to host the annual General Assembly of the OAS (a meeting of foreign ministers) in June 2000 and Prime Minister Chrétien offered to host his counterparts at the third Summit of the Americas in Québec City in April 2001. During this period, and as Permanent Representative, I chaired the OAS Permanent Council in Washington. This flurry of activity was kicked off by a meeting of hemispheric trade ministers in Toronto in November 1999 in what proved to be a vainglorious attempt at establishing a Free Trade Area of the Americas.

The test case was the fragility of democracy in Peru, reeling from the authoritarian rule of President Alberto Fujimori who had staged an "autogolpe" (self-coup) with the military in 1992. The OAS election observation mission had documented significant if not grave irregularities in two electoral rounds in the spring of 2000 and the mission's report provoked intense debate at the Permanent Council as to whether the time-honoured Resolution 1080 (extraordinary meeting of the Permanent Council in response to a coup d'état) should be invoked. Instead it was agreed that the issue should be kicked forward to the General Assembly in Windsor where a resolution (AG/Res 1753) was passed authorizing a special democracy fact-finding mission to Peru led by the President of the General Assembly, Lloyd Axworthy, and the Secretary General of the OAS, César Gaviria, to determine next steps following meetings with political and civil society actors on the ground in Lima (OAS 2000). I worked the floor amongst delegations to get the resolution passed, ironically with a Peruvian delegation that had dropped its opposition, recognizing that the resolution provided a valuable safety valve against turmoil at home. My toughest discussions were with the Venezuelan and Mexican foreign ministers, who in keeping with traditional doctrine (at least in the case of Mexico), viewed the resolution as unacceptable interference in the internal affairs of a member state. The Venezuelans had stuck to their mantra of the virtues of "democracia participative" as opposed to traditional representative democracy. Resolution 1753 was a creative way of avoiding an intense debate and lack of consensus on invoking Resolution 1080.

Gaviria's Chief of Staff Fernando Jaramillo and I were designated special envoys to lead the pre-mission to Peru. We visited, supported by both the OAS secretariat and our embassy in Lima, meeting with a wide range of political actors and civil society representatives, and hammered out a draft democratization plan of some 29 points, which we refined in the Canadian government aircraft with Axworthy and Gaviria en route to Lima at the end of June. Key was the establishment of a "mesa de diálogo" (round table) for discussion that included all stakeholders, that would be chaired by Eduardo Latorre, the former foreign minister of the Dominican Republic, assisted by OAS and Canadian officials. The scope for dialogue was broad: judicial and electoral reform, media freedom, anti-corruption and Congressional oversight of the military and intelligence services. We added a timeframe for results, but the real value was getting the Peruvian players around one table (Cooper 2001).[1] What stands out in my mind are the pre-mission meetings with then President Alberto Fujimori (we examined Peru's constitution with him whilst sitting in rocking chairs in the presidential palace) his notorious intelligence adviser Vladimiro Montesinos and our secret encounter with opposition leader Alejandro Toledo. He would become President less than two years later. Our work added momentum, both at the OAS in Washington and in the separate Summit of the Americas negotiating track, towards having some form of an Inter-American Democratic Charter ready for leaders to examine at Québec City. That summit has

---

[1] In my view, the best analysis of OAS democratization efforts in Peru can be found in Cooper, Andrew F. Cooper, and Thomas Legler. The OAS in Peru: A Model for the Future? *Journal of Democracy* 12: 123–136.

been well-documented and analysed by academics, with the street protests receiving most of the media attention. The negotiations on the communique, particularly the Charter reference, were arduous with Venezuela and Mexico again being the most difficult delegations to convince. The Americans left most of it to us, since we had established a good record of getting things done and the administration of George W. Bush had only been in office for a few months. In the end, we tried all types of persuasion to convince Venezuelan President Hugo Chavez to sign on. He eventually did but insisted on a footnote recognizing "participatory democracy". The Charter was fittingly signed in Lima (minus the footnote) at an extraordinary meeting of OAS foreign ministers on September 11, 2001, and was totally overshadowed in public terms by the tragic terrorist attacks of that day in the US. Yet the parameters for strengthening democracy in the hemisphere had been set out clearly, Canada had played a significant role and had been recognized for it. Nonetheless, as we have seen recently, democracy in Peru and indeed other countries continues to remain fragile.

It is a delicate two-step working with the US on hemispheric questions on democracy. The US approach tends to be binary, driven as much by ideology, diaspora politics with a whiff of a history of interventionism, which the Americans tend to ignore but their regional partners remember all too well in the context of their history with the US forming part of their own nationalism. Decrying imperialism in the western hemisphere (whether mythic, historic, or imaginary) can get you votes and public attention. Also, the US democracy brand, whilst apparently resilient, tends to be a bit tarnished today following the tumult of the Trump administration. As the second largest ODA donor in the hemisphere and with a usually good communications channel to Washington, Canada can and does play a significant role. Others know this and appreciate it, even as the Canadian public and to some degree the media remain unaware. For Canada, the most successful approach has been the direct, creative one, whether as a convenor (a much-maligned term in some circles but accurate in terms of others' expectations) or as a guide and initiator. Canada's regular engagement on critical issues dealing with Haiti, the other French speaking country in the hemisphere, has covered the gamut from strengthening democratic institutions, peacekeeping, police training to outright humanitarian assistance in the wake of earthquakes and hurricanes. Canada's role in the "Lima Group" in the context of the recognition of Venezuelan National Assembly President Juan Guaidó as the interim President was formative and creative (Canadian consultations even took place with Cuba on the subject), but the overall objective of the initiative, new democratic elections in Venezuela, ultimately collapsed.

As has often been the case when established international institutions are seen as either too cumbersome, too diverse or large in their memberships to achieve goals set out by the US, other informal entities are developed. President Bill Clinton pushed for a hemispheric summit in Miami in 1994, bypassing the OAS. President George W. Bush established a "coalition of the willing" to deal with Iraq for the second time, knowing that the UN Security Council would never endorse such a move. Canada has generally been uncomfortable with weaponizing democracy and using it as a goal in the context of military action. President Barack Obama pushed for a series of nuclear security summits, sensing that the UN's IAEA was not up to the task. And so, recognizing that there was a demonstrated but also political need to bolster democracies in the face of increasing competition from autocratic governments particularly in both China and Russia, President Joe Biden convened a virtual Summit for Democracy in December 2021, featuring the participation of some 100 leaders that resulted in 750 commitments. Invitations and participation attracted some controversy in the sense that the list seemed to reflect specific US interests. Such democracy summits look to continue and there is also a move towards more regional, "mini-summit" conclaves. As in all forms of summitry, the key to any perceived progress will be visibility of follow-through and transparency on commitments. Recognizing its political purpose in both domestic and international terms, this summit series should not re-invent the wheel in terms of what other, more formal organizations have already done. If there could be some attention devoted to money in political advertising and support, transparency of data initiatives, clear support for real investigative and local journalism (would a fraud like George Santos have been elected to the US House of Representatives had the national media heeded the warnings of the Long Island media?) and efforts to keep corruption out of politics in democratic countries, this would be a boon to support for democracies throughout the world, be they fragile, threatened or tarnished (Foti et al. 2022). Interestingly, amongst those not invited, including NATO members Hungary and Turkey, China's reaction was perhaps the most forceful. I and undoubtedly many others received a paper from the Chinese embassy, entitled "China: Democracy that Works". If there was a geopolitical target to hit, President Biden's aim was true.

There is a narrative on social media, amongst the far right and the far left, fuelled by various conspiracy theories, that democracy, particularly in those countries rated high on democratic indicators by Freedom House, IDEA, and other non-governmental organizations that rate democratic observance in governance and human rights terms, is in peril. These views were clearly expressed by the "Freedom Convoy" which occupied downtown Ottawa in January and February of 2022, whose basic tenets were opposition to COVID-19 vaccination policies and the view that governmental actions, chiefly at the federal level, transgressed the Canadian Charter of Rights and Freedoms. It was beyond ironic for me that a manifesto circulated by the occupiers called upon the unelected Senate of Canada, working with the unelected Governor General, to overthrow the elected government. Whilst there is a history in Canada of peaceful and not-so-peaceful protest against perceived government overreach: the Winnipeg General Strike of 1919, the "on to Ottawa trek" and the Regina riot of 1935 during the great depression, anti-conscription riots, international summit protests, this was the first occasion of a prolonged multi-venue massive protest that featured on-line organization and execution. Moreover, the federal government invoked the Emergencies Act on February 14, 2022, for the first time to deal with the Ottawa occupation and border paralysis in Windsor, Ontario, and Coutts, Alberta. Polling indicated that many Canadians exhibited a more centrist view and did not approve of the demonstrators' actions. Some politicians sought to exploit the crisis for political gain. Social media provided a multiplier effect in terms of both misinformation and disinformation, the latter apparently also pushed by some malign state actors. Whilst COVID-19 vaccination mandates may have proven to be the catalyst, it was also evident, not just in Canada but in other countries with perceived unshakeable democracies, that the pandemic, restrictions on individuals' movement outside of Canada, rising prices, pressures on supply chains and amongst some a decreasing faith in democratic institutions, had contributed to the malaise. This was a global phenomenon, not just confined to Canada, although the form of its expression here (i.e., occupation by truck), given our relatively peaceful domestic history, generated much attention. The debate about whether by who and whom democracy was usurped in our country will continue for some time, certainly on social media. But it comes down to facts versus feelings: the government acted lawfully in imposing both vaccine mandates and reacting with the Emergencies Act. The Rouleau

Commission of Enquiry eventually concluded that the threshold required for the federal government to invoke the Emergencies Act had been met. Debates in the House of Commons on the introduction of the Emergencies Act were both desultory and laden with histrionics; in the Senate, over two days of debate on February 22 and 23, 36 senators spoke to the motion to confirm the Emergencies Act before its invocation was revoked and the motion withdrawn (Boehm 2022). A public enquiry (mandated under the Act) and a joint parliamentary committee (also mandated under the Act but really only for the duration of the imposition of it) were convened. The fact that these reporting and accountability measures are included in the legislation does underscore fundamental democratic principles. It would be incredibly premature and inaccurate to suggest that Canadian democracy is at great risk by either the occupation of the centre of our country's capital or the response. Nonetheless, some of the underlying ideas and overarching goals of the organizers indeed suggest a great and insidious risk to democracy. Perhaps better cases could be made that the invocation of the "notwithstanding clause" (Section 33 of the Constitution) by some provinces as a heavy measure to quash any opposition to new legislation or the introduction of provincial legislation that would allow choice in accepting federal legislation, constitute more of a threat to the pillars of our Constitution. Some might even ask whether Canada should be promoting democratic development abroad when it should really get its own house in order, reconciliation with its indigenous peoples being a prime example.

We have learned in our own adaptation of the Westminster system that our democracy has moved along incrementally, from Confederation in 1867, to the Statute of Westminster in 1931, the passage of Canadian Citizenship Act of 1947, to the "repatriation" of our Constitution in 1982. Any effort to exact constitutional change in Canada is complex. What is required for an amendment to pass regarding both the powers of the Senate and the method of selecting senators is the general amending procedure (Section 38.1): the agreement of a minimum of two-thirds of the provinces representing at least fifty percent of the population of all the provinces in addition to the consent of both the Senate and the House of Commons. The changes to the Senate appointments process were developed by the current government in 2016, upending a process that had been in effect since 1867. It probably represents the furthest the government could go without crossing the line into formal constitutional change. To the extent that Canadians care about these changes, polls have indicated support for the reforms but those who also think abolishing the institution might be worth considering have not gone away. From 2015 to 2019, one-third of government bills were successfully amended in the Senate, as opposed to work under the previous appointments system when only one out of 61 bills was amended between 2013 and 2015 (Dean 2022). Time will decide whether our parliamentary system has become more democratic through these reforms. Also, despite the restrictions over two years imposed by the pandemic in terms of requirements for virtual, hybrid, and a reduced number of hearings by Senate committees, reports and studies have still been produced. In addition, two current studies, one on security in the Arctic undertaken by the Senate Standing Committee on National Security, Defence, and Veterans Affairs, and a study on the "fit for purpose" nature of Global Affairs Canada being pursued by the Senate Standing Committee on Foreign Affairs and International Trade, potentially represent significant contributions to public policy, assuming the government heeds the recommendations in some measure. The evolution of our upper house continues along its own path, but it is interesting how some countries with a similar heritage have changed their upper houses going from outright abolition (New Zealand) to proportional representation elections and fixed terms (Australia) to the ongoing struggles in the British parliament on reforming the House of Lords in terms of size (currently 784) crossbench/independent members, terms, and accountability. Should a future Canadian government wish to return to the status quo ante in terms of Senate appointments, any change involving a return to traditional partisan political appointments would, given current demographics in the chamber, take a generation to be palpable.

Apart from the often valuable committee work undertaken in both houses of parliament, expressions to support democracy or criticize the lack thereof tend to take the form of motions. Motions may have symbolic value in terms of signalling the will of parliament for the government or a foreign state to undertake certain commitments. They can be unanimous, contested through votes, but inevitably fulfill the purpose of quick gratification, sometimes reflecting a politically partisan or diaspora-infused position (sometimes for political gain, given Canada's very diverse electorate). They are often wide off the mark in terms of the feasibility of the implementation of their demands. At the end of the day, the government will take its international positions under the Royal Prerogative, regardless of the wishes or demands expressed through parliamentary motions.

A different approach is the promotion of democracy through the work of inter-parliamentary groups and associations across the globe. Canada's parliament can boast of 8 multilateral and 5 bilateral parliamentary associations, 4 inter-parliamentary groups and approximately 60 friendship groups. The longest standing entity is the Inter-Parliamentary Union, founded in 1889, which under its motto, "For Democracy, For Everyone" brings together some 178 parliaments, including many from dictatorships. Whilst meetings of all groups were either curtailed or undertaken virtually during the pandemic, the value of interaction, exchange of best legislative practices and discussion of themes ranging from security, human rights, gender to bilateral, and regional issues cannot be underestimated. Canadian groups are comprised of both members of parliament and senators and overall management falls under the umbrella of the Joint Interparliamentary Council. In my view, greater attention should be given to targeted funding and cohesion amongst these groups and with a clearer enunciation of the Canadian national interest, in supporting democratic development, for example. Substantive preparation is vital to the credibility of these groups as they meet with their counterparts. If not, we will come across as well-intentioned but parochial when interacting with our foreign counterparts, either in Canada or abroad. My bias is clear: Canada is one of the world's oldest and most durable democracies. We should look at greater parliamentary engagement abroad, with the hope that some of our "political osmosis" might have an impact on legislators in other jurisdictions. All should recognize that the process of what will be a lengthy period of reconciliation with our indigenous peoples, as painful as it is and will be, is a sign of democratic maturity.

The promotion of democracy remains an important tenet of Canadian foreign, trade, and international development policies. The past few years have featured a greater correlation between international development and democratic governance goals through the amalgamation of the Canadian International Development Agency (CIDA) into the then Department of Foreign Affairs and International Trade in 2013. Whilst the bureaucratic culture has been slow to change, particularly with respect to project management, the advent of the Feminist International Assistance Policy in 2017 provided opportunity for greater emphasis on more agile definition of local requirements and targeted expenditures. However, the evolution continues: the recently released Indo-Pacific Strategy features democratic development as a pillar, and one to be included in discussions with authoritarian governments in the region. The speech by Deputy Prime Minister and Finance Minister Chrystia Freeland at the Brookings Institute in November of 2022 made references to "friendshoring", in the context that global actions by authoritarian actors, Russia and China in particular, should be countered by efforts amongst like-minded countries to pool resources and act on the basis of shared democratic values (Buck and Manulak 2022). The chapter on how such an approach could lead to either strengthening or changing the international rules-based order has yet to be written. That order was more or less established in 1945 on a statist, multilateral framework. Since then, globalization and the technological revolution that has brought us the internet and with it social media has given more scope for civil society interaction, for good or ill, including in autocracies. The rapid Chinese policy changes in pandemic management and Russian men voting with their feet to avoid conscription serve as examples. Iron curtains and lines of control have been relegated to the past, despite efforts to control access to the world wide web through outright system control or the spreading of misinformation and disinformation through troll and bot farms. So new or revised forms of democratic interaction amongst the "likeminded" should not ignore the value of maintaining if not enhancing people to people contact.

Canadian efforts to support democracy around the world have been determined and well-intentioned over the past few decades, regardless of who was in power in Ottawa. We are a middle power that can, if it wishes, kick consistently on the democracy file. Our efforts through international organizations such as the Commonwealth and the OAS have had some lasting impact, regardless of current challenges. Our work on electoral reform, observation, and strengthening parliamentary institutions, promoting gender equality, space for diverse voices is probably without peer. We have successfully pressed for consensus (the adoption of the Inter-American Democratic Charter) and demonstrated creativity in establishing and chairing a G7 Rapid Response Mechanism launched by leaders in Charlevoix in 2018 that promotes coordinated responses to evolving threats to democracy (Boehm 2019). But the challenges are huge. The economic impact of the pandemic has resulted in some countries slipping back from their "emerging economies status" to qualify again for official development assistance. This against a backdrop of food insecurity, more displaced people and climatic disasters. These are often interrelated factors. Other international actors have stepped in to offer cheap credit, infrastructure development, and/or mercenary forces to struggling countries. It is more than time for richer democracies to up their game, to redefine assistance for democratic development, coordinate better, and increase funding. Given its record, Canada is well-placed to initiate and to lead. But the will amongst all political actors must be mustered to address this unprecedented challenge. And that is not an easy task.

Consistency of approach and delivery on democracy-strengthening initiatives is and will continue to be Canada's greatest challenge. Various governments have made spectacular announcements of institutions that were to have global reach, such as the Canadian Institute for International Peace and Security (CIIPS), the Pearson Peacekeeping Centre (PPC), and the Canadian Foundation for the Americas (FOCAL). All eventually faltered through diminished funding, an inability to set priorities or a change of flavour in the government's focus. The most obvious example was the closure of Rights and Democracy by the Harper government in 2012. The position of an ambassador for religious freedom at the then Department of Foreign Affairs and International Trade was also abolished by the Liberal Government in 2015. In announcing the intention to establish a Democracy Centre in 2021 and including this initiative in the foreign minister's mandate letter, the Trudeau government has Canada charting a course in advancing democracy abroad. As it moves forward, it should look at successful examples. In the US, both the National Democratic Institute (NDI) and the International Republican Institute (IRI) are celebrating their fortieth anniversaries of international non-governmental activism for democracy. The two largest German "Stiftungen", the Konrad Adenauer and Friedrich Ebert Foundations, have been around much longer. The German foundations operate in association with but are independent of political parties and use public funds as determined by the Bundestag. Canada's own but somehow little-known Parliamentary Centre has existed since 1968. It remains underfunded but has done excellent work in Armenia and Ukraine. In addition to setting out clear priorities and focus for the Democracy Centre, close scrutiny should be given to appropriate and durable funding models and accountability structures. If not, Canada may well reflect on its previous successes, express its altruistic intentions, and continue its good, but too often episodic approach in its support for democracy around the world.

REFERENCES

Boehm, Peter M. 2019. De l'utilité du G7: témoinage d'un sherpa [The Value of the G7: Reflections of a Sherpa]. *Politique étrangère*.

Boehm, Peter. 2022. Imposition of the Emergencies Act. Debates of the Senate, February 22. www.sencanada.ca

Buck, Kerry, and Michael W. Manulak. 2022. Friend-Shoring Canada's Foreign Policy? *Policy Magazine*, October 29. www.policymagazine.ca.

Clark, Joe, Elizabeth Voeller, and Marinna Ofosu. 2006. Election Observation Missions: Making them Count. Woodrow Wilson International Center for Scholars, Africa Program, Occasional Papers Series 5, January.

Cooper, Andrew. 2001. More Than a Star Turn: Canadian Hybrid Diplomacy and the OAS Mission to Peru. *International Journal* 56 (2): 279–296.

Foti, Joseph et al. 2022. *Inflection Point: Making the Summit for Democracy Matter at the IACC*, December 2. https://www.brookings.edu/blog/fix gov/2022/12/02/inflection-point-making-the-summit-for-democracy-mat ter-at-the-iacc/

Dean, Tony. 2022. The Senate's Longstanding Duopoly Has Finally Faded. Policy Options. IRPP, February 16.

Lippert, Owen. 2021. The Problem with Election Observation Missions. Canadian International Council, August 4.

Organization of American States. AG/Res 1753, Mission of the Chair of the General Assembly and the OAS Secretary General to Peru. www.oas.org/jur idico/english/agres_1753.

CHAPTER 3

In Search of Democratic Revival, at Home and in the Lives of Others

Jeremy Kinsman

The world today: news for democrats remains disconsolate, though there are some recent signs of recovery of confidence in democracy in a few countries. But the central questions remain: what happened to the euphoria of 1989 after the fall of the Berlin Wall? How can democracies recover traction and best contribute to democratic governance and human rights defence going forward?

In March (2023), V-Dem (p. 6) reported that "the level of democracy enjoyed by the average global citizen is down to 1986 levels." There are now more dictatorships than liberal democracies. True liberal democracies have declined to 32 from 41. 72% of the world's population live in autocracies (a number that is magnified, of course, by China and now India.)

J. Kinsman (✉)
Konrad Adenauer Stiftung Canada, Ottawa, ON, Canada

© The Author(s), under exclusive license to Springer Nature Switzerland AG 2023
M. A. Cameron et al. (eds.), *Democracy and Foreign Policy in an Era of Uncertainty*, Canada and International Affairs, https://doi.org/10.1007/978-3-031-35490-8_3

But the trend is stark. Ominously, "the number of democratizing countries is down to only 14 with only 2% of the world's population. There have not been so few since 1973, fifty years ago."

V-Dem's prior 2022 Democracy Report data found that the "last 30 years of democratic advances are now eradicated…35 countries suffered significant deteriorations in freedom of expression at the hands of governments—an increase from only 5 countries 10 years ago."

Put another way, but in the same direction, Freedom House noted that 2022 represented the 17th straight year of democracy decline in the world. But by late 2022, some encouraging signs emerged. In the US, 2020 Republican election-deniers generally failed to win election in 2022 midterms, indicating a possible moderation of US polarization. Autocratic Brazilian president Bolsanaro was narrowly defeated by Lula da Silva and conceded the transfer of power. Other autocratic populists—Rodrigo Duterte of the Philippines, Gotabaya Rajapaksa of Sri Lanka, and Andrej Babis of the Czech Republic—had their wings clipped.

But the stressed preoccupations of established democracies tend to be inward-looking. To the extent they include external relations, they are crisis-driven, as is the case for the war in Ukraine. The effect is to demote democracy support for others down the list of priorities. The impression this conveys of gradual withdrawal of official interest and solidarity has been demoralizing to human rights defenders and civil society proponents in repressive non-democracies.

Democratic recession mostly occurs by stealth. Once majoritarian populists win power by exploiting anxiety, they use their majoritarian support to eliminate the effectiveness of democratic and human rights checks and balances in courts, tribunals, and legislatures. Backsliding incrementally erodes civil liberties, inclusivity, and openness, consistently subtracting from tenuously established democratic space, polarizing opinion, often against minorities as well as against outsiders.

Nationalism again has propulsion, as it did in the Nineteenth Century, or in the 1930s. Its ascent has been at the expense of globalism and multilateral cooperation. Russia's invasion of Ukraine is driven by Putin's expansive nationalism, and challenges bedrock international norms from the post-war consensus to eliminate nationalist aggression. V-Dem's (2022: 9) "State of the World" summarizes it thus: "A war began in Europe…the doing of the same leader who triggered the third wave of autocratization when he began to derail democracy in Russia 20 years ago. The invasion seems like a definite confirmation of the dangers the world faces as a consequence of autocratization around the world."

Some argue that this confirmed trend means that democratic allies should face up to the reality that major autocracies, particularly China and Russia, are immutably hostile, and to concert in oppositional recognition that the world is again divided. Democratic concertation can indeed favour coordinated positive policies in support of democracy. However, creating a closed democratic circle to confront what is seen to be an outside threat is a leap to the wrong conclusion. Most countries are "in-between" democracy and autocracy. Most need and want support from all sides.

Multiple meetings of Canadian, German, and other scholars and experts over the course of the last two years under the Canada-Germany civil society project "Renewing Our Democratic Alliance" (RODA) advised that the "silent majority" of the world's nations, especially the poorest countries that are most vulnerable to exogenous adversities in global trends, do not want to be coerced into one side or the other in a renewed cold war. That reticence clearly emerged at recent meetings of the G-20, ASEAN, APEC, La Francophonie, and other multilateral groupings. Globally, we are at an inflection point when the existential nature of transnational challenges of health and climate and other inter-connected ongoing crises underline the reality of universal inter-dependence. The necessity of an effective international response requires protecting the potential for cooperation on vital challenges to the global commons. Despite the vexed China–US relationship, Presidents Xi Jinping and Biden recognized their special joint responsibility at their Summit in Bali, Indonesia in late 2022.

Every country has the responsibility to be attentive to and engaged by collective challenges and responsibilities. Most democracies have committed to protect the rules-based order by supporting Ukraine's defence of its national sovereignty "for as long as it takes." But they should simultaneously encourage the international community to mobilize for its common global agenda of necessity. At home, they need to reinforce their own institutions, intensify links with trusted partners, and provide exemplary inclusive and effective governance. And our democratic societies should re-boot concern for the eroding positions of human rights defenders and others seeking open government elsewhere. Citizens everywhere share expectations: for stability, security, and well-being, but also for fairness and transparency, opportunity, and the impartial rule of equitable law.

Democracies should renew confident support for this quest that has continued wherever humans live—for human rights, dignity, and accountability. The support needs to be more than declaratory. But to enable support for others to have practical impact, democracies need to know much better what is needed, what is feasible, and what works best. That is the theme of this essay.

Disappointment in Washington, 2014

What remained of 1989s confidence that democratization would be the prevailing global outcome was decisively depleted by the Arab Spring's burn out in the early 2010s. Brutally repressed in Syria, it subsided in disarray elsewhere, especially Egypt, where democratic reformers couldn't unite sufficiently to sustain public confidence they would deliver stable governance. By 2014, President Obama confided private advice that NGO advocates of support for democracy development should first figure out what succeeds. His impression was that we had got it muddled. At the Washington-based but internationally inclusive Council for a Community of Democracies (I had been since 2007 inaugural Director of its program of democracy development support), we experienced first-hand the waning of donor backing in the wake of similarly disenchanted questions as President Obama's. Human rights defenders and political activists in increasingly self-confident autocracies abroad felt orphaned by this apparent weakening of concrete solidarity as authoritarian illiberal regimes cracked down on their rights, tendencies which have deepened since, especially in China and Russia.

Today, when public opinion in established democracies has become increasingly preoccupied by polarization at home, 71% of American voters believe their own democracy is at risk (New York Times/Siena College poll). But in early 2023, only 7% identified that as "the most important problem in the country," in comparison to the worst inflation since 1982, the withdrawal of federal abortion rights after 50 years, and an uncertain perception of surging crime. Additionally, whilst foreign policy and budgetary agendas of established democracies have now re-geared to meet the need to help Ukraine protect its sovereignty, managing this support and its considerable costs to treasuries has further narrowed the political and budgetary band width available for support of democracy development elsewhere, and for lightening the impact on poorer countries of the world's systemic "polycrisis."

In order to relate more effectively to the needs of other countries, citizens of democracies need first to understand better how democracy develops—*why it succeeds and why it fails*. The broad design needs first to focus on conclusions from empirical review of the decades since 1989 that urges concentration on the building blocks of democratic behaviour and competence. The building blocks are essentially:

1. The consolidation and protection of *civil liberties*, that are foundational to openness and inclusion, and which
2. Allow *civil society*, which is the incubator of democratic *behaviour*, to develop and flourish.

President Vaclav Havel's Advice

It is axiomatic that elected governments need to be able to execute governance and program delivery in order to retain public support. But delivery has been where neophyte democratic regimes often fell short. Democracy needs to be an all-of-society effort. The human factor is paramount. *Successful inclusive democracy relies as much on human behaviour as it does on process and institutions.* It does, however, need the anchor of acknowledged rule of law. To proceed with transformation to freedom without first cementing the rule of law, as Russia did in the early 1990s, is to invite chaos. But the rule of law depends on more than establishing courts and statutes. As Carnegie legal scholar Thomas Carrothers has argued, "it's what's in citizens' heads that matters."

Vaclav Havel whose trajectory from dissident advocate of freedom to President of Czechoslovakia he later summarized as a journey "from the prison cell straight into the presidential palace" (Havel 2014: xv), understood this imperative, but also its difficulty. Thanks to my wife Hana, a political refugee to Canada from Prague, I met Havel shortly after Civic Forum's Velvet Revolution had displaced in November 1989 what had been viewed as the most hardline communist regime in Europe. To Hana's question, "Pan President, what is the first thing you think of on waking up in Prague Castle?" the ex-playwright sighed, "Oh, God, I'm the President." His enduring worry was whether people could learn to "be nicer" to each other, because democracy relies on civic cooperation. To Hana's remonstration he could inspire positive civic behaviour, because the people loved him, he riposted "Sure, they love me now! Wait till they find out we don't know what we're doing." Havel's friend and spokesman Ambassador Michael Zantovsky recalls (in his biography, "*Havel*") the President warned his team, "We are coming in as heroes, but in the end, when they realize what a mess we're in and how little we can do about it, they will railroad us, tarred and feathered, out of town" (Zantovsky 2015). Having realized that "the velvet was wearing thin," Havel anticipated "the hunt for villains, scapegoats and culprits would start soon" (Zantovsky 2015).

It often did, once people who had celebrated 1989s recovery of freedoms in expectation that democracy was synonymous with prosperity, began to realize that, as Fareed Zakaria wrote, "democracy is a long, hard, slog." Havel's was one of several untried democratic governments facing enormous challenges of repairing and transforming societies broken by generations of totalitarian rule. Porter (2010) reported in "*The Ghosts of Europe*" that Polish reformers Kiron, Geremek, and Michnik "confessed" to "shock therapy" proponent Jeffrey Sachs fears "that when they came into power, they would not be able to make enough of a difference in the desperation of people's lives…that they would be held responsible for the crisis."

The post-communist democratic revolution in ex-USSR and Warsaw pact countries became subsumed in Western economic advice of "shock therapy" to enable transition to market economies, in line with neoliberal economic theory that was part of the "Washington consensus" then current. It urged open markets, privatization, de-regulation, and budgetary austerity. But it wrought havoc to pension, welfare, and the bedrock social safety net, causing hyperinflation and vastly wider disparities. A backlash indeed inevitably followed, especially when it became apparent that many "former prisoners of conscience turned out to be ineffectual administrators" (Porter 2010). Populist nationalists soon emerged to exploit voters' discontent, promising to protect the public from accelerated change and disrupting transformation.

When President Havel visited Moscow in 1995, he asked how I estimated the Russian democratic experiment's progress. To my fairly optimistic report, he replied sardonically, "Sixty years. Sixty." After Havel's death in 2011, Michael Zantovsky clarified the source of his cryptic response. In 1990, Havel had read an essay by Ralf Dahrendorf which predicted that a democratic transition could design a new political order in six months, but that it would take six years to change the legal system, economy, and institutions—and *60 years* to change the people's ways of thinking. *It is the people who make democracy work through their civic behaviour. It is civil society that enables them to learn how.*

Civil Society

Civil society—what citizens do together in shared endeavours, often non-political—forms the building blocks of democratic self-realization. It enables citizens to learn from and work with each other towards shared policy and delivery outcomes, developing the necessary habit of achieving consensus in self-governance. In apartheid-era South Africa the Black population was denied the opportunity to organize in civil society, with the exception of churches and football clubs that became in time self-governing incubators of solidarity whose political face was the ANC (African National Congress), the clandestine party of opposition that ultimately prevailed in the historic struggle.

On a reporting trip to Cuba in 2012, I met with the late Cardinal Jaime Ortega who urged I visit a parish day-care centre the Church had instituted at the request of President Raul Castro to relieve over-burdened and inefficiently top-down government day-care facilities. I saw the formation of essential behavioural building blocks in real time, young women for the first-time making decisions about matters vital to their own lives. It wasn't organized as an act of dissent from state-run governance that habitually controlled peoples' lives. But in awarding these young women unaccustomed agency it had the effect of preparing citizens for genuine self-governance.

Hard-line autocracies suppressed civil society's development, especially in the communist bloc. In Poland, the originally union-based "Solidarity" became in 1980 the first mass movement in the bloc outside state or party control. It gave the subsequent transition to democracy a head start. In Tunisia, an active women's movement, unions, and professional societies that had existed for decades provided in 2010 the social capital to enable the revolution that ignited the Arab Spring (though buoyant popular expectations in Tunisia would be disappointed by the daunting economic challenges that remained).

Understanding the Past: What Went Wrong?

Uninformed Advice for the Newly Free in Europe

The transformation expected of formerly communist regimes and societies was unprecedented in scale and depth. The prevailing assumption in both West and East was that the burden of adaptation rested on the new regimes, whilst Western economic and social perspectives could remain more or less intact, as the aspirational norm for all. International financial institutions prescribed the prevailing "Washington consensus" based on faith in the market economy, that favoured de-regulation and severe austerity, but that almost everywhere was accompanied by growing inequality. The economic impact in the transforming countries of this neo-liberal advice and influence was almost universally disruptive. Neophyte democratic governments began to lose popular support, even in the post-communist states of eastern Europe that had an advantage over the USSR, having been modernizing market economies only a few generations prior. The evacuation of communism as a national belief system left a void. New democratic leaders soon concluded that the import of western democratic institutions would not suffice as a replacement belief system. But there was little support for a social revolution to accompany the vivid political changes.

Jacques Rupnik of the Sciences Po points out that imitation cannot provide the authenticity required to meet identity and nation-building needs of newly independent nations. EU and NATO membership for Central and Eastern Europe did offer attractive identity affirmation to peoples that had been cut off from their European family. But accession would require a lengthy process. As populist leaders sought to fill the empty belief space vacated by communism, they plumbed national pasts for ways to ground identity in reformulated traditional national values, often appealing to emotive majoritarian ethnic and tribal bonding that in Milosevic's Serbia, and later, in Hungary and Poland, morphed into nationalist "illiberal democracies."

Global Events, from 1989 to January 6, 2020

China's crackdown on protest at Tianamen Square on June 4, 1989, was a warning that the rush to democracy would not be universal. But globalization proceeded optimistically throughout the 1990s until the jihadist attacks of September 11, 2001, abruptly interrupted the extended belief in "one-world" outcomes. The March 2003 US/UK invasion of Iraq on contrived grounds of securing "democracy" (when other justifications of Iraqi WMD and complicity in the 9/11 attack came up empty), conflated democratic solidarity with an agenda of forceful regime change, undermining the credibility of well-intentioned democracy support, creating *en passant* a transatlantic democratic rift as well.

The negative impact of the financial crisis of 2008 cannot be overstated. It deepened depletion of confidence in Western leadership (and in what Obama called "an economic philosophy that has completely failed.") But little effort was made to reform it; the focus of crisis coordination was on preventing financial collapse. Though industrialized governments stabilized the world economy, the insecurity and loss experienced by many ordinary people by reckless banking practices remained largely unaddressed in substantive effect. Economic disparities continued to widen in almost every country. Populist illiberal nationalists exploited the disrepute of neo-liberal laissez-faire economics and associated it with liberal democracy. In established democracies, working-class income stagnation deepened hostility to globalization that was blamed for the export of jobs.

Increasingly, tribal, nationalistic, and even racial and sectarian identity issues held sway with significant portions of populations, driven by what they wanted to believe no matter the facts. Ubiquitous, unmediated, polarizing, and destabilizing social media that empowered and amplified extreme voices, including those projected into the democratic arena by outside adversaries, grew in global influence. Nonetheless, the ignition in 2010 in Tunisia of the "Arab Spring" spurred hope in autocratic Middle Eastern societies that reform, indeed revolution, was possible. In Cairo's Tahrir Square, it inspired demonstrators who proclaimed impatience, not primarily for other peoples' "democracy" but for an end to autocracy and for fairness, and dignity.

Clearly, non-violent protestors lacked coherence and cooperation. They were either easily outmaneuvered by organized Islamist opponents, as in Egypt, or were crushed by ruthless autocratic clans in power, as in Syria, where the catastrophic costs of civil war claimed more than 400,000 lives, and displaced more than 11 million, including several million refugees. In Tunisia, elected democratic governments couldn't cope with economic challenges. Tunisians would lose optimism that the advent of democracy promised swift prosperity.

Authoritarians Took Their Cues

The autocratic use of massive violence to retain power quashed dissent in Daraa, Moscow, Hong Kong, Caracas, Yangon, Minsk, Iran, and elsewhere. Backsliding democracies weakened judicial and other safeguards to protect human rights, eventually from Budapest to Brazil and even to Washington. After 2016, the impact of the Trump Administration was toxic. Trump applauded nationalistic trends whilst scorning human rights. US assertion of "America First" provided autocrats with exemplary permissive license. They followed its divisive playbooks, stoking and exploiting polarization rooted in economic and cultural resentments. Even in democratic Europe "conspiracy theories, driven by the global health crisis, are taking root … drawing inspiration from the QAnon movement in the US" (AFP 2021). A backlash against refugees and migrants fomented nativist alienation, islamophobia, and populist nationalism, deepening loss of confidence in government spurred by the 2008 financial near collapse.

Such trends were cheered on by Chinese and Russian leaders, by now open adversaries of liberal democracies, philosophically, and geopolitically, especially after the "Colour revolutions" in Belgrade, Tbilisi, Kiev and elsewhere, and mass protest in Hong Kong. As Clover (2015) put it in *Black Wind, White Snow* about Russia's experience under Putin, "liberalism replaced capitalism as the enemy of the people." In consequence, authoritarians today outlaw foreign support for local democracy advocates and human rights defenders, hobbling the ability of the global democracy community to provide more than moral solidarity.

The Force of Disappointment

Though Havel seemed pessimistic in the 1990s about the timeline he expected for transition, he correctly anticipated what he described to President Obama as "the curse of people's high expectations. Because it means they are easily disappointed." Such disappointment has been a major factor in making personalist "false democracies" the prevalent form of governance. These regimes diligently appropriate the facade of democracy—all but 5 non-democracies since 2000 have held elections to acquire the veneer of legitimacy and popular mandate—whilst incrementally undermining the checks and balances, judicial independence, and media freedom on which democracy relies. Authoritarian leaders of EU member Hungary and NATO member Turkey now respectively control 90% and 85% of national media. Autocrats increasingly throttle civil society's value as democracy's incubator, thereby stifling experience of agency and the reflex of compromise, essential to democratic outcomes. Factually interfering in western democratic processes, whilst rebutting as illegitimate any criticism of their own internal repression, Russia and China became self-appointed champions for the revived doctrine of non-intervention in internal affairs, dear to Brazil and India, even though Russian credibility should by now be shattered by its attack on Ukraine. The central question for liberal democracies is "what is to be done?" Human rights are paramount.

Since 1989, much has been grasped about best practices for transit to democracy. The forefront conclusion is that each national trajectory is different. Neither is there a single systemic model nor organizational template for a successful democratic transition. *But the availability of universal human rights remains an essential precondition.* In our international democracy development support project's outreach over a decade 2007–2016, we encountered pushback from friends and officials of the Government of France, who argued that the primary emphasis should be on the essentiality of human rights rather than on the effort to *promote* democracy. It was a long-standing French belief that the perception of US-led democracy promotion had conflated it into being a perceived surrogate for US-led influence and economic doctrine. Democracy promotion became as apt to divide countries as to bring them together, being seen by many non-democracies as an unacceptable intrusion on national sovereignty. But by contrast, human rights are in principle litigatable internationally. Almost all countries are signatories of the relevant foundation covenants of the United Nations and other international bodies.

The differentiation is not one of sequence but instead of interdependence, because democracy and human rights are integrally linked. Without human rights, civil society has little chance to breathe. Without the breath of civil society, democracy has little opportunity to grow. Human rights are therefore basic to democratic evolution. If they are present, inclusive democracy development has a way to gain traction, provided that democratic aspirants, once in office, are able to deliver effective government to the electorate. The question is how democracies can best contribute. Ambassador Pierre Vimont, inaugural head of the European Union's External Action Service posed as a primary obligation of democracies the protection of human rights defenders, but also asked, "How far can you go?" (Kinsman and Bassuener 2014: 4). Democracies should begin by holding all countries—beginning with themselves—to their commitments to international human rights covenants.

Democracies have the leverage of favour and influence. Foreign relations form concentric circles. Inner circles of close relationships with corresponding benefits will necessarily be reserved for trusted partners. Evidence of human rights abuse should inevitably affect the quality and intensity of bilateral relationships. This principle *must be consistently applied,* irrespective of country-specific transactional. commercial, and geo-political interests. There is some merit in preferential "friend-shoring" theses that urge democratic solidarity in supply chains and economic security, provided they don't again divide the world into two opposing camps. But democratic governments have to pay attention to the fact that everywhere, governments are struggling with the effects of change, much of it adverse and exogenous.

The very stressed conditions in much of the world need the consistent and if possible concerted attention of the world community, where alignments are to some extent changing. India's Foreign Minister S. Jaishankar sees a "very very deeply Western world order being hurried out of existence by the impact of the war in Ukraine, to be replaced by a world of *multi-alignment*" (Cohen 2022). He accused western leaders of believing that "Europe's problems are the world's problems, but the world's problems are not Europe's (Cohen 2022)."

Thomas Homer-Dixon has used Adam Tooze's phrase "polycrisis" to encompass "the underlying natural and social stresses contributing to today's multitude of crises. Often called "systemic risks, they include climate heating, zoonotic disease outbreaks, biodiversity decline, worsening economic inequality, financial system instability, ideological extremism, cyber-attacks, mounting social and political unrest, and geopolitical imbalances" (Homer-Dixon and Rockström 2022). Democracies can't successfully advertise the merits of rights and democracies without addressing these overwhelming exogenous issues.

They are inter-related in cause and effect. As the UNDP Report (2022) spells out, 54 developing countries (representing 3% of the global economy) accounting for 1/2 of the world's population, face such high debt burdens that without relief they have little hope of financing an energy transition." Their governments are against the wall from such exogenous forces, which is often bad news for fragile democratic regimes.

As Pippa Norris (2021) argues, "Sometimes, people really do want leaders who prioritize order and security from outside threats, adhere to traditional norms, and promise to defend the tribe." But autocratic populist governments rarely do deliver outcomes on substantive public issues more effectively than democracies. To compensate, they pitch their populist appeal to divisive overriding identity-based cultural and patriotic issues, scapegoating "enemies" within and without. Emotive causes supersede sober analyses.

How Can Democracies Best Support Democracy Development?

Can democratic diplomacy and political engagement be viewed in new ways to enable better partnering to support democratic development?

We Need a New Paradigm for Democracy Support. Old Donor Country-Recipient Country Development Models don't Apply. A Spirit of Mutual Learning is Essential

Initially, programs to assist post-Cold War transitions in ex-Iron Curtain countries assumed a symmetry of intentions, and placed the focus on institutional mentoring, and election mechanics. A review of the experience of the UK Know-How Fund that was the response to the transformational challenges that followed events in Europe in 1989 concluded that "reform assistance only works when reformers want to reform" (*Learning From History Seminar, 30 October, 2013: From the Know-How Fund to the Arab Partnership*). As a US Ambassador cited put it, "the over-riding lesson is that without some degree of consensus and political reform, the input of assistance in political and economic eforms is limited." Beneficiaries end up being primarily donor country contractors.

The UK experience—familiar to Canada's—was summarized by Mark Lowcock, Permanent Under-Secretary of the Department for International Development: "if the success measure is how fast we are spending the money, we are doing quite well. If the success measure is the breadth of the smiles on the faces of British consultants, we are doing fantastically well." We need to choose the most effective vehicles for the transfer of capacity that succeeds with the partners in advancing their democracy.

Democracy development assistance needs to be de-bureaucratized and increasingly delegated. The most helpful route is via civil society. The country-case studies in *A Diplomat's Handbook* revealed that "the best vehicles for outside support (for civil society actors) are rarely government programs, however well-intentioned." They are not good at it. Outside support for democratic capacity-building potential comes best from international civil society partnerships, with the lead partner being the one inside the country. "The partnership support budgets of democracies should show as much support for civil society as possible. There are calls to apportion 25–30% of development support funds to civil society to administer directly. Juxtaposing beneficial connective tissue via direct civil society-to-civil society links, often for functional non-political and local civil society projects needs to be enhanced.

Democracies Should Share Assessments and Agree on Basic Principles

Can democratic countries cohere basic principles of concept and operation?

1. Conceptually, without proposing that there is a single theory of transitional success, Western democracies should acknowledge basic normative assumptions about conditions needed for democratization, such as:
   – Democracy cannot be exported.
   – Democracy needs to emerge authentically from within the country in question.
   – There is no single theory or preferred template, but respect for civil liberties and human rights, gender equity, and an open environment for media commentary and reporting are foundational.
   – Inclusivity is essential—unless citizens enjoy equal rights, the country's status is not democratic.
   – Fairness and respect for human dignity are paramount; corruption corrodes conclusively.
   – Democracy's building blocks are bottom-up, lodged in civil society, where participants experience agency and the essential facility of compromise.
   – Civic behaviour needs time to become second nature to citizens, though some societies (e.g., Taiwan, and the Republic of Korea) show a faster track than others.

- Each trajectory is different, and outcomes vary, including truth and reconciliation efforts linked to respectful pacting between old and new orders.
2. Operationally, working together with civil society partners, democracies should:
   - Share needs analyses, audits, best practices, to enable comparisons of benefit:
   - Divide labour, and leverage national contributions to maximize comparative advantage, often cooperating on country-specific projects.

Multilateralism

Democracies are generally, by disposition, multilateralists. They help build democratic capacity and norms into multilateral functional organizations which radiate them outward. They should:

Ensure the democratic value standards of multilateral "clubs"—the EU, NATO, OECD, Council of Europe/ECHR, the Commonwealth, La Francophonie, OAS, etc.—are actually applied;
Use sanctions selectively and judiciously to encourage correct international behaviour only after considering the alternative of positive incentives (as in the JCPOA with Iran);
Cooperate via diplomatic missions, which should maintain local encouragement for civil society and support of independent media if possible, and demarche collectively incidents of unaddressed human rights abuse.

Other Actors, Policy Imperatives, and Positive Messaging

International business investments can play an important role in channeling inclusive and equitable governance. If corporate practices of outside investors consciously align local activity with governance norms that are obligatory in industrialized democracies, it can embed in the local workplace ethics such as transparency, accountability, meritocracy, sustainability, and gender equity that can transfer to civil society more broadly. Democratic countries (indeed all countries) should prosecute vigorously evidence of corrupt practices abroad and end the competition to offer profitable havens to oligarchic and criminal wealth. Arms sales to dictatorships and repressive regimes are a toxic insult to the professed beliefs and credibility of democratic countries.

THE FAKE NEWS PHENOMENON

Whatever democratic governments do to support democracy development and human rights would be semi-futile without parallel attention to the Internet's contribution to polarization and illiberalism. Clearly, the early notion the Internet would bring people together and enable sharing of evidence-based information has been overtaken by the pernicious phenomena of (a) fabrication and dissemination of alternate realities through ubiquitous and unregulated social media, and (b) suppression of free media and commentary.

a. *Platform Governance*: Dr. Ulrike Klinger, Professor of Political Theory and Digital Democracy at the European New School of Digital Studies points out that social media are not an exogenous factor; they "are" society. Social media platforms themselves do not threaten democracy, but their business models have harmful collateral effects. "They did not invent disinformation, hate speech, radicalization or propaganda, but they make it worse. Their business models and the design of their largely intransparent and non-accountable algorithmic systems reward and fuel negativity, hate and anger, reinforcing the overblown impact of aggressive, abusive hyperactive users and groups…They are built for profit, not to promote rational discourse…Their lack of transparency and accountability are fundamental obstacles to the functioning of democratic public spheres." (Paper presented to RODA conference, Montreal, Sep 30, 2022). To "ensure public values, and rights, are kept in the forefront," Dr. Klinger stresses it is up to society to force change in platform behaviour. Currently, platforms are optimized for profit maximization only. "While technologies are neither 'good' nor 'bad,' they are not neutral either, but must be re-designed to not wreak havoc on the public sphere. Like with any technology, societies need time to find ways to regulate it, and the time is now."

Dr. Klinger urges the EU and countries such as Germany and Canada to provide leadership in platform regulation by shoring up human agency as the driving factor—to take control, via formal legislative initiatives.

b. *Freedom of the Press*: To defend freedom of the press, without which democracy cannot flourish, and to diminish the destructive effect of disinformation and propaganda, Antoine Bernard, Research Director of Reporters Without Borders (RSF), urges support for the *Forum on Information and Democracy,* that was created by RSF and 10 civil society organizations to propose regulatory frameworks and public policies. At the United Nations General Assembly in 2021, the Forum announced the formation of a coalition of democracies to enable the safeguarding of a "democratic information space" via an International Observatory on Information and Democracy. To support Russian journalists in exile, RSF created the JX Fund whose first project has been the launch of *Novaya Gazeta "Europe."* To counter the blocking in Russia of trustworthy news producers, RSF initiated "Collateral Freedom" that enables continued access to censored websites, such as Meduza, Deutsche Welle, "Rain TV," Radio France International and France 24 TV. Canada should be a leader in advancing the above precepts and initiatives amongst democratic nations. Democracies should increase funding to the non-governmental International Fund for Public Interest Media.

Recommendation for a Solidarity Network

The Renewing Our Democratic Alliance project (RODA) between Canadian and German civil society actors concluded in 2022 two years of consultation by urging pro-democracy actors to establish a new like-minded group of governments and international civil society to concert to protect democracy, defend human rights, and strengthen international cooperation to enable effective outcomes on the inter-connected challenges facing humanity today. A Network for Democratic Solidarity would aim to strengthen and protect global commitment to universally acknowledged civil liberties and human rights and concert against the systemic export of malicious disinformation.

The Network would also provide a channel for participating states and civil society organizations to coordinate policy responses on inter-linked multilateral issues, to build traction for effective decision-making in international fora that are today polarized. The group will promote the sort of overall oversight and coordination of a system that is currently siloed by often negotiating solitudes, that compete sector-by-sector. The new likeminded group would begin with a core group of inclusive and globalist democracies, plus international civil society, from the South and North, and operate in the spirit of mutual learning in a pluralistic world. The group will start from the perception that constant vigilance in the quality of their own democracy is essential to the credibility of efforts to support democracy elsewhere.

Overall, democratic publics need to pay more attention to the lives of others. In developed countries, and notably in Canada, global and international issue gets short shrift from mainstream media.

An eternal debate in the conduct of foreign policy is how to calibrate the right mix of "values" and interests. Canada's internationalist vocation and the view that human rights are indivisible made the "lives of others" an enduring preoccupation of Canadian globalist policy for decades, in keeping with democratic values and other principles that guide our Charter of Rights and Freedoms. They are not an ideological end in themselves but constitute "a form of government relying on the consent of the governed… a means of fulfilling individual lives and pursuing common purposes" (Kinsman and Bassuener 2014). In 1989, Vaclav Havel wrote to the PEN International Congress in Montreal (which he was not permitted by Czechoslovak authorities to attend in person) of the "venerable practice of international solidarity." "In today's world, more and more people are aware of the indivisibility of human fate on this planet, that the problems of anyone of us, or whatever country we come from -be it the smallest and most forgotten—are the problems of us all; that our freedom is indivisible as well, and that we all believe in the same basic values, while sharing common fears about the threats that are hanging over humanity today."

It rings as truly now as it did then. But as a country, and as people, we have to do more than just declare our indivisibility in sentiment and attachment to values. We have to find ways to provide concrete solidarity through practical support and cooperation, not as just a sidepreoccupation of government, but as a core concern of foreign policy, as internationalist leaders in democracy development support.

REFERENCES

Agence France Presse. 2021. Conspiracy epidemic, born in US, spreads in Europe. *France 24*, May 17, 2021. https://www.france24.com/en/live-news/20210517-conspiracy-epidemic-born-in-us-spreads-in-europe

Clover, Charles. 2015. *Black Wind, White Snow*. New Haven: Yale University Press.

Cohen, Roger. 2022. The Ascent of India. *New York Times*, December 31, 2022.

Havel, Václav. 2014. Preface to *A Diplomat's Handbook for Democracy Development Support*, eds. Jeremy Kinsman, and Kurt Bassuener, xv-xvi. Ontario: The Centre for International Governance Innovation in Partnership with the Council for a Community of Democracies.

Homer-Dixon, Thomas, and Rockström, Johan. 2022. What Happens When a Cascade of Crises Collide? *New York Times*, November 13, 2022. https://www.nytimes.com/2022/11/13/opinion/coronavirus-ukraine-climate-inflation.html. Accessed 23 Jan 2023.

Kinsman, Jeremy, and Bassuener, Kurt (eds.). Introduction to *A Diplomat's Handbook for Democracy Development Support*. Ontario: The Centre for International Governance Innovation in Partnership with the Council for a Community of Democracies.

Norris, Pippa. 2021. Voters Against Democracy, Roots of Autocratic Insurgence. https://www.foreignaffairs.com/reviews/voters-against-democracy. *Foreign Affairs*, May/June 2021. https://www.foreignaffairs.com/reviews/voters-against-democracy. Accessed Jan 2023.

Porter, Ann. 2010. *The Ghosts of Europe: Journeys through Central Europe's Troubled Past and Uncertain Future*. Vancouver: Douglas & McIntyre.

V-Dem Democracy Reports. 2022. *Autocratization Changing Nature*. Gothenburg: University of Gothenburg. https://v-dem.net/media/publications/dr_2022.pdf

V-Dem Democracy Reports. 2023. *Defiance in the Face of Autocratization*. Gothenburg: University of Gothenburg. https://www.v-dem.net/documents/29/V-dem_democracyreport2023_lowres.pdf

UNDP Report. 2022. *Avoiding 'Too Little, Too Late' on International Debt Relief*. New York: UNDP. https://www.undp.org/sites/g/files/zskgke326/files/2022-10/UNDP-DFS-Avoiding-Too-Little-Too-Late-on-International-Debt-Relief-V3_1.pdf

Zantovsky, Michael. 2015. *Havel: A life*. New York City: Grove Press.

CHAPTER 4

Democracy and Foreign Policy: A Retrospective

Maxwell A. Cameron

INTRODUCTION

Democracy and Foreign Policy, the 1995 edition of the Canada Among Nations series, was written at a time of shifting policy frames. With the end of the Cold War, scholars and policymakers began to rethink the role of democracy both *in* foreign policy and as an objective *of* foreign policy. In the realist conception of global politics that dominated international relations theory in the Cold War era, domestic institutions were regarded as secondary to the structure of anarchy—understood as the absence of government—in international affairs. Although the Cold War had been framed as a contest between capitalist democracies and totalitarianism, realists argued that in crucial respects all states behaved similarly: they sought at a minimum their own defense and, at a maximum, to dominate other states (Waltz 1979). This viewpoint lost credence with

M. A. Cameron (✉)
Department of Political Science & School of Public Policy and Global Affairs, University of British Columbia, Vancouver, BC, Canada
e-mail: Max.Cameron@ubc.ca

© The Author(s), under exclusive license to Springer Nature Switzerland AG 2023
M. A. Cameron et al. (eds.), *Democracy and Foreign Policy in an Era of Uncertainty,* Canada and International Affairs,
https://doi.org/10.1007/978-3-031-35490-8_4

the collapse of the Soviet Union and the prospect of another "wave" of democratization in the post-Soviet successor states.

Already in the 1980s, scholars like Michael Doyle (1983) were noticing that democracies do not engage in warfare with other democracies. Hobbes fell out of fashion and Kant was back in; the conflict between friends and enemies was replaced by competition among rivals. Scholars like Bruce Russett et al. (1995) suggested that democracies are governed by norms, including publicity that promote peace. Since democratic governments need to secure the support of domestic public opinion before they launch an attack on another country, and since mobilization for war in a democracy tends to be very public, it is hard to surprise other states with unilateral aggression. The data also showed that democracies *do* fight non-democracies—and with considerable regularity. An obvious implication of this finding was that democratic states have a security interest in preservation of democracy in the inter-state system.

Influenced by such findings, we began the 1995 edition of *Canada Among Nations* with the question of democracy as a foreign policy aim or objective. If democracies do not fight one another, can they work together to strengthen democracy globally? Moreover, might such a logic foster an interest in promoting democracy at home as well as abroad? Indeed, might foreign policymaking itself be more democratic? We postulated that the imperative to strengthen democracy globally might encourage nations to reinforce their democratic institutions at home, building public support for democracy through the recognition of its critical importance to international peace, and thus using foreign policy not just as an instrument for advancing national interests but also as an expression of democratic values. This gave rise to a discussion of a values-based foreign policy. It also generated a debate over whether expert consultations in foreign policymaking was a meaningful from of public engagement or mere window-dressing. An optimistic view of the role of democracy in foreign policy was outlined in the Liberal Party's Red Book (see discussion in Cameron and Molot 1995b: 9–10); it called for strengthening the role of parliament in foreign policymaking and public consultation on the direction of foreign policy—in short, the "democratization of foreign policy-making" (Liberal Party of Canada, 1993).

The optimism about a democratic peace and the suggestion that foreign policy could be made more democratically seem out of step with the present moment in global politics. As the world reels at Russian aggression against the Ukraine, it is worth returning to these issues. Russia has engaged in the kind of aggression that is possible in a secretive, tightly-knit authoritarian regime where power is concentrated in the hands of a single autocratic individual or small group. It is almost inconceivable that the invasion of the Ukraine would have occurred had Russia achieved a successful transition to democracy. That did not happen in part due to the failure to create a politically regulated market economy. In her thoughtful essay on "Democracy and the Problem of Government in Russia" in *Democracy and Foreign Policy*, Andrea Chandler (1995) cautioned foreign policymakers that Russia was having serious difficulties establishing democratic institutions and the transition to markets via shock therapy was creating violence, instability, and hardship.

China represents a different problem. By achieving economic transformation under an authoritarian regime that systematically violates human rights, China demonstrated not only that rapid economic growth can be achieved without the kind of free market policies advocated under the "Washington Consensus," but also that authoritarian regimes can be durable as incomes rise (as noted by Przeworski and Limongi 1997). Perhaps even more troubling from the perspective of neoliberal globalization is the erosion of democracy in the United States. Trump's complaints about the "carnage" caused by bad trade deals and job-stealing migrants tapped into grievances arising from an increasingly unequal and polarized political system (Edsall 2022). As the US political system has become more oligarchic (Bartels 2008; Foweraker 2021), the commitment of its leaders to democracy abroad has waned. The election of Joe Biden in 2020 temporarily reversed this trend, but Republican extremism eliminated the bipartisan consensus on democracy in foreign policy that took root under the Reagan presidency.

These trends invite renewed reflection. That democracy is vital for countries like Canada to defend is a proposition I accept, but needs to be nuanced. The trends I have just noted point to a deeper intellectual crisis of liberal democracy. The end of the Cold War not only failed to produce a more harmonious world based on a comity of liberal democracies: it failed to do so precisely because of an over-confidence in the inexorable advance of liberalism and democracy despite the highly uneven effects of market-led globalization. In addition, emerging global issues like climate change, reconciliation with Indigenous peoples, and the management of pandemics have intersected with globalization in ways that challenge liberal democracies to address human needs beyond the immediate interests of voters and politicians within the confines of the nation state.

Consider some of the key challenges facing the world in the third decade of the twenty-first century. Liberal democracies need to find ways to include the needs of future generations in policy decisions (Shue 2022). In 1987, the Brundtland Report harshly criticized the "spendthrift ways" in which current generations "overdraw" environmental resources that cannot be repaid: "We act as we do because we can get away with it: future generations do not vote; they have not political of financial power; they cannot challenge our decisions." Decades later, the message from the Intergovernmental Panel on Climate Change (2022) is essentially the same: the window is closing on a livable future for humanity.

Liberal democracies also need to supplement abstract and individualistic notions of citizenship with recognition of diverse cultures, histories, and systems of knowledge (Lightfoot and MacDonald 2017: 35). In coming to terms with the harms caused by ongoing colonialism—a process facilitated by a Royal Commission, a Truth and Reconciliation Commission, an Indian Residential Schools Settlement Agreement, and the adoption of the United Nations Declaration on the Rights of Indigenous Peoples—Canadians are beginning to realize that repairing the relations with First Nations cannot be achieved without decolonizing institutions and practices. Finally, the COVID-19 pandemic has taught us that demagoguery and nationalism can be an impediment to achieving global common goods. Liberal democracy may be the best system of government we have, but it is still insufficient. At the conclusion of this chapter, I suggest ways it can and must be supplemented.

Policy Frames: Conflict, Competition, Crisis

Setting aside "alternative facts" peddled by demagogues, public policy controversies rarely revolve around disagreements over facts. Instead, they involve contrasting frames, which can be understood as mental maps that help us to interpret patterns and regularities in an often-chaotic world (Schwartz and Sharpe 2010; Rein and Schön 1996). Like all maps, policy frames provide pictures that highlight what we consider most worthy of attention. They engage our capacity for making decisions based on the discernment of relevant facts and relationships (Schwartz and Sharpe

2010: 61–62). Often frames involve narratives—stories we tell ourselves that imbue actions with meaning and purpose.

Linguist George Lakoff (2004) notes the crucial role of language in framing. The use of certain evocative words can conjure particular frames and thereby influence our understanding of the world and our attitudes toward it. A parent walking with a child might describe a forest as enchanted and magical, or evil and dangerous. The choice of words in that context are likely to influence the experience of the child. The words we use to describe global politics are likewise evocative of alternative frames.

Framing matters from a democratic perspective because the activity of self-government demands that we work through deliberative processes to achieve decisions to act collectively in the public sphere. Framing aids decision-makers as they make the leap from analysis to action; it assists them in breaching the gap between what there is and what we ought to do about it. Since policy frames often work by providing the implicit or unstated narrative arc that gives meaning and coherence to action, competing frames can lead to different decisions and actions even as decision-makers agree about the relevant facts on the ground. The source of disagreement needs to be excavated through analysis of implicit frames.

I suggest three competing frames for thinking about democracy in foreign policy. The first emphasizes conflict and calls itself realistic. In a world of states, where there is no overarching authority to punish aggression, all states must look out for their own interests. This frame evokes a Hobbesian world of war of all against all. A contrasting neoliberal frame emphasizes competition and suggests that states and non-state actors are motivated by the desire to maximize their interests, and this can be harnessed by institutions that foster competition. A third frame is critical in the sense that it emphasizes crises, the unviability of the status quo, and the need for change. It highlights the accumulation of wicked problems derived from over-population, unrestrained growth, the limits of environmental carrying capacity of the planet, the collapse of ecosystems and species diversity, climate change, pandemics, mass movements of peoples, and violence and polarization.

Each of these policy frames has distinct implications for democracy, which will be explored below. Whereas realists question the relevance of democracy to foreign policy, neoliberals embrace democracy as a foreign policy goal, and critical theorists warn us about the capacity of democracy to respond to the multiple, overlapping crises of our times. I begin with the much-noted crisis of liberal democracy.

The Freeland Doctrine: A Neoliberal Frame?

For the purposes of this analysis, a good place to begin a discussion of the way in which Canadian foreign policy framing intersects with the current crisis of liberal democracy is with Deputy Prime Minister Chrystia Freeland's October 2022 speech to the Brookings Institution in Washington D.C. I argue that the "Freeland Doctrine" represents a continuation of neoliberal foreign policy thinking—complete with the same flawed assumptions—but under new circumstances.[1]

Freeland stated that "The past 33 years were guided by an idealism that was both high-minded and—for the countries of the transatlantic alliance—supremely comfortable. We were fat and happy, assured in our belief that we could do good by doing well." Freeland insists that the intentions of the West were benevolent: "With hindsight, it is easy to mock the hubris and the naiveté which animated that era. But as we set about building its successor, it is important to start by remembering how generous and humane our intentions were." But she acknowledges that the announcement of an End of History (see Fukuyama 2006) was not accompanied by effective and consistent efforts to put the West's the universal rights and values into practice. She does not, however, question that these values are universal. "The End of History was founded on the profoundly liberal and egalitarian conviction that everyone in the world had the right and the ability to live as well as we do. That is why it was such a powerful and promising idea."

Later, I will return to the implications of the claim "everyone in the world had the right and the ability to live as well as we do." Here, I merely note the irony that Gerald Butts, former Principal Secretary to Prime Minister Trudeau (2015–2019), when he was President and CEO of the World Wildlife Foundation, argued that four planets like earths would be required if everyone consumed resources the way Canadians do (World Wildlife Foundation [WWF] 2010).

Freeland argued that the "End of History had an economic corollary": as countries became prosperous through trade, democracy would become inevitable and war would become an anachronism. The democratic peace

---

[1] The speech assumes considerable import since last major comprehensive review of Canadian foreign policy was undertaken by the government of Pierre Trudeau in the late 1960s. The most recent review was interrupted by 9/11, completed several years later, and was largely ignored by the Harper government (Mulroney 2020; Levin Bonder 2019).

was, in this view, reinforced by the "Golden Arches Theory": no two countries in which McDonald's operates would wage war on each other. In short, democracy and prosperity were seen as mutually reinforcing, both contributing to international harmony. Freeland acknowledges that this view was mistaken. Authoritarian regimes will not inevitably decline, and "economic interdependence" does "not always prevent war." In short, "We need to assume that in the decades to come we will be sharing the planet with rich and powerful countries who do not share our values—who, in fact, often see our values as both hostile and inferior to theirs."

Another way to think about the corollary of the End of History is in terms of competition as a driver of institutional change. Francis Fukuyama (2011) argues that institutional change is the result of competition. Competition among societies produces processes of institutional change that lead to winners (good institutions) prevailing over losers (bad ones). The end of the Cold War was interpreted by Fukuyama as a victory of good institutions over bad ones. Freeland acknowledges that liberal democracies have not prevailed but does not depart from a competitive view of international politics.

Her critique of the End of History leads to three propositions. First, "the world's democracies, must strengthen our connections with each other, "including 'friendshoring'" (by which "democracies must make a conscious effort to build our supply chains through each other's economies"). Second, the "in-between countries" (that is, those neither in the friendshoring alliance nor among its adversaries, primarily from the global South) must be welcomed if they are prepared to play by the rules and "share our values." Ultimately, "our own success" will be key to "victory" which will be achieved "by delivering widespread prosperity for our own people." Finally, democracies must be firm with autocrats: "authoritarian regimes are fundamentally hostile to us…Our success is an existential threat to them." Democracies must avoid vulnerabilities and ensure they cannot be blackmailed by autocrats.

The first proposition appears at a glance to be consistent with a Kantian vision of democratic peace. Democracies have every right to engage more closely with other democracies and to shun autocracies. Moreover, building preferential economic linkages is a good way of creating incentives for other regimes to seek inclusion in the club of democracies. Such a logic has informed diverse market-driven integration projects. Moreover, Freeland explicitly advocates the inclusion of democracies that are not among the wealthy nations of the "non-geographic West." Yet her analysis side-steps rising inequality, exacerbated by market-driven globalization. She notes but does not articulate an alternative to what she calls the "turbocharged globalization of the past 30 years."

And yet, this turbocharged globalization has contributed to the existential crossroads that Freeland has described in several ways. First, the global economy is a victim of its own success. The rise and occasional alignment of the BRICs—Brazil, Russia, India, and especially China—has deadlocked international trade negotiations, undermining the hegemony of the United States as a rule-maker in the global economy (Hopewell 2020). Second, globalization has produced a backlash, consistent with what Karl Polanyi called the "double movement" in which the market-led globalization produces countervailing pressures for social protection (Evans 2008). The rise of the Latin American left since 2000 can be seen as a reaction against the neoliberal model of development enshrined in the institutions that promote globalization. Finally, globalization contributed to the rise of nativist and nationalist leaders like Donald Trump, Vladimir Putin, Viktor Orbán, Giorgia Meloni, and Jair Bolsonaro.

Freeland rightly seeks to avoid a return to Cold War era conflict but proposes to do so by reinforcing the institutionalized competition of neoliberal globalization. Freeland notes it was a mistake to assume "that we could do good by doing well." And yet, instead of interrogating this connection, she reaffirms it by arguing that "our own success" will be key to "victory." The contemporary crisis of democracy will not be resolved through intensifying or reconstituting the competitive market forces that created the crisis in the first place. Global conflict is to be avoided but liberal thinkers, especially neoliberals, often miss the ways in which liberalism itself contributes to generating conflict. As classical realists are fond of noting, conflict is often the product of liberal idealism. The Wilsonian idea of "making the world safe for democracy" is an example, and Freeland's "friendshoring" has similarly belligerent implications. By contrast, realism emphasizes the importance of prudence: a hard-headed appreciation of the role of power and violence in politics and the necessity of minimizing their evils effects. It is not my goal to offer a defense of classical realism, however, but rather to offer a critical perspective on the assumption that we might "do good by doing well" competitively.

A Critical Perspective on the New Policy Frame

Liberalism is an insufficient bulwark against today's polarization and extremism, as indeed it was in the 1930s. We tend to forget that one of the great lessons of the 1930s was precisely that in a context of globalization liberal democracy was vulnerable to extremism, and therefore, government had a role in balancing the inequalities created by market forces. As David Harvey (2005: 9) has written: "The restructuring of state forms and of international relations after the Second World War was designed to prevent a return to the catastrophic conditions that had so threatened the capitalist order in the great slump of the 1930s." This created conditions conducive to the class compromises that historically underpinned the social welfare state.

The Bretton Woods institutions were designed to allow states to provide for welfare because Keynes and others of his generation understood that without a flexible system of regulation of markets the backlash against an open global economy would be inevitable. This was aptly described by John Ruggie (1982) as the "compromise of embedded liberalism." The breakdown of this compromise happened for reasons that are too complex to address here. Suffice it to say that, beginning in the late 1970s and early 1980s, the global marketplace became increasingly dis-embedded from social or political regulation. Neoliberal thinkers rose to prominence precisely at the historic moment that the USSR collapsed, thereby contributing to the triumphalism and hubris mentioned by Freeland.

A return to the embedded liberalism of the past is unlikely. The power of globally mobile financial capital and the erosion of democratic regulation places social democracy at risk or out of reach in most countries, especially the most powerful driver of global capitalism, the United States. There are, however, powerful forces at work in the current crisis that offer a glimpse of what the future might hold in terms of disrupting existing policy frames. Two are mentioned by Freeland, and one is neglected; confronting them seriously calls into question the viability of her three propositions.

The first is the climate crisis. Freeland notes that "even as we are more cautious and more limited in our economic ties with authoritarian regimes, we need to work with them to preserve the global commons. That means, first and foremost, continuing to work together on tackling the preeminent threat of climate change." Freeland recognizes that the climate crisis cannot be addressed without China. "We cannot save the planet today without working with Beijing."

It is unclear how a strategy of isolation or containment of authoritarianism offers hope for global cooperation on climate change. Freeland argues that "A more overtly suspicious attitude toward the world's dictators need not preclude, or even imperil, cooperating on common goals." Yet, it seems likely that with regard to China "common goals" will involve contributing to rather than fighting climate change. Although the Trudeau government promised action on climate change, and a nationwide price on emissions was created, Canada is far from achieving its targets. The fight against climate change has not prevented Canadian contributions to emissions through its exports. Coal was Canada's top export to China in 2022. Despite its commitment to limiting global warming to 1.5 degrees Celsius, the Trudeau government will spend an estimated $21 billion to expand the Trans Mountain Pipeline with the goal of exporting more crude oil to Asia. Already most of the Canadian crude that gets re-exported after being refined in the US Gulf Coast goes to China (Jaremko 2021). Freeland's vision of friendshoring would not reduce Canada's efforts to ship fossil fuels to China. It is small wonder elements of the business community responded enthusiastically to the speech, pressing for more subsidies and regulatory changes to foster mining and energy projects (Corcoran 2022).

Cooperation with China would require an effort on the part of the Quad to understand that country's legitimate developmental goals. But to do this implies recognizing that the economic model advanced by the rich countries cannot be imposed on the global South. A "win–win" relationship with China seems a remote possibility unless the "non-geographic West" can re-design the global economic order to allow wealth to be shared with the global South. The South will need a global redistribution of wealth in order to adapt to climate harms that they have contributed little to creating, and rich countries will need that redistribution of wealth to secure their contributions. Yet, we are far from a world in which the global redistribution of wealth is given serious consideration.

The second doubt expressed by Freeland concerns "my country's original sin against Indigenous Peoples." Yet, Freeland seems primarily concerned to avoid self-doubt that would make the defense of liberal democracy vulnerable: "an awareness of unredeemed historical crimes, and of our serious fresh challenges, in no way contradicts my equally profound conviction that the liberal democracy we are so lucky to enjoy in Canada is the best way humans have found, so far, to organize a society. Self-criticism is a feature of democracies—not a bug. But it is a pitiless mirror that can rattle our self-confidence when we measure ourselves against tyrants and their armour of oblivion."

There is much to unpack here, starting with the challenge of accommodating Indigenous self-determination within the framework of liberal democracy. This demands legal pluralism and recognition of Indigenous land and title. It also demands giving land back to Indigenous communities where treaties were not signed and negotiating nation-to-nation on the terms of a new relationship. It is hard to see how a genuine process of reconciliation is possible without a fundamental rethinking of liberal democracy and the market economy. In fact, the opportunity provided by reconciliation is precisely that we acknowledge the harms caused by colonization and embrace the possibility of repairing our relationship not only with Indigenous peoples but with ways of life that offer a better balance between human activity and nature. A democracy that found ways of decolonizing itself and allowed for Indigenous self-determination would look rather different from "the best way humans have found" to govern themselves. A renewed nation-to-nation relationship with Canada's First Nations was promised, but most of the calls to action from the Truth and Reconciliation Commission remain unfulfilled.

Finally, since the election of the Liberal government in 2015, there has been a gradual shift from a progressive domestic democratic reform agenda to a defensive preoccupation with external threats to democracy. For example, a comprehensive catalogue of the Government of Canada's commitments to strengthening democracy in its National Action Plan on Open Government (see Government of Canada 2023) reveals an overwhelming focus on defensive measures: combatting online disinformation, especially among marginalized and vulnerable groups; supporting local news in the face of the erosion of traditional media ecosystems; raising awareness of foreign interference; developing a critical incident electoral protocol; countering cyberthreats; ensuring electoral management bodies are the leading source of authoritative information on where to vote; and defending journalists and freedom of speech worldwide.

In part, this reflects concern about the rising assertiveness of authoritarian regimes and evidence of meddling in Canadian and other elections by countries like China and Russia. These concerns came to a head in early 2023 when leaked intelligence reports suggested Beijing had sought to influence Canadian elections, resulting in a decision to appoint a special rapporteur to investigate and determine whether a public inquiry was necessary. Today, democracy intersects with foreign policy in ways that reflect not only a weakened global liberal order, but also a loss of domestic democratic reform momentum. We can see these trends in the promises made during election campaigns in 2015, 2019, and 2021.

As in the 1990s, the Liberal Party came into office in 2015 promising sweeping democratic reforms, only to cool their ardor after the election. Justin Trudeau's path to electoral victory was paved with promises of democratic reform, including electoral reform, Senate reform, more free votes in parliament, improvements to Question Period, more power to parliamentary committees, and less in the Prime Minister's office. Although considerable progress was made on Senate reform (see the chapter by Peter Boehm in this volume), and a Leaders' Debates Commission was created to discourage the gamesmanship around participation in leaders' debates (McKay 2019), the single most important democratic reform that could have been undertaken by the Liberal government was to fulfill the promise to make 2015 the last election under the First-Past-the-Post electoral system. A more proportional system would have weakened the tendency to form false majority governments; it might have encouraged more cooperation in parliament and less hyper-partisanship. Yet, the excellent work of the cross-partisan electoral reform committee was peremptorily abandoned when its final report tilted toward electoral systems that did not appear to be favored by the Prime Minister (who later acknowledged his preference for the alternative vote system). In other words, the process was abandoned for partisan reasons.

In the 2019 election, many of the promises made in 2015 were reiterated: private members bills were to be given more time and committees were to be better resourced. A Canadian Centre for Peace, Order, and Good Government would be created. The promise to govern more democratically rang increasingly hollow, not only in light of the failure to pursue electoral reform, but also after the SNC-Lavalin scandal and the dismissal of Minister of Justice and Attorney General Jody Wilson-Raybould (2021). Moreover, the election of Donald Trump absorbed much of the attention of the government and contributed to a growing concern about electoral integrity at home and abroad. In addition, parliamentary reform was complicated by the COVID-19 pandemic, which altered the functioning of the parliament, as much of its activity moved online. To some degree, parliament was sidelined by the pandemic; many members of parliament were overwhelmed by the specific, often-pandemic-related demands by their constituents.

The 2021 election was widely seen as unnecessary; there was no compelling reason to drop the writ other than the hope of winning a majority. The PM bet that relatively successful pandemic management would be rewarded at the polls. In the course of the campaign, the issue that emerged was the highly divisive matter of vaccine mandates, the politicization of which created a wedge in the Conservative Party and contributed to the rise of the Freedom Convoy. The occupation of Ottawa weakened the moderate leader of the official opposition, Erin O'Toole, and paved the way for the rise of one of the most partisan politicians in Canadian politics, Pierre Pollievre (the former Harper Minister of Democratic Institutions responsible for the anti-democratic "Fair Elections Act").

The 2021 Liberal election platform placed stress on democracy and human rights as foreign policy objectives: "With foreign threats and interference on the rise and the impact of authoritarian trends more widespread, now more than ever, itis time to place the promotion of democracy, human rights, and rule of law at the centre of our foreign policy." The meant, *inter alia*, support for emerging democracies, the creation of an anti-corruption court, protection for persecuted minorities, and support for human right, feminist, and LCBTQ2 activists. Again, the Liberals reiterated their promised to establish a Canadian Centre for Peace, Order, and Good Government. Even in the most modest way in which the Liberal government might have democratized foreign policy, little action was taken.

The Liberals did not initiate broad-based foreign policy consultations nor put in place a meaningful public engagement strategy (although a study of foreign policy is being undertaken in the Senate, as noted by Peter Boehm). Civil society has largely filled the gap: an innovative participatory process of examining Canada's place in the world was conducted by the Canadian International Council (2021), a well-established non-governmental organization. The lack of public engagement by government went hand-in-hand with a lackluster diplomatic record. Canada acquired a reputation for rhetorically espousing progressive values but doing little to take or support diplomatic initiatives. On the democracy file, despite the opportunities created by multiple democracy summits, Canadian foreign policy rhetoric has not been met by commensurate action.

To be fair, the Canadian government was forced to commit substantial resources to the NAFTA renegotiation process demanded by the Trump administration and by most accounts was successful in protecting domestic economic interests. For that, of course, Freeland in particular gets considerable credit. But this may also explain why, despite ending her talk on an ostensibly inspiring note, Freeland's vision is ultimately a grim one. She exhorted her Washington audience to "build a world where we can save the planet and ensure that working people have good jobs and lead comfortable lives. A world where we look after our friends. A world where democracies depend on democracies, rather than despots." This is a foreign policy frame that divides the world into friendly democrats, authoritarian enemies, and in-between nations that have to be cajoled and corralled into supporting rich democracies. It does not appear to be a world in which the prospects for global climate action, reconciliation, and the deepening of democracy at home and abroad have a bright future.

Concurrent and Intersecting "Polycrises"

In this penultimate substantive section, I want to offer a third frame for thinking about current foreign policy challenges. Instead of emphasizing either conflict or competition, I want to suggest that the dramaturgical metaphor of crises is more appropriate (Habermas 1976). I use the plural to capture what some are calling the contemporary "polycrisis" (see the discussion in the chapter in this volume by Jeremy Kinsman). The idea is meant to capture the severity, the acceleration, and the overlapping of multiple crises facing humanity which may derive from climate change, collapse of ecosystems, loss of biodiversity and wilderness, pandemics and contagious diseases caused in part by human encroachments into wilderness and global mobility, inequality and its politically corrupting effects, polarization and extremism, misinformation, disinformation, war and conflicts caused by dispossession and migration, demands for decolonization, and the proliferation of identity politics as ways of life as the planet becomes increasingly connected but also uprooted. These forces spread and multiply, often exacerbating one another with astonishing intensity and speed. In this context, not only democracy but governance generally may be overwhelmed and unable to cope.

The observation that democracy is in a worldwide recession or crisis has to be accompanied by a recognition that contemporary political regimes function under unprecedented circumstances. This is neither to deny the erosion of democracy, nor to suggest it must fail, but rather to insist that the biggest challenge to democracy may be endogenous: the limit of the capacity of democratic governments to meet the urgent problems humanity faces. These problems implicate all political systems, but they generate democratic crises in a specific sense: institutional features of contemporary democracies may be a hindrance to their resolution.

For example, electoral democracies are good at aggregating the preferences of specific groups of individuals at particular moments in time. Elections are less useful for weighing the interests of future generations, non-citizens, other species, or non-human life. This makes democratic institutions, as currently configured, ill-equipped to respond to the climate crisis and ecocide, the costs of which are borne most heavily by future generations, people living in vulnerable environments, and endangered species, none of which have legal standing or voting rights in contemporary liberal democracies. Even the challenge of reconciling liberal democracy with Indigenous self-government largely eludes contemporary democracies. Although the climate emergency is the most urgent and existential crisis humanity faces, similar problems of exclusion and non-enfranchisement afflict democratic governance in the spheres of conservation, public health (including disease and substance use), migration, the protection of the public sphere, domestic violence, and international conflict.

In many of these global issues, we suffer from what biologist Garrett Harden (1968) called the tragedy of the commons—namely the tendency of individuals to burden the commons as a result of individually rational strategies of maximizing welfare. Using the example of shepherds employing common pasture for cattle, he argued that when the carrying capacity of the commons was reached, collapse would follow. Harden specifically stressed "tragedy of *freedom* in the commons" (my italics). It was individual freedom to pursue and individually rational but collectively ruinous strategy that was at the heart of the dilemma. "Freedom in the commons brings ruin to all" (Harden 1968: 1244). This helps explain the contested status of freedom in the contemporary political debates on global issues, as well as the challenges this poses to democracies that rely on a public philosophy that values individual freedom to maximize utility.

There can be little question that human freedom has, to paraphrase Hegel, continued its march through history. What is less clear is whether the march is tantamount to progress. Certainly, the struggle for freedom constitutes a deep, often imperceptible social force for democratization.

Citizens have more choices, more resources, and more capabilities to choose how they want to live and what they want to be than ever before—even, to some degree, in non-democratic regimes. The world's most authoritarian regimes—China, Iran, Cuba, and Venezuela—struggle to contain pressure to allow greater freedom. But this powerful human insistence on freedom may well be the cause of our ultimate downfall. We seem to lack the capacity as citizens, as communities, and as a species to make sacrifices even for the sake of our own individual and collective survival. The pandemic has revealed our impatience with the slightest restrictions, imposed for our own good, and government is paralyzed when faced with emergency situations both natural and social. This bodes ill for our capacity to adapt to and mitigate tragedies of the commons.

Can our systems of government demonstrate their relevance or even minimal capacity to deal with our most pressing collective needs? To answer this question, we need to more thoroughly probe what it means to recognize the difference between doing well and doing good. We need to reimagine the global common good.

Modest Proposals

I end with three modest proposals to address our current democratic crises. These suggestions are offered not as concrete action plans, but as an attempt to glance at the horizon and take our bearings for the path ahead. It is a call to end our blind rush into catastrophe, and it is informed by Hardin's (1968: 1243) view that our challenges are not technical but require "a fundamental extension in morality."

First, democracy today, as in the past, demands civic virtue—both from leaders and citizens. Only citizens capable of concern for all other citizens, non-citizens, human, and non-human life are fit for self-rule in the Anthropocene. To echo Jeremy Kinsman's reflections in his excellent essay in this volume, democracy demands more than institutions; it demands citizens capable of behaving (I would say functioning) democratically within those institutions. They put the common good ahead of narcissistic and materialistic self-interest that markets promote and ahead of the office-seeking and partisan interests that elections promote. Civic virtue is learned through practice, and through practice the habits of self-government in a political community are acquired. A community capable of placing collective survival and flourishing above individual egocentrism can avoid the tragedy of freedom in the commons.

Second, democracy today, as in the past, demands leadership with moral authority. Without moral authority, leaders are incapable of demanding (and modeling) sacrifices for the greater good. Pandering and demagoguery have always afflicted democracies, and cannot be avoided, but the price of such irresponsibility is today higher than ever before. The specific nature of the problem, which in the past would have been called the mischief of faction, today takes the form of hyper-partisanship. The strength of democracy depends on the ability of citizens and rulers alike to embrace moderate partisanship, which leads to politics as a practice of collective self-government of equal citizens, not the practice of domination which involves the imposition of the will of one party over another. There are many ways to attenuate partisanship, including electoral reform, participatory innovations, the cultivation of reflection-in-action in politics, and public education.

A third crucial defense of democracy is the preservation of knowledge and trust in expertise. Shared knowledge—indeed language itself—is a fundamental common good and must be protected against misinformation, disinformation, deliberate falsehood, and plain nonsense (Gessen 2020). This involves careful balancing acts, since I have already noted that we face moral and political rather than technical challenges. We should not turn to experts to make public decisions for us but *with* us; and we need to find ways of agreeing on factual truths while acknowledging that the decision to act on what we know demands political skill and knowledge—what the Greeks called "practical wisdom" or phronesis (Schwartz and Sharpe 2010). The protection and strengthening of a professional public service is critical to the collective ability to deliberate and act on the basis of shared knowledge and evidence.

Each of these proposals points not only to ways of making democracy a more effective instrument of policy, but also of improving the functioning of democracy itself. The strength of democracy depends on its ability to address our greatest collective challenges, and democracy's ability to meet those challenges is the best guarantee of its future prospects. Canadian foreign policy in particular, although it merits some praise for its contribution to a more democratic world, may also be taken to task for doing too little to meaningfully engage citizens in the global struggle for a more democratic world.

References

Bartels, Larry M. 2008. *Unequal Democracy: The Political Economy of the New Gilded Age.* Princeton: Princeton University Press.

Cameron, Maxwell A., and Maureen Appel Molot, eds. 1995a. *Democracy and Foreign Policy: Canada Among Nations 1995.* Ottawa: Carleton University Press.

Cameron, Maxwell A., and Maureen Appel Molot. 1995b. Does Democracy Make a Difference? In *Democracy and Foreign Policy: Canada Among Nations 1995b*, eds. M. A. Cameron and M. A. Molot, 1–25. Ottawa: Carleton University Press.

Canadian International Council. 2021. *Foreign Policy by Canadians: Conclusions and Implications.* Toronto: CIC. https://thecic.wpenginepowered.com/wp-content/uploads/2021/07/FPBC_Conclusions-and-Implications-ENGLISH-VS-FINAL3-1-32.pdf

Chandler, Andrea. 1995. Democracy and the Problem of Government in Russia. In *Democracy and Foreign Policy: Canada Among Nations 1995*, eds. M. A. Cameron and M. A. Molot, 235–256. Ottawa: Carleton University Press.

Corcoran, Terence. 2022. The 'Freeland Doctrine's' Unfree Plan, *Financial Post.* October 28. https://financialpost.com/opinion/terence-corcoran-the-freeland-doctrines-unfree-plan

Doyle, Michael W. 1983. Kant, Liberal Legacies, and Foreign Affairs. *Philosophy & Public Affairs* 12 (3): 205–235. http://www.jstor.org/stable/2265298.

Edsall, Thomas B. 2022. When it Comes to Eating Away at Democracy, Trump Is a Winner. *The New York Times*, August 24. https://www.nytimes.com/2022/08/24/opinion/us-democracy-trump.html

Evans, Peter. 2008. Is an Alternative Globalization Possible? *Politics and Society* 36 (2): 271–305.

Foweraker, Joe. 2021. *Oligarchy in the Americas: Comparing Oligarchic Rule in Latin America and the United States.* New York: Palgrave.

Freeland, Chrystia. 2022. *Remarks by the Deputy Prime Minister at the Brookings Institution.* Washington, DC: Brookings Institution.

Fukuyama, Francis. 2006. *End of History and the Last Man.* United Kingdom: Free Press.

Fukuyama, Francis. 2011. *The Origins of Political Order: From Prehuman Times to the French Revolution.* New York: Farrar, Straus and Giroux.

Gessen, Masha. 2020. *Surviving Autocracy.* New York: Riverhead.

Government of Canada. 2023. *Canada's National Action Plan on Open Government 2022–2024.* https://publications.gc.ca/collections/collection_2022/sct-tbs/BT22-130-2022-eng.pdf

Habermas, Jurgen. 1976. *Legitimation Crisis.* Cambridge: Polity Press.

Harden, Garrett. 1968. The Tragedy of the Commons. *Science* 162 (3859): 1243–1248.

Harvey, David. 2005. *A Brief History of Neoliberalism*. Oxford: Oxford University Press.

Hopewell, Kristen. 2020. *Clash of Powers: US-China Rivalry in Global Trade Governance*. Cambridge: Cambridge University Press.

Intergovernmental Panel on Climate Change. 2022. Climate Change: A Threat to Human Wellbeing and Health of the Planet. Taking Action Now Can Secure Our Future. https://www.ipcc.ch/2022/02/28/pr-wgii-ar6/

Jaremko, Deborah. 2021. Canadian Oil Deliveries to Asia Confirm Opportunity for Trans Mountain expansion: Oil Sands Crude Now Competes in China Head-to-Head with Iraq's Basrah Heavy. Canadian Energy Centre, June 7. https://www.canadianenergycentre.ca/canadian-oil-deliveries-to-asia-confirm-opportunity-for-trans-mountain-expansion/

Lakoff, George. 2004. *Don't Think of an Elephant: Know Your Values and Frame the Debate—The Essential Guide for Progressives*. White River Junction, VT: Chelsea Green Publishing.

Levin Bonder, Jennifer. 2019. Redefining Canada's Foreign Policies: Canada's Last Review of Its Foreign and Defence Policies Was Completed by Pierre Trudeau in 1970. Is It Time to Conduct Another One? *Policy Options*, July 22. https://policyoptions.irpp.org/magazines/july-2019/redefining-canadas-foreign-policies/

Liberal Party of Canada. 1993. *Red Book: Creating Opportunity*. https://web.archive.org/web/19961109134016;http://www.liberal.ca/english/policy/index.html

Lightfoot, Sheryl, and David MacDonald. 2017. Treaty Relations between Indigenous Peoples: Advancing Global Understandings of Self-Determination. *New Diversities* 19 (2): 25–39.

McKay, Spencer. 2019. Literature Review—Canada's Leaders' Debates in Comparative Perspective. Appendix 7, Leaders' Debates Commission, *Democracy Matters, Debates Count: A Report on the 2019 Leaders' Debates Commission and the Future of Debates in Canada*. Ottawa: Government of Canada. https://www.debates-debats.ca/en/report#fnb1-ref

Mulroney, David. 2020. Fifty Years After Canada's Last Foreign-Policy Review, Our Identity Is More Precarious Than Ever. *The Globe and Mail*, February 17. https://www.theglobeandmail.com/opinion/article-fifty-years-after-canadas-last-foreign-policy-review-our-identity-is/

Przeworski, Adam, and Fernando Limongi. 1997. Modernization: Theory and Facts. *World Politics* 49 (2): 155–183.

Rein, Martin, and Donald Schön. 1996. Frame-Critical Policy Analysis and Frame-Reflective Policy Practice. *Knowledge and Policy* 9: 85–104. https://doi.org/10.1007/BF02832235.

Ruggie, John Gerard. 1982. International Regimes, Transactions, and Change: Embedded Liberalism in the Postwar Economic Order. *International Organization* 36 (2): 379–415. http://www.jstor.org/stable/2706527.

Russett, Bruce, Christopher Layne, David E. Spiro, and Michael W. Doyle. 1995. The Democratic Peace. *International Security* 19 (4): 164–184. https://muse.jhu.edu/article/447382.

Schwartz, Barry, and Kenneth Sharpe. 2010. *Practical Wisdom: The Right Way to Do the Right Thing*. New York: Riverhead Books.

Shue, Henry. 2022. *The Pivotal Generation: Why We Have a Moral Responsibility to Slow Climate Change Right Now*. Princeton: Princeton University Press. https://doi.org/10.1515/9780691226255.

Waltz, Kenneth N. 1979. *Theory of International Relations*. Addison-Wesley Publishing Company.

Wilson-Raybould, Jody. 2021. *"Indian" in the Cabinet*. Toronto: HarperCollins.

World Wildlife Foundation. 2010. WWF: Canadians' Footprints Among the World's Heaviest. https://wwf.ca/media-releases/wwf-canadians-footprints-among-worlds-heaviest/

CHAPTER 5

Policy and Practice in Canada's International Democracy Support

David Gillies

This chapter examines Canadian policies to support democracy abroad. It sets out key policy milestones and looks at aspects of Canada's current international engagement, including at the Summit for Democracy and plans to establish a Canadian Centre for Democracy. Observations are shared on the domestic environment for democratic policy making and the demise of publicly funded institutions such as Rights and Democracy.

Canada's policy commitments for democracy support have had three peaks of activity, under both Conservative and Liberal governments. The first two peaks were in the late 1980s and between 2006 and 2009 (Schmitz 2013). Renewed policy activity today is driven by democratic backsliding and growing authoritarianism abroad and some impetus for democratic renewal at home to address external interference in our politics and electoral system, converging governance challenges, and signs of polarization.

D. Gillies (✉)
Queen's University, Kingston Ontario, Canada
e-mail: david.gillies9@gmail.com

© The Author(s), under exclusive license to Springer Nature Switzerland AG 2023
M. A. Cameron et al. (eds.), *Democracy and Foreign Policy in an Era of Uncertainty*, Canada and International Affairs, https://doi.org/10.1007/978-3-031-35490-8_5

Parliament has been instrumental in each period of policy activity. However, since the end of the Cold War, the commitment of Canadian governments to international democracy support has been inconsistent. Beyond Parliament it is not clear whether there has ever been much of a democracy support policy community in Canada. Governments have shown only episodic and short-lived commitment for regularized forms of public input and consultation. Planning to establish a Canadian democracy support centre underscores that the foreign policy process is filled with stops and starts, broadly top-down, driven by external prompts, such as alliance commitments, and by careful political management. Whilst the sum is still not greater than its parts, elements of a democracy ecosystem are in place. The proposed Canada Democracy Centre provides another opportunity to galvanize a more coherent, networked, and whole-of-society approach to democracy support. Time will tell whether domestic governance and security compulsions, geopolitical shifts, and threats to the 'ruled-based international order' can prompt the sustained political will and resources Canada will need for durable investments in democratic renewal at home and democracy support abroad.

Policy Milestones in Canada's International Democracy Support

Prompted by external factors, the late 1980s mark the first period of policy activity. A third wave of democratic transitions led to a doubling of the world's democracies by the end of the 1980s, culminating in the November 1989 fall of the Berlin Wall. Unable to meet the demands of performance legitimacy, numerous authoritarian regimes collapsed or gave way to democratic transitions. In America, the Reagan government established a National Endowment for Democracy. In Canada, a Special Report of the House and Senate took note of the US approach with its focus on support to political parties, but visualized a Canadian agency anchored in international human rights (Axworthy 2019). An effective cross-party Parliamentary initiative made all the difference. The Mulroney government appointed two special rapporteurs to tap public opinion and consider a mandate. Against the resistance of some career diplomats and NGOs but with the support of then Minster of External Affairs, Joe Clark, the Mulroney government put forward Bill C-147 to establish a centre supporting institutions that 'give effect to the rights and freedoms enshrined in the International Bill of Human Rights.' Royal assent was given in September 1988 and the International Centre for Human Rights and Democratic Development (ICHRDD) was established in Montreal with an initial budget of $15 million over five years.

In 1990, after nearly three decades as an Observer, Canada became a member of the Organization of American States (OAS). From the outset, as part of a commitment to the OAS democracy pillar, Canada supported the 1990 establishment of a Unit for the Promotion of Democracy which 'signalled a more embedded institutional concern with the *process* of democratization' (Cooper and Legler 2001).[1]

The 1990s was also a period of policy and program development inside government. Influenced by the new 'good governance' thinking at the World Bank, bilateral aid agencies acknowledged that political variables such as pluralism, voice, accountable public institutions, and the rule of law contributed to economic development. Canada's international cooperation programs in human rights, democratic development, and particularly good governance rapidly expanded. By one estimate, between 1996 and 2006, Canada disbursed about $3.8billion on governance programming of which $1.3 billion was for 835 democratization initiatives (Schmitz 2013).

After 9/11 democracy promotion went mainstream. In 2001, DFAIT created a Democracy Unit and by 2006 the Canadian International Development Agency (CIDA) established an Office of Democratic Governance. There were also government efforts to regularize public input into policy making. The Martin government made good on its 2005 international policy statement by setting up a Democracy Council in 2006 that brought key institutions of government together with implementing partners like the Parliamentary Centre, Rights and Democracy, and the National Judicial Institute. But these bureaucratic innovations and outreach efforts were not sustained. By 2010 the Democracy Council was closed, the CIDA Office for Democratic Governance was disbanded, and the DFAIT Democracy Unit was absorbed into another bureaucratic structure. Whilst Global Affairs Canada has an Office for Human Rights, Freedoms, and Inclusion and some capacity on digital and cyber policy, there is limited in house expertise on democratic governance and limited prospects of attracting and retaining specialized knowledge.

---

[1] My italics. The OAS 'Unit' was later renamed the Secretariat for Strengthening Democracy.

After the financial crisis of 2008, the need to rein in discretionary government spending meant that organizations largely dependent on public funds, from Rights and Democracy and the Pearson Peacekeeping Centre, to FOCAL and the North–South Institute, fell out of favour and closed. It did not help that some groups were slow to innovate and diversify their sources of funding. Since the demise of these groups, it is not clear whether Canada has anything approaching a mature policy community for democracy support.[2] One consequence may have been a relative exodus of home-grown expertise attracted away in the main to US organizations or to the UN system. However, the survival of older institutions, such as the Parliamentary Centre and the Forum of Federations, together with newer players like the Centre for Global Pluralism, the Centre for Governance Innovation (CIGI), Citizen Lab, the Munk School's Policy, Elections and Representation Lab and the McGill Centre for Media, Democracy and Technology suggest that elements of a more durable democracy ecosystem are in place. The proposed Canadian democracy centre could usefully conduct an audit of what kind of expertise currently exists in Canada to support its mandate.[3]

Democracy Support in an Era of Uncertainty

In contrast to the optimism of the late 1980s, democracy support today must take shape in more pessimistic and difficult times. Russia's invasion of Ukraine has shaken global security. The other key geopolitical shift is the rapid rise of China and a rival governance model of managed, market-driven growth with few of the civil, political, and cultural rights embedded in international law. The Xi Jinping era has strengthened the grip of the Chinese Communist Party (CCP) as China's economic, military, and soft power is projected globally, becoming a pole of attraction not only in the Indo-Pacific region, but also in Sub-Saharan Africa and Latin America.

---

[2] In the sense of a densely networked group of actors who *regularly* interact and share information around a set of issues and a common technical language. Parameters such as the degree of integration, openness or insulation, stability, continuity, and influence can impact the vitality and durability of a policy network. Amongst others, see Pal (2014) and Coleman (2001).

[3] An audit would confirm the balance between democracy program implementing organizations, which may be thin on the ground in Canada, and democracy research groups, such as the Samara Institute and small centres at Queen's University, University of British Columbia, and Simon Fraser University.

Democracy, meanwhile, is on the backfoot across much of the globe, and to an extent not seen for decades. Trust in democratic institutions has waned as high-income democracies face challenges from climate change, pandemics, energy, and cost-of-living crises to cultural forces such as inequality, populism, and polarization. Whilst a 2019 Pew Research Center survey found that Canadians remain broadly satisfied with the state of their democracy, there are also persistent deficits to address such as income inequality, inclusion, and reconciliation with indigenous groups.

The Summit for Democracy

Calling the defence of democracy 'the challenge of our time,' President Biden hosted the two-day virtual summit 'to renew democracy at home and confront autocracies abroad.' Organized around the themes of defending against authoritarianism, combating corruption, and advancing human rights, the summit brought together governments, multilateral institutions, human rights defenders and journalists, mayors, parliamentarians, business, and labour leaders. With an invitation list mired in politics, the summit saw trade-offs between values and interests. But it also usefully convened like-minded countries, took stock of the global democratic recession, and prompted action.[4]

At the December 2021, Summit Canada made commitments for follow up in the 2022 'year of action' and as a basis for discussion at a second summit slated for March 2023. The 35 separate commitments include efforts to renew democracy at home and protect and advance democracy abroad. Canada's key international commitment is a plan to establish a Canadian centre for democracy support. There were also promises to strengthen support for elections abroad, 'advance digital inclusion,' promote transparency and open government, and combat corruption and illicit financing.

---

[4] To address the perception of the first Summit for Democracy as an exclusionary and US-led process, the second Summit is co-hosted by a variety of countries, from Zambia to the Netherlands, and will ensure that discussions are more regionally based. Whilst officials thought it unlikely that there would be another Summit or any long-term institutional arrangement to focus the efforts of a loose alliance of democracies, South Korea has now agreed to host a third Democracy Summit in 2024. The results of the issue-specific 'cohorts' could also find their way into extant multilateral or regional institutions (Personal communication with Canadian officials, January 2023).

To protect human rights on the home front, the government commits to a National Plan on Combatting Hate and an LGBTQ Action Plan. It also commits to working towards accepting and resettling more Afghan refugees and to diversifying the types of refugees Canada accepts. To address corruption, the government commits to organizing a high-level roundtable, developing a beneficial ownership registry, incorporating human rights and Economic, Social and Governance (ESG) principles in public procurement, whilst continuing to support more open government. These Summit commitments reinforce other domestic actions to develop a National Action Plan on Open Government, bolster an anti-money laundering regime and address democracy concerns, notably the 2017 Justice for Victims of Foreign Officials Act—the so-called Magnitsky laws. Following concerns during the Trucker convoy protests about unregulated crowd funding, the beneficial ownership registry is now being fast-tracked for 2023.

A few of Canada's 2021 summit commitments are novel, requiring additional resources. Others are vague, recycled, still to be developed or already underway. Not a single new dollar was announced for a Canadian implementing organization. Instead, the small sums announced include support for the UK's Westminster Foundation and the UN Office for the High Commissioner for Human Rights. Canada's preferred way to project its soft power is distinctly low cost. In the 2022 Year of Action, Canada was part of three Summit for Democracy 'cohort' groups: on media freedom, information integrity, and civic space. Also in 2022, Canada chaired three inter-governmental democracy support forums: International IDEA, the Freedom Online Coalition, and the Community of Democracies.

Cutting through Canada's sunny declarations, when stacked up against our laggard approach to domestic data privacy, our contrasting response to Ukrainian and Afghan refugee claimants, the timid implementation of public sector whistle blower protections, or the slow, opaque and quite possibly broken access to information system, were the Summit for Democracy announcements anything more than window dressing? In preparation for the March 2023 second Summit for Democracy, the government will need to ensure that progress has been made to implement actions to sustain and renew democracy at home that are both credible and line up well with its international commitments.[5]

RIGHTS AND DEMOCRACY: A CAUTIONARY TALE OF MISALIGNMENT AND REPUTATIONAL RISK

The road to establishing a new democracy centre has been filled with stops and starts. In 2006–2007, the House of Commons foreign affairs committee examined Canada's democracy assistance. Its key recommendation was to establish 'an arm's length Canada foundation for international democratic development' to be resourced by multi-year funding following all-party consultations (Canada 2007). In the 2008 Throne Speech, the government pledged to create such an institution and in 2009 Democratic Reform Minister Steven Fletcher set up a four-person advisory panel led by Tom Axworthy to recommend a way forward. The advisory panel supported the creation of a Canadian Centre for Advancing Democracy with a focus on support for political party development but also small grants in areas such as human rights, electoral systems, legislative bodies, and local government.

Why did the Harper government want a new democracy support centre when it was already funding Rights and Democracy? One reason is that Rights and Democracy put more emphasis on its support for human rights organizations whilst parliamentarians saw a need for a democracy 'foundation' to assist political parties abroad. But the more telling reason was that the Conservative government lost confidence in Rights and Democracy which was perceived as 'not delivering'[6] and at odds with the Tories approach in the Middle East, particularly its unequivocal support for Israel. The government took steps to change the organizational culture and appointed three new board members, notably the Chair of the Board, University of Toronto academic Aurel Braun.

The nub of the conflict at Rights and Democracy was that new board members challenged staff decisions to fund three organizations known

---

[5] As at early 2023, there was no publicly available summary of Canada's implementation of its Summit for Democracy commitments.

[6] Interview with a former Harper government policy advisor, Ottawa 2022.

to be critical of Israel. The board cancelled grants enabling these organizations to investigate alleged rights violations in the Gaza strip. More than forty staff then signed a letter criticizing the Board. Which in turn led to the suspension of three senior managers. These managers were finally let go, prompting labour relations litigation. Not only did these actions not achieve the hoped for reset, but they also helped to further polarize Rights and Democracy set the stage for a show down between some Board members, and between the board and staff.

On one side, new board members pointed to a dysfunctional management culture, questionable program choices, and accounting practices, with a staff and President operating outside board oversight. On the other side, staff backed by some board members complained of a board that had overstepped its role and was micro-managing and undermining the President and staff. Especially contentious was a board-initiated negative performance evaluation of the Rights and Democracy President, Remy Beauregard. Two board members resigned, at odds with the actions of board Chair, Aurel Braun. Tragically, Remy Beauregard was to die of a heart attack shortly after a particularly tense and difficult board meeting.

With Beauregard's untimely death, the lid came off the internal disputes at Rights and Democracy. Following damaging media stories, the House of Commons Standing Committee for Foreign Affairs and International Development initiated its own investigation. Its lengthy report (Canada 2010) and recommendations to help Rights and Democracy move towards a stronger future included actions to enhance transparency and accountability. Others addressed governance, calling for reconstituting the board, training board members in corporate governance, and having the Board apologize to the family of the late Remy Beauregard. In its response, the government agreed with some suggestions, such as training in corporate governance, considered others such as bringing in the Office of the Auditor General 'in the future,' disagreed with reconstituting the board, and side-stepped the recommendation of an apology to the Beauregard family. Unfortunately, the Committee's prescriptions for a viable reset at Rights and Democracy were both optimistic and short lived.

Despite government assurances to the Committee about the future of Rights and Democracy, within two years it had changed its mind. The appointment of a new President failed to right the sinking ship. And in April 2012, then Foreign Minister John Baird closed the agency and brought its programs within the Department of Foreign Affairs and International Trade. Citing austerity 'efforts to find efficiencies and savings' as the immediate reason, Baird also conceded that it was 'high time' to put the 'well-known problems [of Rights and Democracy] behind us and move forward.' Reeling from the bad press, moving forward in fact meant shelving any plans for its own alternative to Rights and Democracy. And finding work arounds to support the embattled and fledgling democracies, notably in Ukraine. In the perceived absence of large Canadian implementing organizations, the Harper government quickly funnelled much of its $220 million package for democracy, good governance, and economic development in Ukraine through American and European organizations.

In its twenty-four-year history, ICHRDD (subsequently called Rights and Democracy) had some notable successes. It was particularly vocal and well aligned in reinforcing Canadian government advocacy on women's rights, gender equality, and combatting gender-based violence.

Ed Broadbent, ICHRDD's first president, took on several issues which the government could not directly engage. In meetings with Jean-Bertrand Aristide, Haiti's embattled president, Broadbent discussed establishing a Truth Commission to address rights violations during the Duvalier era and ongoing gang related violence. The Centre engaged a prominent human right lawyer to share with President Aristide a potential framework for a truth and reconciliation process. Broadbent also met Gerry Adams, leader of Sinn Fein, and a key figure bringing the republican movement into a peace process culminating in the 1998 Good Friday Agreement in Northern Ireland. With the peace process, Adams was finally allowed to visit Canada. In Myanmar, following the house arrest of Aung San Suu Kyi, ICHRDD gave financial and technical assistance to the democratically elected government-in-exile which was prevented from assuming office by the military junta. Finally, the Dalai Lama, recipient of the 1989 Nobel Peace Prize, visited the Centre in the early 1990s. Facing pressure from China, neither the Mulroney nor the Chretien governments were willing to meet him officially. His visit to the arms-length ICHRDD to discuss human rights was a practical compromise on a sensitive issue in an era when Canada sought to improve bilateral relations strained after the Tiananmen Square killings, and to rapidly amplify Canada–China trade.

Having a former Canadian political party leader head up a non-partisan public institution was a winning formula. Under the Liberals, the

Centre was also led by another retired national politician, former Solicitor General Warren Allmand. But there is no guaranteed formula to 'politics proof' an arms-length democracy centre from funding or existential crises. Certainly, no government would want to preside over the rift between Board and staff, to wade through the forensic audit by Deloitte, to read the report of the Parliamentary Standing Committee, or try to restore normalcy after the tragic death of Remy Beauregard.

Creative tension was always embedded in ICHRDD's governance arrangement. Handled well, ambiguity can be an asset for action at the margins of what government can hope to achieve. It works if all the key stakeholders—senior management, officials, and the government of the day—maintain close links and periodically test assumptions and directions for action. With Rights and Democracy over time the different perceptions of its role became more pronounced. Some of the Centre's staff saw themselves increasingly as human rights activists whilst officials saw the Centre as more of an adjunct of the public service, taking on issues that diplomats could not.

These painful events suggest that any design for a publicly funded democracy support institution cannot fully safeguard it from controversy at home or abroad. There may well be situations where the Centre is not well aligned with the foreign policy of a future Canadian government. Managing those situations will call for regular dialogue, good will, and adroit leadership from all stakeholders: CEO, Board, partners, and the government. There is also no sure way to future proof the Centre. Governments come and go and priorities change. Unfortunately, Canada's support for institutions reliant on the public purse is filled with examples where governments have launched initiatives with a flourish of enthusiasm to be followed some years later by their closure for lack of funds, for perceived lack of impact, following controversy, or following a shift in priorities. Rights and Democracy is the most extreme example. But there are others, including the short-lived Canada Corps, the Canadian Institute for International Peace and Security (CIIPS), the Canada Consortium on Asia–Pacific Security, the Canada Foundation for the Americas (FOCAL) and the Pearson Peacekeeping Centre (PPC) which was established by the Chretien Liberal government in 1994, partially funded by the former CIDA and closed in 2012 by the Harper government.

The demise of Rights and Democracy is a cautionary tale as the Trudeau Liberals plan a new democracy centre and search for a governance model that can minimize politics and assure longevity. The whole sorry affair revealed an ugly underbelly in Canada's foreign policy. It damaged Canada's brand. And it underscores the reputational risks for any government when an arm's length, but publicly funded institution is not aligned with the foreign policy priorities of the day.

Establishing a New Democracy Support Centre

Prime Minister Justin Trudeau's announcement to establish a Canadian Centre to promote 'democracy and good governance around the world' dusted off earlier plans to establish a 'Canadian Centre for Peace, Order, and Good Government.' The idea first surfaced at a Trudeau Foundation event in 2012. The idea resurfaced in 2019 Liberal Party Platform and shorn of its throwback to the British North America Act, was included in mandate letter for Foreign Minister, Francois-Philippe Champagne.

Foreign Minister Melanie Joly's December 2021 Mandate Letter reiterated the call to set up a 'centre to expand the availability of Canadian expertise and assistance to those seeking to build peace, advance justice, promote human rights, inclusion, democracy, and deliver good governance.' Alongside these areas of potential activity was the need to 'expand fast and flexible support for fragile and emerging democracies, increasing Canada's diplomatic presence in regions of strategic importance, and working closely with democratic partners to promote open, transparent and inclusive governance around the world.'

The proposed democracy centre is one practical way for Canadians to engage partners around the world on the governance challenges of our time. The new centre's credibility and staying power will be improved by also asking hard questions about Canada's own democracy. By engaging widely with Canadians, and by linking its work abroad to challenges at home, the centre can carry out its mandate with a degree of humility, acknowledging missteps in our own democratic journey, and a willingness to share experience and learn from others.

A few value propositions may help guide the centre's activity. First, long-term success in supporting rights, democracy, and good governance depends on efforts within societies and cannot be externally imposed. Second, whilst democracy is a demanding political ideal and not a universal prescription there is growing recognition that the legitimacy of any governing order should include respect for human rights. Third, given the complexity and variety of political regimes, drawing a binary division of democracy versus autocracy is best avoided. Finally, all human rights (civil and political, economic, social, and cultural) have equal importance; they are interdependent, indivisible, and mutually reinforcing.

A significant issue for any democracy support institution in this era of global uncertainty, is navigating the intertwining of democracy with geopolitics and security as politicians and media divide the world into a binary struggle for freedom versus tyranny. In his State of the Union address, President Biden said that 'in the battle between democracy and autocracy, democracies are rising to the moment, and the world is clearly choosing the side of peace and security.' And in Canada, Deputy Prime Minister Chrystia Freeland has described the Ukraine crisis as a 'struggle between democracy and authoritarianism' and a 'direct challenge to the rules-based international order.'

In times of polarizing turbulence, moving beyond binary divisions can enable a more flexible response to ambiguity. Amongst the worlds' sovereign states, there is a huge variety of political regimes. Most are hybrid systems with elements of both democracy and autocracy. Many are in a grey zone where competitive elections, liberal constitutions, and a degree of pluralism exist alongside strong state control. Others are fragile, conflict-prone, and vulnerable to democratic backsliding. Still other regimes emphasize political unity through religion or legitimacy through economic performance. Democratic values, institutions, and practices can be supported in a variety of regimes. Canada's contribution to supporting democracy abroad will come from sustained and serious engagement and not an on–off switch set by the exigencies of the moment.

In a turbulent world, establishing an independent Canadian centre to support human rights and democracy abroad may seem a daunting if not quixotic undertaking. But a world in flux also means that much is in play and weighing in the balance. The challenges include supporting frontline democracies like Ukraine and Taiwan and voices for peace in Russia itself, engaging a rising and assertive China, combating the technologies of repression, helping fragile democracies, and slowing the drift to authoritarianism. At this inflection point in history, human rights, democracy, and good governance need clear-eyed champions who can take the long view.

Planning to establish the centre is well underway with an announcement and further details potentially timed to coincide with the second Summit for Democracy, currently slated for late March 2023. There are several ways to organize the centre: integrated within the bureaucracy with its own funding stream and programs; as a publicly funded but arms-length institution reporting to Parliament; or as a fully independent non-profit that relies on significant public funds. Each approach has its advantages and risks. The key issues to be resolved are the mandate and governance structure, the degree of independence from government, and accountability for the management of public funds.

It will be for the board and staff to set the initial direction, priorities, and activities of the fledgling centre. With the modest resources potentially at play, taking on the full range of issues described in Minister Joly's Mandate Letter will be a tall order. Choosing a few areas of demonstrable expertise will help focus the centre's activities. At issue here is balancing expertise across government and in Canadian civil society with international demand and burden sharing that minimizes duplication. A distinctive niche is not only one that sets Canada apart from its international peers but that also one that avoids duplication of the much larger program investments Canada makes through its Official Development Assistance. Whilst there is no single reliable figure for Canada's overall democracy support, investments by government departments dwarf the funds a democracy centre would receive. At Global Affairs Canada, our diplomatic efforts are supported by about $10 million per year for 'democratic inclusion' and $7.5 million for international human rights. Much larger investments are channelled through Canada's development programs and a few other government departments. Based on OECD Development Assistance Committee data, in fiscal year 2018–2019 alone, Canada disbursed approximately $100million to human rights, $123million to democratic development, and $200million to good governance initiatives. One way to avoid duplication with these larger investments, is to work in countries and situations where Canada has less manoeuvrability through regular development programming.

There are globally engaged Canadian institutions in fields as diverse as federalism, strengthening parliaments, pluralism, elections, the rule of law, and municipal governance. Programmatic areas where the centre could help build and share Canadian expertise include strengthening digital democracy and cyber security, key issues in the struggle for open and plural societies; engaging political leaders at all levels by supporting political party assistance; defending human rights organizations; and facilitating dialogue and mediation in fragile or emerging democracies.

As the government considers the most appropriate business model, it can take stock of how others have gone about establishing their own democracy support institutions. In America, the National Endowment for Democracy (NED) is a grant-making, non-profit foundation established in the Reagan era 'to foster the infrastructure of democracy.' Funded with bipartisan support through annual Congress appropriations to which it reports, NED is uniquely structured. It works with and through US business, labour and political parties, including the National Democratic Institute and the International Republican Institute, which receive half of its funds. The other half is disbursed through grants to NGOs-based abroad. Despite the much larger scale of NED, its controversial history, and the currently tarnished image of American democracy at home and abroad, the NED model may be attractive for Canadian planners, including as it does a structured outreach to both business and labour and a grants-based funding window.

In Europe, the Dutch, British, Swedes, and Danes all have global democracy support institutions. The Westminster Foundation for Democracy was established by the UK government in 1992 to support 'the universal establishment of legitimate and effective, multi-party, representative democracy.' Its focus has been on political elites through three main ways of working 'parliamentary assistance, political party strengthening, and by a combination of these such as supporting the work of parties in parliaments.' Each UK political party runs a foundation-funded program sharing experiences with politically similar parties abroad. The downside is that each political party tends to operate in its own silo rather than integrated into a larger framework or strategy for UK engagement in a particular country. As a non-departmental public body sponsored by the Foreign, Commonwealth and Development Office, the Westminster Foundation is also vulnerable to the generic criticism of UK 'quangos' as unaccountable users of public funds by special interests, in this case political parties. In Holland, The Netherlands Institute for Multi-Party Democracy is also focused on political leadership, dialogue, and capacity building. It works with politicians from all levels of governance and across the political spectrum to enhance their competencies to cooperate on 'issues that affect them, their country, and their region.' Finally, the mission of the inter-governmental, Stockholm-based International IDEA is to 'advance democracy worldwide ...through support to the building, strengthening, and safeguarding of democratic political institutions and processes at all levels.' In practice, its efforts fall into three broad areas: electoral processes, constitution building, and political participation and representation.

Organizational Model

A publicly funded but arms-length institution established by an Act of Parliament and reporting perhaps bi-annually to Parliament through the Minister of Foreign Affairs may take time to establish but is one viable option for Canada.[7] A quasi-independent, para-statal institution working at the creative nexus of government, the legislature and civil society would call for sound convening skills and judgement to navigate controversial issues and choices. Its board would help set strategic direction, review activities, and approve budgets and would include both independent Canadian and international experts. Senior management and professional staff would ideally be drawn from diverse cultural backgrounds. Funds would be drawn from the international assistance envelope giving the Minister of Foreign Affairs final accountability. As the front lines of democracy support include middle income countries (MICs), a case would need to be made to direct some Canadian aid, which normally prioritizes low-income countries, towards selected MICs or else identify other sources of public funding.

However, if speed is of the essence to have the Centre up and running by the March 2023 Summit for Democracy follow up meeting, the government could channel new democracy support funds through an established non-profit, such as the Parliamentary Centre or one based at a Canadian university. Or it could establish a new standalone, independent non-profit, an approach which was used to establish the former Canadian Institute for International Peace and Security (CIIPS) and the Pearson Peacekeeping Centre (PPC). But there are risks. As an independent non-profit, PPC was not immune from politics. Whilst distant from government, it was also gradually starved of funds in a post-cold war,

---

[7] In principle, all party support for a democracy support institution is already available through the endorsement of the idea by the Standing Committee on Foreign Affairs and International Development (Canada 2019). However, the September 2022 election of a new Conservative Party leader, Pierre Poilievre, could plausibly still confound the assumption of all party agreement.

'peace dividend' world and then wound up in 2012. CIIPS was abruptly cancelled after less than eight years in operation. Moreover, not having Canadian parliamentarians more closely linked to the work of a democracy support institution would be a missed opportunity.

FINANCIAL RESOURCES

Proposed funding levels of $25 million for the initial year with $50 million annually thereafter would improve on allocations to the former Rights and Democracy which was starved of funds and eventually of policy influence. The proposed levels would be about one third of the public funds disbursed by the International Development Research Centre (IDRC), a crown corporation now entering its sixth decade. If confirmed, the proposed funding levels would put Canada in good standing with other government supported democracy promotion institutions, such as the Westminster Foundation and International IDEA which are funded at about $25 million and $45 million per year respectively. The Canadian Centre would be much smaller than the National Endowment for Democracy (but still proportional based on population), which will likely take the lion's share of the U.S. 2021 Summit for Democracy announcement of USD 414 million per year to support democratic institutions and practices.

To reduce its dependency on public funds, the enabling legislation should ensure that the centre has the flexibility to diversify its resource base. IDRC's Think Tank Initiative has public–private partnerships with the Bill and Melinda Gates Foundation and the Hewlett Foundation. The Forum of Federations, an Ottawa-based non-profit, was established by the Chretien government to reaffirm Canadian federalism in the wake of the 1995 Quebec referendum. It has become a centre of global excellence on comparative federalism and multi-level governance. And its business model has evolved from an early reliance on public funds to a growing ability to attract project-based funding from other governments and international organizations. The Westminster Foundation leverages additional funds on a case-by-case basis through fee-for-service activities on behalf of selected UK embassies and missions. The former Rights and Democracy selectively drew on Canadian embassy financial and in-kind resources for some field-based activities. And there may also be scope for partnerships with like-minded Canadian foundations, like the Centre for Global Pluralism, as well as philanthropic foundations based in the Global South.

The Question of Scale

Democracy support covers a spectrum of approaches. At one end are elaborately planned, large-scale multi-year investments with well-established partners managing complicated donor results, value for money, and accountability frameworks. At the other end of the spectrum are modest grants directed to a multitude of small-scale organizations where managerial systems are more rudimentary but where nimble, administratively light, and fast disbursing funds can make all the difference to individual activists and embattled civil society organizations. Working with fledgling partners is demanding, time-consuming, and higher risk. Local partners may lack or need support for internal accounting expertise that Canadian contracts typically require. The key point is that there is no need for an either-or approach to issues of scale and fiduciary risk. There is merit in a spectrum of funding windows with larger-scale initiatives balanced by an administratively light fast-disbursement window and a significant small grants program.

Balancing Ways of Working

Experience shows that new democracy promotion institutions take time to establish their competencies and credentials. One set of issues will be to determine the balance amongst programming, convening and public outreach, and knowledge generation. Done right, these are complementary rather than competing values. Disbursing funds and managing programs either directly or through Canadian and international partners may draw the lion's share of resources. But the level of skill and effort to be an effective convenor or to facilitate dialogue in complex and conflicted settings will be considerable and could grow as the Centre's credentials are established. Public outreach is likely to be an important strand of activity to ensure that the Centre is anchored through public education and dialogue on Canada's democratic practices at home as well as situations abroad. Whilst it may be unlikely that the Centre would invest in a landmark research niche, such as NED's flagship *Journal of Democracy* or International IDEA's annual *Global State of Democracy* report, it could commission country analyses to help underpin its programmatic support. Rights and Democracy established an annual human rights prize which brought public recognition to the work of front-line rights campaigners. Finally, some in house monitoring and evaluation capacity would also serve the Centre well, not only to address value for money and accountability requirements, but also to generate and share practical knowledge about what works, what doesn't, and why.

The Centre's Mandate

The proposed centre currently lacks a clear and unambiguous statement of what Canada will and will not emphasize. Minister's Joly's Mandate Letter sets out opportunities from building peace and advancing justice to promoting human rights, inclusion, democracy, and delivering good governance. Whilst there is overlap, these distinct issue-areas have their own complexities, models of practice, and communities of interest. The Mandate Letter does not say whether the list is a comprehensive set of priorities or merely intended to illustrate the range of interests to the government. Nor is there any clear indication where and to what extent Canada has genuine expertise and a clear niche with something of relevance to bring to the global agenda. As it stands, there is a risk of having the Centre be too many things to too many constituencies blunting its potential impact by thinly spreading its resources and expertise. A narrower mandate with a clear niche will help focus staff efforts and allow the Centre to develop its brand.

Outreach and Consultation

The government has reached out for external input to the policy process. In addition to selectively inviting written input, in May 2022 Global Affairs Canada organized three by-invitation online consultations. Two focused on domestic viewpoints and one was held with international partners. Minister of Foreign Affairs, Melanie Joly, chaired one meeting whilst the parliamentary secretaries for foreign affairs and for international development chaired the others. The consultations helped identify niches for Canada based on our strengths and expertise, gaps in international support and emerging priorities for engagement. Whilst officials reportedly tried to ensure equality of access with diverse and inclusive voices, final participation was a political decision and included numerous Liberal party insiders. There were only two experts from the global South.

Participants reaffirmed strong domestic and international interest in Canada playing an active role in democracy support. Whilst there was consensus on leveraging existing Canadian strengths and on support for local groups and local ownership, thematic proposals were diverse: ranging from protecting human rights and civic spaces, to gender inclusion, and the intersection of democracy and technology, including combatting digital disruption. There was broad support for engaging communities not traditionally represented in democratic institutions or processes—from youth and indigenous groups to LGBTQ2I. International participants emphasized the need for new ways of working that go beyond the siloes of policy, programs, and advocacy and for flexible responses to emerging global challenges. Officials must now try to narrow the priorities, objectives, and niche and prepare a submission to Cabinet.

In the absence of a mature democracy ecosystem, one of the most valuable contributions of the new Centre could be to facilitate dialogue between the Canadian government and civil society. It could bring together strategic thinking amongst Canadian implementing partners, locally-based experts and partners, and the government contributing to a whole-of-Canada approach to our democracy support whether by country focus, thematic issue or in multilateral forums.

Programmatic Priorities

Choosing a few areas of demonstrable expertise will help focus the Centre's activities. Examples of niches where the Centre could leverage Canadian expertise include digital democracy and cyber security, political party assistance, human rights, and mediation for peacebuilding in deeply divided societies. The ability of citizens to communicate without fear is a keystone of democracy. But repressive states are increasingly adept in their use of technologies for repression and social control. In the murky corners of the digital world, shadowy companies sell spyware enabling states to carry out cyber surveillance, hacking, online harassment, and digital targeting. Civil society organizations are especially vulnerable to digital threats and most have few resources to deal with them. Citizen Lab is a leading Canadian public interest research hub focused on digital threats, including exposing spyware and targeted espionage. Its work should be shared or replicated wherever freedom of expression is under threat. As digital attacks shrink civic space, Canada's democracy centre could make a difference helping human rights and other civic organizations enhance their cyber security. Such efforts would build on Canadian digital know how and reinforce growing Government of Canada activity in the digital democracy space, both at home and abroad.

Support for political parties would engage Canadian parliamentarians and help reinforce the legislature's buy in for the work of the proposed centre. By itself, however, political party assistance is quite narrowly focused on political elites. And like-minded organizations in the US, UK, and Europe all have significant expertise in this area. However, promoting *women's political leadership and participation* is one area where a Canadian democracy support centre could make a distinctive difference that is also aligned with our current 'feminist foreign policy.'

Active in every kind of political system, human rights defenders are on the front lines in the struggle for human dignity, the rule of law and more open societies. Repressive governments use a range of tools to attack them from defamation, threats, and intimidation to surveillance, judicial harassment, arbitrary detention, and violence. Our development dollars not only help build schools and health clinics, wells, and irrigation systems. They can also help empower marginalized groups to know their rights, access services, hold governments accountable, and fight injustice and corruption. Through support for human rights defenders and legal literacy, the new centre could help address not only civil and political rights, such as freedom of expression or combating gender-based violence, but also poverty-related problems such as legal identity, land disputes, displacement, and access to basic services.

Support for the rights of indigenous peoples, including indigenous women, would engage Canada's own difficult history by potentially reaching out to our First Nations to share their experience. Canada has finally adopted the UN Declaration on the Rights of Indigenous Peoples. The challenge now is to align government legislation, policies, and services with the minimum standards set out in the Declaration (Jody Wilson-Raybould 2019: 98–106). Implementing the Declaration is an area where the proposed centre could facilitate a sharing of experiences amongst jurisdictions with indigenous populations.

Including *peacebuilding* amongst the potential areas of work for the new centre speaks to our peacekeeping traditions and to the aspirations of the Trudeau government to restore Canada's liberal internationalist legacy. One aspect of the peace agenda is dialogue and mediation in fragile, conflict-prone societies. Whilst our political culture is built on compromise and accommodation these skills have not often found expression internationally. As a core member of security alliance and trade structures, Canadian governments may be constrained to serve as an impartial mediator. They may also have little appetite to engage outlawed groups or odious states that violate international norms and fundamental human rights. Finally, as Peter Jones underscores, the peacebuilding space, including within the government of Canada, is divided over the seemingly mutually exclusive roles of norm advocacy and impartial mediator (Jones 2019, 2023). The Liberal government's singular recent foray into the mediation space is not encouraging. A premature public announcement of Canada's role as a 'facilitator' in the Cameroonian conflict suggests that domestic public relations rather than discretion and quiet diplomacy were in the driving seat at Global Affairs Canada and the Prime Minister's Office. But an arms-length Canadian democracy support centre may have more room for manoeuvre. It could support back channel and unofficial civil society dialogues sometimes called Track Two diplomacy or fund research and training in mediation both in Canada and through international partners.

Conclusion

The Summit for Democracy has brought to the forefront the Liberal government's commitments to establish a well-resourced democracy support institution, work with other democracies to address growing authoritarianism, and help renew democracy at home. It will be a 'heavy lift' for a mid-mandate minority government to make good on its plans. It is not enough to establish a Canadian democracy centre simply because most of our G7 partners have one. Our comparative advantage needs to be well articulated and is still by no means clear. Longevity is by no means certain. There are difficult choices to be made about the proposed democracy centre's business model, sustainability, focus, and governance arrangements. Canada's record of fitful support for globally engaged national institutions speaks to a lack of staying power at odds with our role in global alliance structures. At the second Summit for Democracy, in contrast to Prime Minister Rishi Sunak's announcement of a UK 'centre for expertise in democratic governance' there was no update on plans to establish a Canadian democracy centre in Prime Minister Trudeau's statement. The Prime Minister merely noted that Canada 'will be investing in fifty million more for projects and initiatives' that promote and protect democracy at home and abroad. If the government does still move ahead, an institution established through legislation with all party support, embedded in civil society, reporting to Parliament but with ministerial accountability remains a viable way to ensure that Canada's proposed centre is durable and adds value to global efforts to strengthen democratic norms, practices, and institutions.

The author would like to thank Gabrielle Bardall, Max Cameron, Catherine Hecht, Ian Hamilton, and Rupak Chattopadhyay.

REFERENCES

Axworthy, Tom. 2019. Now More than Ever: The Case for Canada Advancing Democracy and Human Rights Abroad. Presentation to the House of Commons Standing Committee on Foreign Affairs and International Development, Ottawa, ON, February 7.

Biden, Joe. 2021. Remarks by President Biden at The Summit for Democracy Opening Session. Washington, DC. Retrieved at https://www.whitehouse.gov/briefing-room/speeches-remarks/2021/12/09/remarks-by-president-biden-at-the-summit-for-democracy-opening-session/.

Canada Parliament House of Commons. 2007. Standing Committee on Foreign Affairs and International Development, Advancing Canada's Role in International Support for Democratic Development.' Ottawa, July

Canada Parliament House of Commons. 2010. Commons Standing Committee on Foreign Affairs and International Development, 'Situation at Rights and Democracy.' Ottawa, June 15.

Canada Parliament House of Commons. 2019. Standing Committee for Foreign Affairs and International Development, 'Renewing Canada's Role in International Support for Democratic Development.' Ottawa, June.

Coleman, W.D. 2001. *International Encyclopedia of the Social and Behavioral Sciences*. Editors-in-Chief. Neil J. Smelser and Paul B. Baltes. Amsterdam: Elsevier.

Cooper, Andrew F., and Thomas Legler. 2001. The OAS Democratic Solidarity Paradigm: Questions of National and Collective Leadership. *Latin American Politics and Society* 43 (1): 103–126.

Government of Canada. Various years. Global Affairs Canada. Statistical Report on International Assistance.

Jones, Peter. 2019. Middle Power Liberal Internationalism and Mediation in Messy Places: The Canadian Dilemma. *International Journal* 74 (1): 119–134.

Jones, Peter. 2023, forthcoming. Quiet Helpful Fixer or Noisy Norm Advocate? Canada as Mediator. In *Democracy and Foreign Policy in an Era of Uncertainty*, ed. Max Cameron, David Carment, and David Gillies. New York: Palgrave Macmillan.

OECD, Development Assistance Committee Creditor Reporting System Code Lists.

Pal, Leslie. 2014. *Beyond Policy Analysis: Public Issue Management in Turbulent Times*, 5th ed. Nelson Higher Education.

Pew Research Center, Global Attitudes Survey. Spring 2021. See also the Pew Research Center Survey.

Schmitz, Gerald. 2013. *Canada and International Democracy Assistance: What Directions for the Harper Government's Foreign Policy?* Kingston, ON: Occasional Paper Series, Centre for International and Defence Policy, Queen's University.

Wilson-Raybould, Jody. 2019. *From Where I Stand: Rebuilding Indigenous Nations for a Stronger Canada.* Vancouver: Purich Books.

CHAPTER 6

The State of Democracy in the World—Problems, Pitfalls, and Policy

Marshall Palmer and David Carment

INTRODUCTION

This chapter is about the global decline of democracy and Canadian attempts to reverse that trend. Our chapter is empirically broad in scope but specific in purpose: to show that democracy promotion begins at home with a focus on declining accountability, economic inequality, the rise of populism, and systemic corruption.

The chapter begins with an overview of trends and problems in measuring and evaluating democratic performance. Collectively, these trends point towards a global democratic decline. We argue that this decline is even worse than presented as these indexes dilute the outsize

---

M. Palmer
School of International Affairs, Carleton Univeristy, Ottawa, Canada
e-mail: MarshallPalmer@cmail.carleton.ca

D. Carment (✉)
School of Indigenous and Canadian Studies, Carleton Univeristy, Ottawa, ON, Canada
e-mail: DavidCarment@cunet.carleton.ca

© The Author(s), under exclusive license to Springer Nature Switzerland AG 2023
M. A. Cameron et al. (eds.), *Democracy and Foreign Policy in an Era of Uncertainty*, Canada and International Affairs, https://doi.org/10.1007/978-3-031-35490-8_6

role of the United States in democratic decline. They also do not account for concomitant declines in good governance. We furthermore consider why this trend has occurred despite the over $2 billion spent annually by the United States and its allies in the service of democracy promotion (Lawson and Epstein 2019). To illustrate our point, we consider the mixed effects of Canadian democracy promotion policies in Ukraine.

Accordingly, our next two sections advance a comprehensive explanation for the global decline in democracy. Elite capture, the growth of a rent-seeking political class, and the diminished political autonomy of elected leaders all contribute to this decline. These patterns are found in both weak and new democracies. Our third section focuses on the problem in the United States and Canada in particular. Democratic decline is particularly strong in the United States, where a re-emergent white nationalist movement confronts a fragile coalition of social democrats and liberal progressives. Corporate and class-based power continues to assert its influence through both Democratic and Republican parties. In Canada, Prime Minister Trudeau follows the trend of his Conservative predecessor by centralizing power in the Prime Minister's office. As the recent Shaw-Rogers merger shows, monopolistic power in Canada remains a significant threat to Canadian democratic interests.

In our fourth section, we consider the decline of democratic oversight in the context of purported Chinese interference in Canada's electoral process. While acknowledging that China assertively engages in transnational suppression and has attempted to influence Canadian elections, we caution against the emergence of a culture of denunciation, especially when based on snippets of leaked information. We point towards the ongoing consultations of a Foreign Agent Transparency Registry as an example of bringing democracy into policymaking.

Our fifth section considers why the advancement of democracy has proved unable to reverse its decline both at home and abroad, and why an "alliance of democracies" is an insufficient foundation for advancing democratic renewal. We argue that the Canadian government has engaged in dangerous rhetorical over-reach and has subordinated its goals of democracy promotion to the geopolitical containment of Russia.

For our purposes, democracy should be understood in its broadest terms as a political system in which power is shared by competing groups, led by elites in which the degree of their competition and the degree of public participation are relatively high. Institutionally, it means a political system in which the government is responsible to the electorate and in which political opposition has legal opportunities to compete for power. At a minimum, suffrage should be universal, and individuals should hold rights to free association and free expression.

DEMOCRATIC DECLINE: THEORY, EVIDENCE, AND TRENDS

Larry Diamond observed that the number of democracies in the world was on the decline from about 2006 onward. He dubbed this trend the "democratic recession" (Diamond 2015). The claim at the time was disputed by some, but by 2022, the downward trend is unmistakeably clear. Among the major databases and projects that provide quantitative assessments of democratic qualities, there is virtually no dispute that the world is amidst a democratic recession.

A glance at the titles of the most recent annual reports produced by these organizations illustrates the point: "A new low for democracy" (*The Economist* 2022), "The Global Expansion of Authoritarian Rule" (Freedom House 2022), "Autocratization changing nature?" (Varieties of Democracy Institute 2022), "Trend toward authoritarian governance continues" (Bertelsmann Transformation Index 2022). Each of these institutions measures democracy in unique ways but they each point to the same conclusion. The major growth in democracies that occurred following the collapse of the Soviet Union has been reversed.

Turning to how democratic decline has unfolded over the last two decades we see in Fig. 6.1 trends based on empirical research. The figure shows the standardized democracy scores of each of the major indices, over time.

As the figure shows, despite different methods for measuring democracy and different weights of key indicators, each survey points to a similar downward curve over the last ten years or so. The organizations that provide this data also provide cursory explanations for the downward slope. For example, the Economist Intelligence Unit (EIU) points to growing economic disaffection, and the slow growth of real GDP among advanced democracies in recent years (EIU 2022, 29). Freedom House places the blame on the rise of authoritarian-elites, who are able to successfully play on the anger and resentment felt by a partisan base, which similarly emanates from economic and cultural dislocation (Freedom House 2022). Varieties of Democracy focuses on the rise of toxic polarization, which is used by authoritarians to roll back the influence of civil society and attack judiciaries, legislatures, and election

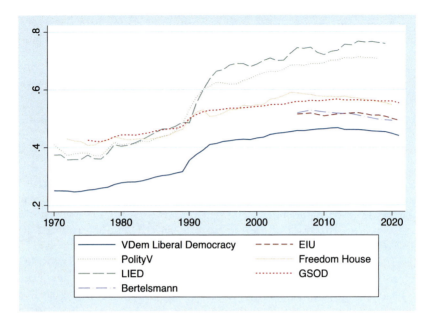

Fig. 6.1 Mean Global Democracy Scores According to Seven Surveys (*Note* All indices are rescaled to the 0–1 interval. Freedom House political-rights and civil-liberties scores are averaged and reversed)

management bodies (Boese et al. 2022). The Institute for Democracy and Electoral Assistance (IDEA) points to the rise of illiberal and populist parties in government alongside growing levels of polarization (IDEA 2022).[1]

The problem with these explanations is that they don't tell us why democratic decline occurs, preferring to assign responsibility to bad actors

---

[1] Independent scholars, like Steven Levitsky and Daniel Ziblatt, point to breakdowns in norms of mutual toleration and forbearance in government (Levitsky and Ziblatt 2019). Each of these reports also notes the role of the pandemic in enabling governments to introduce measures to track, trace, and control the movement of individual citizens. China's growing relative power has also proved an exacerbating factor. China— these reports argue—provides an alternative source of investment to fellow autocrats and can use its economic clout suppress criticism abroad of its own policies and principles (Repucci and Slipowitz 2022, 3–4).

and bad behaviour as opposed to elite preferences and autonomy.[2] This slanted perspective exists for two reasons. One is the heavy emphasis on pro-forma measures of democratic performance or what can be called "process legitimacy" (leading to faulty analysis and policy outcomes as we show below). The second relates to a failure to account for "output legitimacy" which is typically not incorporated into these databases.

Process legitimacy occurs when the state is tied to agreed rules of procedure through which the state takes binding decisions, and which organizes people's participation. In Western states, these rules will be mainly formal (usually enshrined in a constitution). In "traditional" political orders, process legitimacy might be based on customary law or practice. Output legitimacy is defined in relation to the performance, effectiveness, and quality of services and goods that the state delivers.

Explaining Democratic Decline

In order to understand why democratic decline is occurring, it is useful to consider contending explanations. We consider three distinct arguments. The first set of arguments examines pro-forma transitional shifts in political orders as shown in Fig. 6.1 in which democratic consolidation occurs over several decades. According to Freedom House, 59 out of 195 countries were considered "partly free" about ten years ago (Puddington and Roylance 2017). These are countries, which despite moving out of authoritarianism through the adoption of varying degrees of political, social, and economic liberalization, have not fully transitioned to democracy or have reversed in some key areas as they begin to open their economies.

This kind of framing of the democratic process linked to economic development draws from a large body of literature dating back to the 1950s. Lipset's (1959) important work on modernization theory argued industrialization, urbanization, wealth, and education would provide the conditions, rather than the causes, for democracy to flourish. While the positive relationship identified by Lipset has been extensively studied, the

---

[2] Their conceptions of democracy relate to the protection of political rights, the vitality of civil society, and the running of free and fair elections. Excluded, however, are questions of corruption, wealth inequality, and corporate consolidation.

modernization perspective can be deemed deterministic where democratization becomes a by-product of development rather than an outcome of deliberate action (Przeworski and Limongi 1997).

Vanhanen in his 1990 study of democratization argued that the long-term nature of a political system is decisively influenced and determined by power distribution, in particular how much is concentrated in the hands of one group or distributed among many independent groups (see Horowitz for a full discussion in the Balkans context [Vanhanen 1990; Horowitz 2005]).

By the turn of the twentieth century, such political orders could be found across Africa (Kenya, Mozambique, Zambia), post-communist Eurasia (Albania, Ukraine), Latin America (Haiti, Mexico), and Asia (Malaysia, Indonesia, Pakistan) each of which began transitioning with the "third wave" of democratization from the 1970s. Most were expected to transform into full democracies. However, many remained "partially liberalized" having adopted varying degrees of democratization.

These partially liberalized political orders were considered neither completely democratic nor authoritarian. A myriad of labels have been used to describe them including "hybrid" (Diamond 2002; Wigell 2008) "semi-democracies" (Diamond et al. 1989), "illiberal democracies" (Zakaria 1997), "electoral democracies" (Diamond 1999), "competitive authoritarian" (Levitsky and Way 2010), "semi-authoritarian" (Ottaway 2003), "soft authoritarianism" (Means 1996), "electoral authoritarianism" (Schedler 2006), and "anocracies" (Marshall and Cole 2014). The proliferation of terms reflects uncertainty on how to categorize countries that occupy this "political gray-zone" (Diamond 2002).

Huntington (1991) suggested that democratic transitions were caused by five major factors: legitimacy problems in authoritarian regimes, economic growth, religious doctrine to oppose authoritarianism, changing policies of external actors (EU, US, USSR), and "snowballing" based on earlier transitions. Once "transition" began, it was expected to proceed in three sequential stages—an "opening" phase marked by political liberalization and cracks in the ruling regime, a "breakthrough" phase where regime collapse is followed by the emergence of a democratic system, and a "consolidation" phase in which democratic forms become democratic substance (Carothers 2002; Carment et al. 2019).

Today, research linking economic and political development argues that transitional paths need not and do not necessarily reach democratic consolidation. The outcome of a transition is inherently uncertain, where transitions from democracy can lead to liberalized authoritarianism or illiberal democracy as well as full democracy (Carment et al. 2019).

A second causal linkage focuses on "backslides" from openness to regime failure autocracy and civil war, as is the case in West Africa, Eastern Europe, Latin America, and the Middle East (Carment et al. 2019). Writing at the end of the Cold War, Huntington (1991) cautioned that waves of democratization would be followed by "reverse waves". Causal factors include frail democratic values, economic impediments, social and political divisions, and the breakdown of law and order due to insurgency (Carment et al. 2019). Diamond (2015) contends that instead of a reverse "wave", the last two decades have seen a "protracted democratic recession" that has ebbed freedoms in some regions, but has not "reversed" democracy as Huntington predicted.

Both of the above explanations are plausible and helpful in understanding democratic decline. Yet they lack a clear causal path that explains why states backslide or fail to consolidate. With a myriad of potential explanations focused on historical antecedents and institutional path dependence, the precise role of elites is missing. Most studies tend to undervalue the profound link between and the importance of elites in the concurrent development of political, social, and economic orders with the three transforming in relation to one another (Carment and Samy 2019).

In essence, political change requires elite adaptation (Carment and Samy 2019). Democratic transitions are achievable if leaders can and will allocate resources effectively and efficiently. Absent effective leadership coupled with uneven resource allocation and reversal will occur. Conversely, backsliding regimes are purposely designed to look like democracies without exposing leaders to the political risks competition entails. The idea of democracy as "window dressing" is what Andrews and others call "isomorphic mimicry" (2017).

More specifically, elites become entrenched through economic liberalization because governments promote linkages between themselves and different economic groups to avoid becoming beholden to any particular faction (Carment and Samy 2019). States pursue "divide and rule" tactics by playing groups against each other. In such cases, partial liberalization can be seen as a strategy not for democratization, but to sustain authoritarian control.

However, such elite bargaining is in fact not stable (Horowitz 2005; Carment and Samy 2019). As Marshall and Cole (2014: 21) argue hybrid regimes "very often reflect inherent qualities of instability or ineffectiveness and are especially vulnerable to the onset of new political instability events such as outbreaks of armed conflict, unexpected changes in leadership, or adverse regime changes".

We believe a focus on elite choice provides the basis for a more plausible explanation of why states fail to consolidate their democracies or backslide. Backsliding will ensue as a result of elite capture, the process whereby resources designated for the benefit of the larger population are usurped by a few individuals of superior status—be it economic, political, educational, ethnic, or otherwise. Elite capture occurs because, on the one hand, leaders have to establish a power base that is broad and inclusive enough to fend off potential challengers (Carment and Samy 2019).

On the other hand, in order to maintain support from within their narrow political base, leaders have to show they are unwilling to compromise on fundamental issues. For example, leaders who take advantage of government programmes aimed at distributing resources or funds to the general public use their influence to direct such assistance in such a way that it primarily benefits themselves and their supporters. This loss of political autonomy generates outcomes where leaders are often beholden to unelected and therefore unaccountable supporters (Carment and Samy 2019). Unfortunately, a backsliding regime that lacks sufficient resources and political autonomy to retain these supporters is likely to lose their narrow power base, thus becoming vulnerable to challenges that could destabilize it (Carment and Samy 2019).

Increased military spending, which is meant to ensure that military leaders will be satisfied, draws resources away from other state functions, undermining state legitimacy and reducing popular support for the government due to reduced service delivery. In Asia shows that the provision of widely available social goods played a key role in generating legitimacy for governments, while states that limited the distribution of goods ended up suffering greater political instability.

Rent-seeking whether it comes in the form of aid, natural resource extraction, or single commodity production undermines the legitimacy of the state. Such arrangements usually lack legitimacy due to institutions being used for political control rather than popular governance. Sudden shocks to the political system may end up leading to violence if either elites or the general population are dissatisfied with new arrangements in the distribution of resources.

Democratic Decline in Consolidated Democracies: Canada and the United States

While the foregoing analysis helps us understand why weak, unconsolidated states decline in democratic performance, a key question remains: does the same argument regarding elite capture, rent-seeking and loss of political autonomy help us understand decline and backsliding among consolidated economically prosperous democracies? The evidence we provide below suggests that it does.

In this section, we examine democracy trends among these countries with an emphasis on the United States and Canada. For example, all the research units identified in Fig. 6.1 find a decline in the quality of American democracy. The EIU, VDEM, and Polity now rank the United States as a flawed democracy (Haken and Fiertz 2023). However, since each index focuses only on global trends, the respective weight of the United States is discounted in the aggregate analysis. It is therefore useful to re-emphasize the sheer material and social importance of the United States among liberal democracies. 32% of the world's democratic population are American. Americans produce 42% of its GDP and account for 64% of its military spending. America's commercial and cultural reach is enormous. Were the United States to fall into authoritarianism, the democratic recession would become a global democratic catastrophe (democalypse, demogrageddon).[3]

In reflecting on these circumstances within the context of Thucydides' Melian Dialogue, Bruce Clark writes:

> The details of the Greek historian's argument don't matter so much as the fact that he was wrestling in an intelligent way with some problems that are very familiar today. The historian's 'democratic advantage' argument—an insight developed by Stanford Professor Josiah Ober—is an attractive one for western policymakers but it is not obviously true. In an all-out conflict, totalitarian regimes and vertical power structures also have some advantages which western policymakers can easily underestimate. As for the warning that Thucydides gives us about demagogues taking control of democratic institutions, every 21st century reader will be able to suggest modern examples of populism and its abuses. (Clark 2019)

---

[3] Technically the United States is not a democracy. It is a constitutional republic https://www.theguardian.com/us-news/2020/oct/08/republican-us-senator-mike-lee-democracy?CMP=Share_iOSApp_Other.

Clark's point is that Athenian democracy contributed to an unnecessary war against the Melians which in turn precipitated Athens' eventual failure as a democratic state.[4] The Athenian case shows that even powerful democracies can succumb to collapse if the gains they generate aren't broadly distributed across political space (e.g. the people will rise against them) or more importantly if they pursue wars they can neither afford nor justify.[5] The populist leader Pericles set democratic Athens on the road to ruin because he lacked political experience and the inherent risk aversion that comes from a stable (conservative) elite-led polity (Robinson 2017, Schake 2017). Established elites are in essence risk averse (why would they change a system that favours them) and therefore make fewer mistakes (or at least decisions that undermine their hold on power).[6]

Today the United States confronts similar challenges as did Athens under Pericles. The bipartisan neoliberal consensus, which has dominated American politics since the 1980s, has proved fertile ground for the emergence of inward-looking nationalist and populist policies directed outward towards China and Russia. The past consensus—defined by its belief that the market is best left to itself, and that the state should limit the extent to which it redistributes resources—produced clear-cut economic "winners". But today those same American policies have produced "losers" whose need for dignity and voice was and continues to be acutely felt (Gerstle 2022). Enormous gains in American productivity and the continued dynamism of the American technological sector mask both inequitable distributions of those gains and lost opportunities of even greater and more socially responsible technological development.

The recognition that neoliberalism has failed, has produced an enormous shock in American politics. On the one hand, the American right, to some extent led by the same capital interests behind the neoliberal revolution, has adopted the politics of ethnic grievance and xenophobia directed

---

[4] See also: https://warontherocks.com/2017/08/what-thucydides-teaches-us-about-war-politics-and-the-human-condition/

[5] "Pericles was a terrific speaker, but he was also the driving force in Athens' war against Sparta; an elected official who ushered in populist policies (restrictions on citizenship, more aggressive collection of tribute from allies, denying democracy and freedom to Athens's empire) that left Athens in decline". https://www.theatlantic.com/international/archive/2017/07/the-summer-of-misreading-thucydides/533859/

[6] Neither system is completely stable. An elite led system cannot perpetually stay in power (resources will dry up or the people will rise up) while populism lacks purpose.

towards China. Interestingly, according to recent survey data, 61% of Americans do not reject the idea of authoritarianism for their country and 23% would be fine with a leader who does away with elections altogether (Angus Reid 2022).

On the other hand, the Biden coalition binds the social democratic populism embodied by Bernie Sanders and a capitalistic but socially progressive liberalism, whose representatives include Pete Buttigieg and Kamala Harris. This movement is united by a shared revulsion of the racial nationalism of the right (although profound differences remain as to the settlement of economic questions) and by the idea of democracy as a weapon which can be directed towards America's adversaries.

Yet underneath these essential differences between the Democrats and the Republicans there is common ground. As with the GOP, much of the Democratic Party remains ideologically and politically beholden to corporate interests, especially since the 2010 Citizens United decision liberalized campaign finance laws.

Weakening democracy in the United States does not rest solely with the right. Today, some Democrats reject the policies of their own party as the machinations of the "woke left" which leave the country increasingly incapable of informed and coherent domestic and foreign policies.[7] In today's context, the rough equivalent of Pericles' populism are liberal policies celebrating the rights of the individual in which politicians seek political advantage by appealing to all aspects of modern identity. Not surprisingly when liberal democracies seek to protect and advance individual dignity and rights, they often do so at the expense of a collective identity that is necessary to unite society. In the absence of a shared identity, further fragmentation and division accelerates.

In sum, increasing confrontation between Republicans and Democrats has reached a tipping point with the radicalization of the American right on the one hand, and the subsequent weaponization of the democracy agenda by the Biden administration on the other (Moeini and Carment 2022). For example, when Donald Trump declared the 2022 Presidential elections fraudulent and attempted to overturn the results by inciting his followers to raid Congress on January 6, 2021, Republican leaders rallied around the President to prevent him or anyone senior politician from being held to account for their actions.

---

[7] See for example Tulsi Gabbard's position on the war in Ukraine and US support for it.

In response, President Biden warns Americans against the threat of "a different terror," closer to home—from "Donald Trump and the MAGA Republicans", who "represent an extremism that threatens the very foundations of our republic". According to Biden, they promote "political violence" and "undermine democracy itself" (Moeini and Carment 2022). As Carment and Moeini argue, Biden's "rhetoric depicts his administration's war against the amorphous spectre of 'MAGA fascism' at home and its stated goal of militarily defeating autocracies abroad as two sides of the same coin" a point that is repeatedly stressed in his administration's 2022 National Security Strategy (Moeini and Carment 2022).

Evidence of broader patterns in the decline of American democracy over the past decade is in full view. Since the Supreme Court repealed large sections of the 1964 Voting Rights Act in 2012, Republican controlled states have introduced a number of different measures of voter suppression.[8] The intent of these efforts is, in short, to convert the United States from a multi-ethnic democracy to a predominantly white-controlled and white-run ethnocracy.

Already, these efforts are having effects. Most notably, Republican Brian Kemp used a plethora of voter suppression tactics to defeat Democrat Stacy Abrahams in Georgia's 2018 gubernatorial election.[9] More recently, gerrymandering ahead of the 2022 midterms likely gave the Republicans the control of the House (Piper and Mutnick 2022). These tactics may soon reach their logical conclusion wherein it becomes impossible for Democrats to win presidential elections or majorities in the Senate, alongside gubernatorial elections in certain states.

For Canada, these findings are important. Canada is a country which struggles to define itself, perhaps even brand itself as distinct from the United States. Now it must do so in juxtaposition to a divided nation undergoing political transformation. Few remember that democracy reform was high on the Liberal Party agenda before it came to power. That initiative was completely abandoned within one year of the Liberal

---

[8] Voter suppression takes a number of different forms including gerrymandering, restrictive voter ID laws, limiting voter registration, purging voter rolls, criminalizing activities around the ballot box, etc.

[9] It is moot whether Brian Kemp may have won regardless of voter suppression efforts. Perhaps he would have won anyway. His efforts were an attack on democracy.

mandate and, in the face of pressing challenges abroad, is on indefinite hold.

Particularly problematic for both Canada and the United States is the increasing influence of unelected and accountable interference in the democratic process coupled with increasing wealth disparity. In terms of corruption, the corrosive effects of wealth disparity are well documented (Rotberg and Carment 2017). Globally, the World Economic Forum estimates that the cost of corruption, bribery, theft, and tax evasion cost developing countries $3.6 trillion US per year (Johnson 2018). In Canada, tax evasion alone is estimated to cost the Canadian government $15 billion annually, of which $10 billion is through corporate tax dodging (Canadians for Tax Fairness 2018).

Indeed, according to the Corruption Perception Index (CPI), Canada and the United States are breaking away from other liberal democracies by becoming more corrupt over time. A decade-long decline through both Liberal and Conservative governments is underway (Rotberg and Carment 2017) (Fig. 6.2).

When it comes to legally held wealth, the trends are no more encouraging. Since 1984, in Canada, there has been a clear upward trajectory in wealth inequality (Davies and Di Matteo 2021). In fact, by 2018, a mere 87 Canadian families owned as much as 12 million citizens—an amount equivalent to the populations of Newfoundland and Labrador, New Brunswick, and PEI combined (Macdonald 2018). These trends are repeated across the democratic world. The share of wealth held by public actors—those accountable to democratic control—has become close to zero. The vast majority of wealth is held in private hands, and the lion's share of that wealth is held by a minority (6.3).

At the same time, the past thirty years of business in the democratic world have been marked by major mergers in hospital, airline, telecom, defence, retail, and technology industries. The Canadian Competition Bureau has never fully blocked a merger in its 40-year history (Bester 2023). As a result, the global business environment is dominated by vast monopolies, capable of keeping prices high and wages low, while undercutting the economic model of independent small businesses and stifling innovation. Until perhaps very recently, the bipartisan political ideology in the West favoured these moves. Over the past four decades, democratic governments around the world shaped their political economies to the benefit of a few monopolists and financiers, to the detriment of labour and consumers (Gerstle 2022).

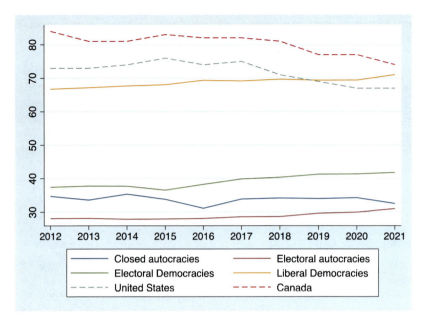

Fig. 6.2 Canada and The United States are losing their status as least corrupt countries. Corruption Perception Index, 2012–2021

Concentrated wealth has political consequences as it drives disenchantment with established parties and leaders, who are seen by many as corrupt enablers of a rigged system. Corruption, and the popular perception of the corruption of leaders whether framed in terms of favouritism, privilege, or back-room dealings all contribute to this decline. In this sense, events like the January 6 insurrection and the so-called Freedom Convoy of 2022 are unsurprising. Elected leaders in Canada and elsewhere have found it increasingly difficult to engage effectively and honestly in global affairs as reality catches up to their rhetoric (Graves 2021).

One unheeded aspect of corruption in Canadian politics is the deepening centralization of power at the federal level. Considering that Canada's key budgets on foreign policy and defence are largely discretionary and vast, there is cause for concern. Not only does centralization privilege unelected political appointments from the Prime Minister's

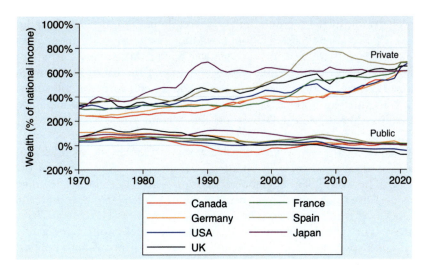

Fig. 6.3 The rise of private wealth and the decline of public wealth in rich countries, 1970–2021 (Data taken from World Inequality Database, https://wid.world/data/)

Office, it also simultaneously closes that office to public oversight and accountability (Rotberg and Carment 2017).

The deepening influence of political machinery on public life in Canada is troubling. For example, political parties now rely extensively on political appointments rather than career bureaucrats to develop and implement foreign policy. The role of political staff and advisers is not to serve the public interest or to sustain the public service. It is a political staffer's job to help re-elect the ruling party.

Whether working as senior advisers, speechwriters or communications specialists, or even quasi-academics with connections back to the political machine, the role of unelected in shaping Canada's foreign policy has only expanded with time. This is corrosive behaviour because these people are not fully accountable to the Canadian public. Couple political interference in public policy with reduced access to information, foreign policies pushed through without proper and full debate and the deployment of Canadian forces on missions that Canadians don't understand, and the promise of more accountable, open government seems uncertain.

The result of these trends is that inherently political decisions—about how resources are allocated, about how often one must work, about gains one makes and where and how they can spend those gains, and about how technology is used—are increasingly out of the hands of sovereign citizens. Instead, these decisions are made by an emergent oligarchic class. Brandeisian notions of "industrial democracy", which underpinned attempts after the Great Depression and Second World War *to preserve democracy*, have all but been destroyed (Stoller 2019).

Taking all the above into consideration, it is clear the world is not looking good for democracy and democracy is not looking good for the world. The world's largest democracy—India—is no longer considered by any measure to be fully democratic. The United States, the most powerful democracy, is trending downward at a disturbing rate (Haken and Fiertz 2023). The outcome of the 2024 US presidential elections may signal a transition towards a more permanently contested if not violent political process.

When an economic focus is introduced, we see that not only is liberty in decline but so, too, are enlightened democratic notions of fraternity and egalitarianism. The consequences for Canada and the rest of the world are severe. The need for improved parliamentary oversight, public debate, and political accountability has never been greater.

Foreign Interference in Canadian Elections: A New Red Scare?

Allegations of Chinese foreign interference in Canadian elections dominated national security news in late 2022 and into 2023. Specifically, news organizations have reported on the existence of CSIS and other intelligence documents reporting Chinese government funding of 11 political candidates in downtown Toronto, a social media influence campaign against MP Kenny Chiu during the 2021 election and coercing of Chinese Canadian students into voting for MP Han Dong.

These reports, which are based on information leaked to the press by members of Canada's intelligence community, raise important questions about what the Prime Minister and other senior elected officials knew and when. Was the Prime Minister willing to take these reports seriously, even as such allegations incriminated members of his own party and as Chinese interference attempts sought primarily to boost Liberal fortunes? Answering that question is not easy. In our view, at the time of writing, there is not sufficient evidence to suggest that the Prime Minister dragged his feet or ignored intelligence reports. Crucially, the reports that have made it to the press do not come with confidence assessments nor without a discussion of the broader context needed to understand the reliability of the base source. Canada's Critical Election Incident Public Protocol (CEIPP) panel, composed of civil servants, did not detect a major threat to the 2019 and 2021 elections. It is almost certain that they saw these same intelligence reports and concluded, based on their differing opinions, that the evidence was not strong enough to warrant public notification.

In any case, public pressure has forced the Prime Minister to request three different oversight reports on foreign election intervention. These reports, run by NSIRA, NSICOP, and the Independent Special Rapporteur on Foreign Interference, will help get to the bottom of this ambiguity. This oversight, in combination with ongoing efforts of Canadian investigative journalists and the lively public debate between national security academics, suggests that Canadians are prepared to ask difficult questions and not simply defer to political elites or remote mandarins.

The more worrying turn for Canadian democracy, however, concerns the ease with which a climate of denunciation has also entered our national discourse. There are ongoing attacks against Chinese Canadians, including a respected Chinese Canadian senator (from Singapore) and a newly elected mayor of Vancouver, who are accused of being agents of the Chinese government. Such allegations result in infringements of people's democratic rights and personal safety. More controversially, Canadian public pressure forced MP Han Dong to resign following allegations that he requested political favours from the Chinese government and advised them to sustain their detention of Michael Kovrig and Michael Spavor. The fact, however, that a press allegation, based on an anonymous source, was able to bring down an elected MP itself bears cautious note.

In the same breath, we also must acknowledge the intimidation foisted upon Chinese Canadians by the action of the Chinese government itself, which has imprisoned Chinese Canadians abroad. Reality, as ever, does not boil down to a black and white dichotomy. Canadians must be diligent to protect their fellow citizens from xenophobic fear domestically and from foreign interference by authoritarian states abroad.

On 10 March 2023, Minister Marco Mendicino announced the launch of consultations of a Foreign Agent Transparency Registry, akin to similar legislation in Australia and the United States. The registry is a good example of a policy instrument that could become deeply politicized if, for example, it does not consider the impact that dual citizen lobbying has on foreign policy and trust in an open society. Democratic states cannot guarantee complete immunity from foreign interference without becoming the enemies of their own open societies. To make vulnerable states fully resistant to foreign influence is to render them closed societies. Promisingly, the Liberal government has made an effort to engage the public and key stakeholders, including members of diaspora groups, in the development of new policy. This is one example of democratic policy building succeeding in the world today.

Democracy Promotion: Past and Present

When it comes to foreign policy, Canada could do worse than having a parliament that is accountable, transparent, and above all, well informed. Perhaps, then, it is troubling to see that the Canadian government is again looking at making democracy promotion a key element of its foreign policy driven in part by a policy of "friend shoring" which would see Canada hitch its bandwagon to those very countries whose democracies are weakening over time. More than ever, it is crucial to learn from the lessons of the past.

Chauvet and Collier's seminal study on the ineffectiveness of aid in inducing reform among weak states and unconsolidated democracies is sobering and relevant (2008). Consistent with our observations above, they conclude that despite massive aid in support of political and economic reform, political development, including democratic processes can be reversed or become stagnant when elite interests deliberately undermine economic and political inclusivity.

The likely sub-optimal outcome in Canada's democracy promotion abroad is borne from a long history of sporadic, uneven, and under-resourced support for such initiatives. Historically Canada's foreign policy approach thrives on "situational ambiguity" and "institutional waffling". Democracy promotion is no different. Far from building effective democratic support mechanisms on comprehensive platforms that align with the national priorities of host governments outcomes have typically been undermined by institutional incoherence, deference to US security priorities, and geopolitical imperatives (Carment and Samy 2016).

For example, the Paul Martin government developed Canada Corps, an inter-departmental body based within CIDA, focused on enhancing knowledge sharing, programming, and coherence on good governance, particularly through two capacities: A whole-of-government coherence mechanism for governance programming; and mobilizing Canadians to participate in governance programming through improved identification of Canadian experience and expertise and improved capacity of the Government of Canada to respond to demands and needs for Canadian technical assistance (e.g. through rosters such as CANADEM). After two years, Canada Corps mutated into the Democracy Council and the Office for Democracy and Governance which were both abandoned in 2007 shortly after Stephen Harper came to power. CANADEM has persisted.[10]

A real problem during the Harper period was the lack of interest in evidence-based decision-making other than that which was narrowly focused on state security and US interests (Carment and Samy 2016). Today, democracy promotion unfolds not within the context of fixing failed and fragile states but as an instrument of war to combat geopolitical rivals. Even before he was elected President of the United States, Joe Biden stressed the importance of building an "alliance of values" based on democratic principles. Biden's goal of democratic renewal has become double edged, defeating political opponents, such as Donald Trump and the Republicans at home and confronting hegemonic challengers abroad.

In a different era, certainly at the height of the Cold War and perhaps shortly thereafter, during the so called "unipolar moment", Biden's polarizing rhetoric might have been a rallying cry for many nations in the developed and developing world. But today, in a multipolar environment, many nations are driven by the pursuit of economic prosperity and are not bound by Cold War values (nor shared threats) (Carment and Belo 2021).

Within this framing, the conventional wisdom underpinning democracy promotion as a foreign policy objective is the idea that all good things, notably markets and liberal democracy, go together. For example, by making the defence of democracy a priority within its National Security Strategy, the United States expects to be a global leader setting itself up for one-sided relationship with smaller, weaker, and more economically

---

[10] Country Indicators for Foreign Policy project developed a democracy and governance methodology for evaluation, and a governance and democracy monitoring tool. Despite being funded by DND, CIDA, IDRC, and DFAIT—there has been no clear discernible impact of its work on operational aspects of policymaking. GAC absorbed some methodologies developed by CIFP. https://carleton.ca/cifp/governance-democracy-processes/data-and-methodology/

dependent states which are not necessarily democracies. This approach is problematic because Western efforts in support of weak states have proven to be relatively ineffective especially in Latin America, the Middle East, and Sub-Saharan Africa.

America's failed policies to sustain and support democracy in Afghanistan Libya, Iraq, and Haiti are perhaps the most notable but so too are challenges in West Africa where Western donors have been compelled to come up with a new approach to democracy promotion there. The failure to prevent an anti-democratic coup in Myanmar underscores the limitations of Western geopolitical reach.

Several decades of democracy support in a variety of nascent political regimes have not enhanced democratic values, institutions, and practices. Indeed, aid policies towards many fragile and conflict-affected states have helped undermine their performance. These states may display all the trapping of democratic institutions such as elections, civilian control of the military, and judicial autonomy but many are, as noted earlier, hybrids engaged in "isomorphic mimicry" that maintain international legitimacy despite structural dysfunctionality. Isomorphic mimicry allows these states to ensure aid flows while creating the illusion of implementing effective developmental policies (Carment and Samy 2019). At the same time, democratic reversals and abuses have become subtler over time (Carment et al. 2019). These abuses are more difficult to monitor. For example, outright military coups have become less common in many parts of the world and those coups which do occur are framed in the context of an effort to restore or improve democracy (for example, Ukraine, Sri Lanka, and Pakistan). Coups in Burkina Faso, Egypt, Guinea, Mali, Mauritania, and Gambia, all of which were led by US trained officers, are considered to be efforts to restore stability and good governance to the country. Such adaptive strategies allow elites to "buy time" to mask non-accomplishment, or actively resist or deflect internal and external pressures for improvement.

Several examples reinforce these points. Afghanistan is a classic case of how foreign aid distribution created distortions, favouring military and security spending over legitimate accountable government. America's primary security objectives in Afghanistan did not change much under George Bush, Barack Obama, or Donald Trump. Instead of securing peace through long-term development, local economic capacity, and improved human rights, the United States largely focused on achieving short-term military objectives (Carment and Belo 2021).

In Egypt, President Obama stood by during General Sisi's military coup in 2013, which overthrew a flawed but democratically elected government. Since then, the American and (Canadian) government have provided billions of dollars in military and security aid to Egypt, while also providing diplomatic cover in the face of rampant human rights abuses. The purported objectives of these policies are to bolster Egypt's counter-terrorism functions and its management of the Sinai-Gaza border. As elsewhere, though, the prioritization of these goals has undermined long-term economic and political development for the Egyptian people.

Ethiopia's ongoing civil war amidst declining democratic accountability, one of the bloodiest in recent history, is driven in part by America's security first agenda which has favoured military aid over good governance. Distortional spending focused on America's security and defence priorities has undermined Ethiopia's commitment to democratic reform by enabling a strong well-armed military more interested in repressing minorities than keeping the peace.

Mali's repeated underperformance is concomitant with an increase in international security assistance. Mali has generally been an aid-dependent country, but that aid increased substantially since its attempts to transition to a hybrid form of democracy. The effects of security support, driven, in part, by promises to reform economically and politically have been remarkably negative.

The problem for these countries is their governments are rarely seen as legitimate by their own citizens and are forced to expend greater resources towards repression and coercion, weakening themselves in the process. Trapped in a low-level equilibrium of weak institutions and poor governance, key factors, which don't maintain the status quo, including democratic oversight, remain under-resourced.

Canada's support for Ukraine is emblematic of the lofty principles invoked by Justin Trudeau, Melanie Joly, and Chrystia Freeland to secure a world in which democracies thrive. Today that goal ranks well behind Russia's defeat on the battlefield, though Russia's withdrawal from Ukrainian territory is one necessary precondition for Ukrainian democracy to flourish. Nevertheless, politicians and the media often fall back on dualistic narratives of the forces and issues at stake. Despite Vladimir Zelensky's highly regarded wartime leadership, it is far from clear that, should Ukraine prove victorious, that he will be able to build a democratic state or even if that is his intention.

As a key ally of Ukraine, Canada has been supporting Kyiv diplomatically as well as through the supply of war materiel and training. However, such support by Ottawa and other NATO members has contributed to more rash and misguided decision-making in Kyiv, making the conflict even more intractable. With respect to democracy support specifically, Canada has two overarching objectives. The first is helping Ukraine develop an inclusive and open democratic society that is tolerant of all minorities and political parties. The second is to find a way to wean Ukraine away from its dependence on an informal economy. These two goals are intertwined and go to the heart of Ukraine's structural problems. Since Russia's invasion of Ukraine in February 2022, Canada has focused on ensuring Ukraine's simple survival as a nation providing loans to service Kiev's sizeable debt, hosting a sizeable number of displaced people, keeping the lights on, and supporting the public sector.

Ukraine remains the only European country deemed essential to Canada's bilateral aid programme. Even before Stephen Harper came to power in 2006, the promotion of democracy in Ukraine was a longstanding area of focus for the Canadian government. But clearly, these efforts have not been enough. Key political obstacles to achieving an inclusive and open political system include deep societal divisions, radicalism on the far right, an increasingly disenchanted and penurious youth, underemployment for women, and an ineffective press that is not free. Aside from Ukraine's lopsided economic performance, the government has trouble protecting property rights, which helps to perpetuate a large informal sector. For many Ukrainian households, in particular, those led by women, an untaxed informal economy is one way of cushioning the impact of economic hardship (Nikolko et al. 2021).

Ukraine's political and economic development has been in decline since 2014 (Carment et al. 2021). The combination of significant capital flight and depopulation following Russia's invasion in 2022 has made the situation much worse (Carment and Belo 2022). The consequences of an unending war are severe. As a rule, protracted conflict marginalizes moderate factions when governance vacuums created by delegitimized politicians are filled by radical leaders. Simultaneously, organized criminal groups move to take control of smuggling operations along borders (Carment and Belo 2022).

Ukraine is already one of the largest arms trafficking markets in Europe, with significant war profiteering and associated criminal elements having grown over the last eight years (Carment and Belo 2022).

In 2021, the Ukrainian government accused former President Petro Poroshenko of war profiteering and involvement in the illegal arms trade. Pundits widely expected Poroshenko to face arrest until Justin Trudeau and Canada's Deputy Prime Minister Chrystia Freeland made personal appeals to prevent Poroshenko's arrest from going to trial.

Looking beyond Ukraine, there is the associated contradiction in the West's desire to build an alliance of democracies, on the one hand, while being a leader on the most pressing global challenges like climate change, the pandemic, and economic recovery, on the other. Each of these "collective action" problems requires a concert of powerful nations—democracies and non-democracies alike—working together. It seems odd that as the United States withdraws from and continues to violate the rules-based agenda, it expects other countries to follow its lead, fall in line and adhere to the international legal system it helped create.

The reality is recent democracy summits are intended to isolate, contain, and separate, not engage. The Lima Group, for example, in which Canada was a leading participant failed to oust Venezuelan leader Maduro from power despite this being a key priority under Donald Trump's presidency. Many countries recognize and oppose this reality in which their political system may soon fall under the watchful gaze of the Biden Administration as a target for "regime change". These concerns were evident in the Summit of the Americas meeting last Spring, in which several key players chose to stay home. Increasingly, states are taking action to sanction proof their economies, wary of American extra-territorial over-reach. The polarization within the Western Hemisphere for example with countries like Mexico, Brazil, and Peru, and others drifting away from American influence is only the beginning.

President Biden's more recent efforts to reach out to "backsliding "nations including Venezuela belies the superficiality of the democratic renewal agenda. For example, faced with an imminent shortfall in oil supplies last Spring, President Biden offered to eliminate a range of sanctions on the country in exchange for access to Venezuela oil. This decision wasn't driven by any lofty goal other than to ensure Americans would not be forced to pay a higher price at the pumps. Indeed, the United States works with many autocracies as needed. Notwithstanding the short-lived Arab Spring, Saudi Arabia, a rights-restrictive absolute monarchy, is a key US ally. Qatar, a country to whom Canada reportedly offered to sell armoured vehicles in late 2021, is another. Other allies in the Middle

East continue to fall back into legitimacy traps, situations where the social contract is weakened in the fate of increasing oppression.

Conclusion

This chapter sought to describe the global state of democracy and situate Canada within that context. As we described, the various institutional indexes that measure democracy are showcasing downward trends. Unfortunately, however, our own analysis points to an even more pessimistic conclusion. There were two main reasons for this. First, these institutions weight each country equally, which dilutes the sea change that would exist should there be an authoritarian transition in the United States. And second, by focusing on the procedural metrics of democracy, these measures neglect questions of good governance and economic fairness. When we turn the focus to questions of economic inequality or outsized corporate power, we see the situation is more dire than even the procedural metrics suggest. The democratic recession is very real. It is a pressing foreign (and domestic) policy challenge for Canada.

Taking these observations into account, we advanced our own argument to explain why these trends are occurring. It is important to distinguish between good governance and democratic processes. Failings in any element of democratic process can result in less-than-optimal governance outcomes, while conditions often associated with good governance can result without democratic process. Democracy is highly fragile and for many states an unobtainable goal. Good governance in contrast speaks to realistic and achievable outcomes, even if part of the ideal outcome is a certain set of processes. When democracies fail at good government, they open themselves to elite capture of political processes and the emergence of rent-seeking economies. Elected leaders will suffer from diminished political autonomy. Anger, distrust, and populism will result. All too often (though not necessarily) this can be taken advantage of by authoritarian actors.

If democracy is in decline, then, the answer may be to rethink how democracy promotion is done and what it means to "promote" democracy. Democracy promotion means something much different now. The shift to instrumentalizing "democratic values" for geopolitical purposes is problematic. Countries, especially those in the Global South, are wary of being used by more powerful nations to support confrontational foreign policies against China and Russia (Carment and Belo 2021, 2022).

Canada's history of democracy promotion has been marred by both deference to US security policies and geopolitical imperatives, as well as by institutional incoherence at home. Dominant political ideologies in Canada—the neoconservatism of the Harper years and the disjointed and often hypocritical liberalism under Trudeau—have not helped. Meanwhile, President Biden's democratic renewal agenda has quickly revealed itself to be a rather transparent political cover for an anti-China and anti Russia alliance (Moeini and Carment 2022).

In our view, a veritable democratic renewal must begin at home. Tackling questions of good governance, of economic fairness, and of political representation are crucial. Abroad, the main challenge to democracy emanates from the United States. Finding ways to disrupt American transition subtly and efficiently to a white-run ethnocracy should be a priority for the Canadian government. Further abroad still, Canada could be an example to tackling wealth inequality and corruption by making a show of tackling it at home first. Doing so would give real credibility to emerging international projects such as the International Corruption Court and the Canadian Centre for Democracy. Canada should likewise emulate the emerging anti-trust trend in the United States, which is one of the brighter aspects of American democracy today.

When it comes to which kind of political orders can deliver economic prosperity there are contrasting examples from which to draw. Rarely do we see good governance enter the discussion. It is troubling that aid programmes still rely on a relatively simplistic benchmark of electoral freedom to gauge which countries are deemed democratically functional or near functional. An obsession with measuring institutional effectiveness based on process legitimacy is problematic (Carment and Samy 2019).

In a deglobalized world caught in an economic slump and recovering from a pandemic where inequality is increasing across and within nations, broadly focused economic outcomes are now more important than ever. This is certainly the message that China brings to the developing world and explains in part why it has achieved great success in delivering that message to the Global South (Carment et al. 2022).

References

Andrews, Matt, Lant Pritchett, and Michael Woolcock. 2017. Looking like a State: The Seduction of Isomorphic Mimicry. In *Building State Capability:*

Evidence, Analysis, Action, eds. Matt Andrews, Lant Pritchett, and Michael Woolcock. Oxford: Oxford University Press.

Angus Reid. 2022. https://angusreid.org/democracy-and-authoritarianism-can ada-usa/.

Bester, Keldon. 2023. Opinion: Canadians Should Be Wary of the Rushed Rogers-Shaw Decision. *The Globe and Mail*, January 1, 2023. https://www.theglobeandmail.com/business/commentary/article-the-rushed-rogers-shaw-decision-shows-canada-is-captive-to-bullying/.

Boese, Vanessa A., Martin Lundstedt, Kelly Morrison, Yuko Sato, and Staffan I. Lindberg. 2022. State of the World 2021: Autocratization Changing Its Nature? *Democratization* 29 (6): 983–1013.

BTI: Trend toward Authoritarian Governance Continues. 2022. BertelsmannStiftung Institute. https://bti-project.org/en/reports/global-report.

Moeini, Arta and David Carment. 2022. The American Security State Comes Home. *Unherd*. https://unherd.com/2022/09/the-american-security-state-comes-home/.

Carment, David, and Dani Belo. 2021. Joe Biden's Bloc Wars and the Next Chapter in the America First Strategy. *Policy Options*. https://policyoptions.irpp.org/fr/magazines/march-2021/joe-bidens-bloc-wars-and-the-next-chapter-in-the-america-first-doctrine/.

Carment, David, and Dani Belo. 2022. *The Ukraine Crisis: More War or Shared Responsibility?* https://iaffairscanada.com/the-ukraine-crisis-more-war-or-shared-responsibility/.

Carment, David, Laura Macdonald, and Jeremy Paltiel. 2022. *Canada Among Nations: Canada and Great Power Competition*. NY: Springer.

Carment, David, Milana Nikolko, and Sam MacIsaac. 2021. Mobilizing Diaspora during Crisis: Ukrainian Diaspora in Canada and the Intergenerational Sweet Spot. *Diaspora Studies* 14 (1): 22–44. https://doi.org/10.1080/09739572.2020.1827667.

Carment, David, Peter Tikuisis, Rachael Calleja, and Mark Haichin. 2019. Backsliding and Reversal: The J Curve Revisited. *Democracy and Security* 15 (1): 1–24.

Carment, David, and Yiagadeesen Samy. 2016. Canada's Fragile States Policy: What Have We Accomplished and Where Do We Go from Here? In *Rethinking Canadian Aid*, eds. S. Brown, M. den Heyer, and D. Black Ottawa: University of Ottawa Press.

Carment, David, and Yiagadeesen Samy. 2019. *Exiting the Fragility Trap: Rethinking Our Approach to the World's Most Fragile States*. Athens: Ohio University Press.

Carothers, Thomas. 2002. The End of the Transition Paradigm. *Journal of Democracy* 13 (1): 5–21.

Chauvet, Lisa, and Paul Collier. (2008). What are the preconditions for turnarounds in failing states? *Conflict Management and Peace Science* 25 (4): 335–348.
Clark, Bruce. 2019. *The Real Thucydides Trap.* London: Chatham House. https://www.chathamhouse.org/sites/default/files/field/field_document/16%20Thucydides%2005.pdf.
Country Indicators for Foreign Policy. https://www.carleton.ca.
Davies, James B., and Livio Di Matteo. 2021. Long Run Canadian Wealth Inequality in International Context. *The Review of Income and Wealth* 67 (1): 134–164.
Democracy Index 2021: The China Challenge. 2022. Economist Intelligence Unit.
Diamond, Larry. 1999. *Developing Democracy: Toward Consolidation.* Baltimore: Johns Hopkins University Press.
Diamond, Larry. 2002. Elections without Democracy: Thinking about Hybrid Regimes. *Journal of Democracy* 13 (2): 21–35.
Diamond, Larry. 2015. Facing Up to the Democratic Recession. *Journal of Democracy* 26 (1): 141–155.
Diamond, Larry, Jonathan Hartlyn, Juan J. Linz, and Seymour Martin Lipset, eds. 1989. *Democracy in Developing Countries. Latin America.* Boulder, CO: Lynne Rienner Publishers.
Gerstle, Gary. 2022. *The Rise and Fall of the Neoliberal Order: America and the World in the Free Market Era.* Oxford: Oxford University Press.
Global State of Democracy Report 2022: Forging Social Contracts in a Time of Discontent. 2022. Global State of Democracy Initiative. https://idea.int/democracytracker/gsod-report-2022.
Graves, Frank. 2021. Polarization, Populism, and the Pandemic: Implications for Canadian Outlook on the World. In *Political Turmoil in a Tumultuous World*, 165–188. Canada Among Nations. Cham: Springer International Publishing. https://doi.org/10.1007/978-3-030-70686-9_8.
Haken, Nate, and Natalie Fiertz. 2023. The United States is Vulnerable: A Flashing Red Light in the Fragile States Index. In *Handbook of Fragile States*, eds. D. Carment and Y. Samy. London: Elgar Press.
Horowitz, Shale Asher. 2005. *From Ethnic Conflict to Stillborn Reform the Former Soviet Union and Yugoslavia.* College Station, TX: Texas A&M University Press.
Huntington, Samuel P. 1991. *The Third Wave: Democratization in the Late Twentieth Century.* Norman: University of Oklahoma Press.
Johnson, Stephen. 2018. Corruption Is Costing the Global Economy $3.6 Trillion Dollars Every Year | World Economic Forum. World Economic Forum. https://www.weforum.org/agenda/2018/12/the-global-economy-loses-3-6-trillion-to-corruption-each-year-says-u-n.

Lawson, Marian L., and Susan B. Epstein. 2019. Democracy Promotion: An Objective of U.S. Foreign Assistance. *Congressional Research Service*, 4 January.

Levitsky, Steven, and Daniel Ziblatt. 2019. *How Democracies Die*. New York: Crown.

Levitsky, Steven, and Lucan Way. 2010. *Competitive Authoritarianism: Hybrid Regimes after the Cold War*. Cambridge: Cambridge University Press.

Lipset, Seymour Martin. 1959. Some Social Requisites of Democracy: Economic Development and Political Legitimacy. *The American Political Science Review* 53 (1): 69–105.

Macdonald, David. 2018. *Born to Win: Wealth Concentration in Canada Since 1999*. Canadian Centre for Policy Alternatives.

Marshall, Monty G., and Benjamin R. Cole. 2014. Global Report 2014: Conflict, Governance, and State Fragility. Washington, DC: Center for Systemic Peace.

Means, Gordon Paul. 1996. Soft Authoritarianism in Malaysia and Singapore. *Journal of Democracy* 7 (4).

Nikolko, M., Sam MacIsaac, and David Carment. 2021. The Impact of Ukraine's Informal Economy on Women: Mobilizing Canada's Diaspora for Growth and Opportunity During Crisis. In *Political Turmoil in a Tumultuous World. Canada and International Affairs*, eds. D. Carment and R. Nimijean. Cham: Palgrave Macmillan. https://doi.org/10.1007/978-3-030-70686-9

Ottaway, Marina. 2003. Democracy Challenged. *Carnegie Endowment for International Peace*. https://doi.org/10.2307/j.ctt1mtz6c5.

Piper, Jessica, and Ally Mutnick. 2022. How Redistricting Shaped the Midterms. *Politico*. https://www.politico.com/news/2022/11/25/redistricting-midterms-00070810.

Przeworski, Adam, and Fernando Limongi. 1997. Modernization: Theories and Facts. *World Politics* 49 (2): 155–183.

Puddington, Arch, and Tyler Roylance. 2017. Freedom in the World 2017: Populists and Autocrats—The Dual Threat to Global Democracy. *Policy File*. Freedom House.

Repucci, Sarah, and Amy Slipowitz. 2022. The Global Expansion of Authoritarian Rule. *Policy File*. Freedom House.

Robinson, Eric. 2017. What Thucydides teaches us about War, Politics and the Human Condition. *War on the Rocks*. https://warontherocks.com/2017/08/what-thucydides-teaches-us-about-war-politics-and-the-human-condition/.

Rotberg, Robert, and David Carment. 2017. *Canada's Corruption at Home and Abroad: At Home and Abroad*. NY: Routledge.

Schake, Kori. 2017. The Summer of Misreading Thucydides. *The Atlantic*. https://www.theatlantic.com/international/archive/2017/07/the-summer-of-misreading-thucydides/533859/.

Schedler, Andreas. 2006. *Electoral Authoritarianism: The Dynamics of Unfree Competition*. Boulder: Lynne Rienner.
Stoller, Matt. 2019. *Goliath: The 100-Year War between Monopoly Power and Democracy*. New York: Simon & Schuster.
The Economist. 2022. A New Low for Global Democracy, February 9. https://www.economist.com/graphic-detail/2022/02/09/a-new-low-for-global-democracy.
Vanhanen, Tatu. 1990. *The Process of Democratization: A Comparative Study of 147 States, 1980–88*. New York: Crane, Russak.
Wigell, Mikael. 2008. Mapping 'Hybrid Regimes': Regime Types and Concepts in Comparative Politics. *Democratization* 15 (2): 230–250.
Zakaria, Fareed. 1997. The Rise of Illiberal Democracy. *Foreign Affairs* 76 (6): 22–43.

PART II

Challenges Ahead

CHAPTER 7

Inclusive Approaches to Multilateral Democracy Cooperation: Challenges and Opportunities for Canada

Catherine Hecht

INTRODUCTION

Two recent Summits hosted by the United States—the Summit for Democracy in December 2021 and the Summit of the Americas in June 2022—resorted to exclusive multilateralism, as the host extended invitations only to those states it deemed "democratic." During preparations and in the wake of these Summits, objections emerged from democratic and non-democratic states alike. The President of Mexico, Andrés Manuel López Obrador, for example, refused to attend the 2022 Summit of the Americas in protest of the exclusion of Cuba, Nicaragua, and Venezuela, sending his foreign minister instead. El Salvador, Honduras, Guatemala,

C. Hecht (✉)
School of Public Policy and Global Affairs, University of British Columbia, Vancouver, BC, Canada
e-mail: catherine.hecht@ubc.ca

© The Author(s), under exclusive license to Springer Nature Switzerland AG 2023
M. A. Cameron et al. (eds.), *Democracy and Foreign Policy in an Era of Uncertainty*, Canada and International Affairs, https://doi.org/10.1007/978-3-031-35490-8_7

and Bolivia also sent lower-level representatives.[1] Among the Heads of State who attended the Summit of the Americas, leaders of Argentina, Chile, Belize, and Barbados added to criticism of the Biden administration's approach.[2] By contrast, Canada largely avoided engaging in the contentious debates about invitations. As Canada designs its future engagement in cooperation for democratic development, however, it is worthwhile to consider the content of some of its allies' critiques and the opportunities and challenges presented by inclusive multilateral approaches.[3]

Political leaders at the 2022 Summit of the Americas emphasized their states' commitment to democratic principles and human rights, yet several argued against excluding states based on regime type and avoiding isolation of countries in the region. Their reasoning combined appeals for deliberation with instrumental and normative elements. For example, President Alberto Fernández of Argentina argued: "dialogue and diversity is the best tool to promote democracy, modernization, and the fight against inequality." President Gabriel Boric of Chile added: "when we disagree… we need to be able to speak to each other face to face."[4] Several connected their criticism of exclusive approaches with the potential benefits of regional integration including supporting peace, pandemic recovery, addressing migration and the climate crisis, development, or improving well-being. Explaining that Cuba provided essential health care experts to almost two-thirds of the countries in the hemisphere during the pandemic, Prime Minister Hon. John Briceño of Belize argued that Cuba should not be isolated because of its cooperation on these issues. Others cautioned against unintended consequences. As Prime Minister Philip

---

[1] See, for example, Kevin Liptak, "Snubs from Key Leaders at Summit of the Americas reveal Biden's Struggle to assert US leadership in its Neighborhood," CNN, June 8, 2022. https://www.cnn.com/2022/06/07/politics/summit-of-the-americas-joe-biden/index.html.

[2] Video recordings of leaders' speeches at the 2022 Summit of the Americas are available at: https://www.youtube.com/watch?v=IKYt4ZTAIMs&list=PLttPZGCY6Nq87YgpPZzBwT9wrY8sa1_3O&index=10, https://www.youtube.com/watch?v=QMfbbGZLkRs&list=PLttPZGCY6Nq87YgpPZzBwT9wrY8sa1_3O&index=20

[3] Maxwell Cameron, The Americas after American Hegemony, Open Canada Podcast #11 with Ben Rowswell, August 9, 2022. https://opencanada.libsyn.com/11-the-americas-after-american-hegemony-with-maxwell-cameron

[4] Citations were transcribed from the recorded speeches available at the links provided in Footnote 2.

Davis of the Bahamas stated, "when we push away those with whom we disagree they often take comfort in one another and deepen their alliances in the face of our hostility…and such alliances can challenge our peace and security." By contrast, a Biden administration official justified excluding Cuba, Nicaragua, and Venezuela based on "concerns about human rights and a lack of democracy in the three nations."[5] A separate and powerful stream of justifications for inclusion, however, invoked states' own prior experiences of exclusion. Prime Minister Davis stated: "for too long, the approach in the region has been about us, without us."[6] Claims invoking fairness, equality, and active participation are frequently recurring counterpoints in these critiques. That these ideas are expressed not only by representatives of excluded states but also by invited (democratic) states speaks to the current salience of less stratified, more inclusive multilateral processes. Among Canada's allies in the Americas, Asia, and Africa, many states seek a range of trading and other partners, which also limits interest in exclusive arrangements.

Yet what opportunities exist for cooperation on democratic development through inclusive[7] multilateral channels? Several global and regional normative frameworks on democracy have stagnated or gone dormant in recent years and in today's contentious international politics, one might doubt that conversations with autocrats can yield democratic outcomes.

North American and European foreign policymakers have tended to underestimate the extent to which democracy has been a symbol of exclusion of states in international society after the Cold War (Clark 2005; Hurrell 2007; Viola 2020; Geis 2013), with potential consequences. More typically, Western diplomats have viewed democracy as unifying and contributing to peace. Having codified by consensus the idea that "democracy, development, and respect for human rights and fundamental freedoms are interdependent and mutually reinforcing" among the 171 United Nations (UN) member states at the Vienna World Conference on

---

[5] Matt Spetalnick and Dave Graham. June 7, 2022 "U.S. bars Cuba, Venezuela from Americas summit; Mexican leader sits out." https://www.reuters.com/world/americas/us-excludes-cuba-venezuela-nicaragua-americas-summit-sources-2022-06-06/ (last accessed 2/2023).

[6] Citations were transcribed from the recorded speeches, see Footnote 2.

[7] Inclusiveness refers here to transcending a particular basis of social stratification in a given multilateral venue, in this case across states with democratic and authoritarian regimes.

Human Rights in 1993,[8] scholars and practitioners optimistically viewed democracy as a core principle underpinning (global) international order. This perception was strengthened in the 1990s and early 2000s as global and regional multilateral institutions bridging states with diverse regime types managed to generate consensus on democratic norm sets. Recurring resolutions on elections and support to new and restored democracies, as well as a resolution on "promoting and consolidating democracy" (A/RES/55/96, 2000) were adopted by the UN General Assembly. Also in those years, frameworks such as the Conference on Security and Co-operation in Europe's Charter of Paris and Copenhagen Document of 1990 and the Inter-American Democratic Charter of 2001 were adopted. Related international cooperation helped some states to improve respect for human rights and the performance of democratic institutions.

More recently, in addition to the well-documented democratic backsliding and decline in the quality of democracy observed across world regions, there has been an upsurge of *status-related contestation* based on democracy and human rights, in which representatives of one or multiple states express claims of unfairness against symbols, institutions, or actors that perpetuate their marginalization in a particular multilateral venue (Hecht 2021). With potentially paralyzing effects, these discursive challenges draw on international law and norms such as sovereign equality. Especially in international organizations (IOs) without formal socio-political prerequisites for participation, if states are stigmatized or excluded for non-compliance with democratic norms (even with codified commitments), this comes into tension with their expectations of sovereign equality as the basis for participation and inclusion.

The reactions of Russia and China to the 2021 Summit for Democracy are examples of status-related contestation unconnected to a particular multilateral venue. They responded, *inter alia*, to the Summit reinforcing the salience of democracy as a basis of social stratification in the (global) international society of states. The Biden administration has argued that the contest between democracy and autocracy is the challenge of our time. Ideological or geopolitical motivations, however, are potentially counterproductive. Excluding Russia and China from the Summit heightened the social visibility of their relative standing among states (and great powers) based on democracy and human rights. Less than two months after

---

[8] Vienna Declaration and Programme of Action 1993, Part 1, ¶8.

the 2021 Summit for Democracy, in February 2022, China and Russia signed a joint statement committing to strengthened cooperation.[9] Three months after the 2021 Summit for Democracy, Russia invaded Ukraine with a 64-kilometer convoy of tanks followed by over a year of unrelenting brutality at the time of this writing. This chapter cannot analyze the complex motivations and histories of Russian or Chinese foreign policies. Several scholars have documented the roles of status concerns and emotions such as humiliation in these cases (Deng 2008; Larson and Shevchenko 2010, 2014; Tsygankov 2012, *i.a.*). Contestation is a consideration as Canada plans its engagement and follow-up to the Second Summit for Democracy held in late March 2023. The geopolitical context presents challenges to international efforts to protect human dignity.

Miscalculation of the appeal of a democratic club led by the United States in 2021 partly stems from underestimating the increased salience of newer policy areas that now co-exist with democracy and human rights as core values in international society. Globally salient normative agendas comprise issues such as addressing the climate crisis, pandemic preparedness and recovery, gender equality, fighting inequalities and discrimination, sustaining peace, and achieving the Sustainable Development Goals (SDGs). In multilateral venues, it can be productive for Canada to pursue new synergies between cooperation for democratic governance and other currently salient ideas and international agendas.

The remainder of this chapter elaborates on these themes. In a first step, I examine advantages and disadvantages of inclusive approaches to multilateral democracy cooperation. I then discuss lessons and potential entry points and propose ideas for Canada's engagement.

Inclusive Approaches to Multilateral Democracy Cooperation: Advantages and Disadvantages

Multilateral support for democratic governance and human rights has been integral to Canadian foreign policy. From John Humphrey's role in drafting the Universal Declaration of Human Rights (UDHR) to Louise

---

[9] https://fm.cnbc.com/applications/cnbc.com/resources/editorialfiles/2022/03/31/Joint_Statement_of_the_Russian_Federation_and_the_Peoples_Republic_of_China_on_the_International_Relations_Entering_a_New_Era_and_the_Global_Sustainable_Development__President_of_Russia.pdf

Arbour's tenure as UN High Commissioner for Human Rights, Canadians have held international leadership roles on these issues, including during specific crises (e.g., Lloyd Axworthy during Peru's transition in 2001; Bob Rae as Special Envoy in Myanmar in 2017–2018). Canada has also advanced important intergovernmental processes, including preparations for the Inter-American Democratic Charter in 2001 (Cooper and Legler 2006: 62–83). At the Summit for Democracy in December 2021, Canadian Prime Minister Justin Trudeau announced the creation of a new "Canadian centre for global democracy."[10] Before discussing the potential place of inclusive multilateral approaches in Canada's democracy cooperation toolbox, this section first considers advantages and disadvantages of such approaches.

Large, heterogeneous organizations like the UN are among several layers in Canada's international engagement to support democratic governance and human rights. While global and regional multilateral arenas may not be the most efficient, they have normative frameworks and comparative advantages that complement Canada's bilateral and multistakeholder partnerships. Global IOs can facilitate communication between actors in different world regions who might not otherwise interact and support non-coercive implementation processes. Norms codified during UN-sponsored summits or in the UN General Assembly have the advantage of collective endorsement by the UN's full membership. Recurring meetings enable negotiators to regularly probe the international political environment for windows of opportunity, while reiteration of codified norms keeps commitments alive during contentious periods (Thomas 2001; Hecht 2016). The UN does not promote a particular model of democracy and is generally seen as less politically motivated and more neutral than bilateral actors, stemming in part from its earlier support for elections in the context of decolonization (Newman and Rich 2004).

Critics of inclusive approaches to multilateral democracy cooperation object, for example, to large, heterogeneous IOs' tendency toward lowest-common-denominator agreements or the election of human rights-abusing states to international leadership positions such as in the

---

[10] https://pm.gc.ca/en/news/speeches/2021/12/09/prime-ministers-remarks-summit-democracy. December 9, 2021. Prime Minister's Remarks at the Summit for Democracy.

Human Rights Council. They raise the important question of credibility, which statements about democracy spoken by authoritarian leaders lack. Negotiations in global or regional multilateral venues ideally lead to action that affirms democratic norms.[11] Inclusive approaches, critics argue, lack clarity about the differences between democratic and authoritarian regimes (Dumitriu 2003).

Along similar lines, not all states at the 2022 Summit of the Americas favored inclusive multilateralism; some highlighted the relevance of denouncing and excluding autocrats. For example, President Iván Duque of Colombia stated: "the genocide that we see today in Ukraine is the product of an autocracy…We can't keep quiet vis-à-vis the dictatorship in Venezuela, in Nicaragua, or... Cuba. Being indifferent to these phenomena is being indifferent to the pain of these peoples." Citing Martin Luther King, he added: "Silence makes us accomplices." He concluded: "We have to maintain our principles; we have to make sure they are clear…Never do we have to make sure that these Summits are a fertile territory for dictators."[12]

Nevertheless, binary (or worse, politicized) judgments of states as "democratic" or "non-democratic" risk overlooking democratic actors in the civil societies of authoritarian regimes who can benefit from and contribute to international partnerships. Excluding some states from participation in summits can adversely affect civil society actors' participation in transnational networks. Conversely, in "established" democracies, non-democratic parties and populist groups have grown. Democracies and autocracies consist of overlapping shades at the sub-national level; political regimes comprise more complexity than judgments about national-level characteristics can capture (Gillies, this volume; O'Donnell 1993). Moreover, normative commitments made in inclusive multilateral institutions are used by civil society actors in their advocacy efforts to increase political pressures on their states for compliance (Keck and Sikkink 1998; Thomas 2001). These advocacy strategies depend on inclusive multilateral venues that codify the international commitments to which the activists appeal, often by consensus, and that do not exclude their states (or civil societies by association) for lack of compliance.

---

[11] Author's interview with Senior IO representative, 10 November 2022, via Zoom.
[12] Speeches available at the link at Footnote 2.

On the operational side, the UN system and other IOs have had widely varied results in supporting democratic governance, yet it is difficult to generalize across cases (Newman and Rich 2004). Critiques that such organizations are prone to using blueprints or, for example, that they have insufficiently integrated processes for meaningful consultation, consent, and ownership (Chesterman 2004), have led to initiatives (albeit unevenly) to improve participation and accountability mechanisms. Limited resources often plague IOs' operations, although some UN programs have adapted in creative ways, such as with innovation labs. Other challenges to implementation have occurred when a state, or group of states, blocks consensus decisions on elaborating agendas or mandates, as has often occurred in the Organization for Security and Co-operation in Europe (OSCE) in the human dimension for several years. David Carment and Yiagadeesen Samy (2016) have argued that Canada's role could be enhanced in working with local, national, and international partners in post-conflict states to improve coordination and cooperation, for example, in early warning efforts, or sharing knowledge and information. Such approaches can thus reinforce multilateral efforts in states where Canada is one of many actors attempting to support peacebuilding and sustaining peace.

Inclusive multilateral approaches have an advantage of pluralism among states yet are vulnerable on the difficult question of what to do about the autocrats and dictators. In the mid-1940s, negotiators employed an exclusive approach: Only those states that had declared war on Germany and Japan were invited to participate in the San Francisco conference to adopt the UN Charter and the Axis powers were not invited to participate in the drafting of the Universal Declaration of Human Rights. In subsequent decades, however, delegations typically sought the greatest possible consensus in global norm-setting and decision-making for legitimation purposes (Claude 1966: 370). Moreover, inclusive multilateral venues provide a space for democracy to speak for itself. As former UN Secretary-General Kofi Annan argued, the best way to help democracies flourish is "to inspire people to import it by demonstrating that democracy works."[13]

---

[13] Kofi Annan (Dec. 6, 2016): Democracy Under Pressure, *New York Times*. https://www.nytimes.com/2016/12/06/opinion/democracy-under-pressure.html (last accessed 3/2023).

How might the content of democracy-related commitments in global and regional organizations evolve? Scholars have documented multiple challenges to democracy in recent years—from internal sources including populist leaders, difficulties improving standards of living, and political polarization, as well as external challenges from authoritarian states' foreign policies (see Carothers 2016a; Youngs 2016; Rich 2017). Canada and democratic allies need to think creatively and use all possible mechanisms to support recommitment to basic democratic ideals.

A potential way forward is to reconnect multilateral cooperation on governance-related topics more explicitly with ideals of political inclusion, yet also to push the envelope in the direction of economic and social inclusion. We might expect *political equality*, a core ideal at the heart of democracy, to resonate more strongly than it currently does in the post-2015 international normative environment. Ideals of political equality have the advantage of procedural legitimacy (Young 2000; Hurrell 2007: 77–92). They resonate with the globally salient concept of *leaving no one behind*. It also seems important to connect support for (components of) democratic governance with other currently salient concepts and issues. Support for democracy as an end in its own right is now more difficult to justify to the broad audience of UN member states and the global public than ideals of inclusive governance (as an independent variable) that support salient collective substantive aspirations such as building peace, fighting climate change, or achieving the Sustainable Development Goals.

Recent conceptual innovations at the global level are bridging procedural and substantive legitimacy in interesting ways. Canada's engagement on democracy would arguably benefit from tapping into such trends. Some related synergies are already contained in Canada's *Feminist International Assistance Strategy* (see Bardall, this volume).[14] For example, the idea of *leaving no one behind* conveys a concern for non-discrimination and greater equality of opportunity and outcomes (Fukuda-Parr and Hegstad 2019). Similarly, the fundamental concept of *dignity* has been rising in salience at the global level (Rich 2017: 58)[15] and bridges multiple forms of inclusion—political, economic, and social;

[14] https://www.international.gc.ca/world-monde/issue_developmentenjeux_developpement/priorities-priorites/policy-politique.aspx?lang=eng.

[15] See the UN's home page and statement: "Peace, dignity and equality on a healthy planet," https://www.un.org/en/about-us.

individual and collective. Whereas advocates of *human rights* in global venues have been criticized for focusing on civil and political rights over economic, social, and cultural rights, and as proponents of *development* have been criticized for the concept's colonial undertones, the increased salience of *leaving no one behind* and *dignity* in large, heterogenous multilateral venues in recent years suggest a global policy window for cooperation that delivers greater equity and equality, both in terms of inclusive governance and (socioeconomic and ecological) outcomes.

Current trends toward increased multidirectionality and partnership in democracy cooperation are also important for relevance in a post-Western international order. This includes expanding recognition of contributions and knowledge from partners in the global South (Koelble and Lipuma 2008; Holthaus and Christensen 2022). In this respect, it can be worthwhile to reframe and update the terminology employed in democracy cooperation. For example, democracy supporters can abandon the dehumanizing metaphor of "carrots" and "sticks" in favor of partnerships. Similarly, language of "democracy promotion," which has come to imply imposition of democratic norms rather than a multi-directional learning process can be replaced with terminology and practices that acknowledge mutual contributions. After all, democracy promotion is a contradiction in terms; imposing democracy goes against the idea that the will of the people should be the basis of the authority of government (see Rich 2017: 46). As Thomas Carothers argues (2016b: 2–3):

> a basic divide between the established democracies and the non-Western countries who are struggling to become democratic—no longer holds. The similarities of democratic challenges across all regions of the world are much greater than the differences... Aassistance should be redesigned and presented publicly as a common entreprise aimed at alleviating democratic deficiencies both here and there, highlighting the value of mutual learning and flows of knowledge in both directions.

In terms of their convening function, large, heterogenous international organizations have a comparative advantage—they offer platforms for a wide range of actors from different world regions to share knowledge, experiences, and good practices on a recurring basis. Strengthening such platforms through the UN system and other (regional) multilateral venues can support mutual learning between representatives of governments, IOs, the private sector, and civil society, among others, for example, on democratic innovations that contribute to equitable outcomes and achieving shared goals. Inclusive multilateralism offers opportunities for actors to showcase and debate how democracies can better deliver for the people and the planet. Such venues also enable reiteration of (democratic) norms and principles, to help keep them alive during contentious periods. In a context of shifting international legitimacy principles and power in global politics, the appeal of democratic governance depends on its ability to deliver on a range of goals, e.g., well-being, socioeconomic development, peace, and environmental protection, which societies define in various ways. The next section considers opportunities and challenges in this context for Canada's engagement in inclusive approaches to multilateral democracy cooperation.

Opportunities and Challenges for Canada

As mentioned above, in 2021 Prime Minister Trudeau proposed to establish a Canadian centre for global democracy. What does the Canadian government mean by *global* democracy in this context? Few clues are provided in recent public statements. An initial step in thinking about opportunities and challenges for Canada in supporting global democracy is to consider visions of what might be the future place of democracy in global politics.

Are we observing, as some suggest, the beginning of a new Cold War, with a democratic bloc on one side? While the international system may become increasingly bipolar, several important dissimilarities with the Cold War between the United States and the Soviet Union are highlighted by Deborah Larson, including differences in the level of ideological competition, more frequent interaction between the United States and China, and a greater connection of their economies. She adds that "because of globalization, it is unlikely that the world will return to the mutually exclusive trading blocs of the Cold War" (2020: 175–178). Instead, with reference to Yan Xuetong's research, Larson underlines *status* as a primary aspect of competition, for which China has sought moral leadership along economic lines (2020: 178–179). Because many states and non-state actors simultaneously seek positive relations with both China and the United States, the international normative environment is likely to be more variegated than during the Cold War.

Another difference is that, although with different meanings, states of all types continue to use the language of democracy in communications to a global audience. The general concept of democracy holds a level of global salience, even if its (liberal) content is contested (Bukovansky 2007; Bridoux et al. 2012). Nevertheless, China, Russia, and other states present headwinds to cooperation on democracy-related issues in global and some regional IOs, as well as at local level in several cases. Their contestation against the *implementation* of bilateral and multilateral programs to support democratic governance and human rights has increased, as has their engagement with non-democratic actors in long-standing and newer democracies, as many analysts have noted. The inauspicious geopolitical context amid widespread democratic backsliding suggests that it may be a challenge to manage public expectations about potential results of a Canadian centre for global democracy.

One interpretation is that Canada intends to mainstream cooperation for democratic governance into its global programs and foreign policy. Contributors to the June 2019 House of Commons Standing Committee on Foreign Affairs and International Development report, *Renewing Canada's Role in International Support for Democratic Development*, note that resource constraints prevent Canada's extensive bilateral democracy support in more than a limited number of countries (e.g., Haiti, Ukraine).[16] Still quite distant from its international commitment to provide 0.7% of GNI in official development assistance (ODA), Canada's ODA increased by 8% in 2021 to 0.32% of GNI, in part due to increased COVID-19 and climate financing.[17] In the above-cited 2019 House of Commons Report, Christopher MacLennan of Global Affairs Canada (GAC) mentioned that because of political sensitivity, it can be challenging for GAC to support the more political aspects of democratic development,[18] which suggests a role for the proposed new Canadian democratic development institution. Given Canada's middle power status, multilateral cooperation would seem even more significant for Canada's aid than for the much larger assistance programs of the United States and United Kingdom, which the report studied as potential examples.

---

[16] https://www.ourcommons.ca/Content/Committee/421/FAAE/Reports/RP1058 0262/faaerp28/faaerp28-e.pdf.

[17] https://www.oecd.org/dac/financing-sustainable-development/development-fin ance-standards/ODA-2021-summary.pdf. OECD, 2022. ODA Levels in 2021 - Preliminary Data, p. 3.

[18] p. 31. See Footnote 15.

In some cases, it can be counterproductive to use the contested language of democracy if the aim is to pursue narrower goals such as supporting elections or fighting corruption, which are generally less contested. Especially since 2015, some actors in the UN system have shifted away from the language of democracy to avoid tensions with China or other states. Actors without a mandate to support "democracy" such as the World Bank have used the language of good governance from the 1990s. While the United Nations Development Programme (UNDP) supported *democratic governance* in the mid-2000s and early 2010s, it now supports "inclusive" governance or drops the adjective altogether, while UN Women encourages women's political participation.[19]

Some components of democratic governance (free and fair elections, participation of women in politics, education for democracy, inclusive institutions, etc.) have stand-alone normative frameworks at the global and regional levels that enjoy notably higher levels of consensus than broader norm sets on democratic governance. An example is the consistently high support for a recurring UNGA resolution, "Strengthening the role of the United Nations in the promotion of democratization and enhancing periodic and genuine elections," which was voted upon by UN member states on 12 occasions—yearly between 1990 and 1995, and bi-yearly between 1997 and 2007—and it received only 13 "No" votes in its history: 8 in 1990, 4 in 1991, and 1 in 1994.[20] Support for this resolution increased from 88% of voting UN member states in 1990 to 93% in 1999, to 99% in 2007. It was adopted without a vote in 1988, 1989, 2009, 2011, 2013, 2019, and 2021.[21] On the basis of these resolutions, UN operations engage in concrete areas of electoral support that respond to expressed needs and work directly with civil society.

The UN Democracy Fund (UNDEF) is an initiative that Canada could consider further supporting. In line with Canada's priorities, UNDEF supports local civil society organizations (rather than working directly with governments as do many other UN funds and programs) on a range of topics related to democratic development, through an annual

---

[19] Author's interview with Senior IO representative, 10 November 2022, via Zoom.

[20] Voting record search, UNBISnet.org.

[21] A recorded vote was requested by the Russian Federation in 2015 and 2017. In 2015, it was adopted by 155 votes to 0, with 15 abstentions (A/C.3/70/SR.48, pgs. 7–8). In 2017, it was adopted by 148 votes to 0 with 14 abstentions (A/C.3/72/SR.44, p. 13).

competition for grants of up to $300,000 USD.[22] Countries that have provided funding to UNDEF over the years are a diverse and fluctuating group from all world regions and levels of national income. Financial contributions range from $5,000 to several million USD in given years. Although UNDEF has been operating since 2005, Canada neglected it for thirteen years until 2017, with contributions only in 2017, 2021, 2022, and 2023.[23] Canada's contribution of $1,562,840 USD was UNDEF's third largest of 2022, and it donated $743,716 USD as of March 2023. In 2022, Canada also held the Chairship of the International Institute for Democracy and Electoral Assistance (International IDEA), an intergovernmental organization with headquarters in Stockholm that aims to strengthen and safeguard democratic institutions at all levels. It remains to be seen if Canada's recent support signals a shift toward a stronger commitment to inclusive multilateral approaches to democracy cooperation.

One of the most inclusive multilateral venues for cooperation on democratic governance, the International Conferences on New or Restored Democracies (ICNRD) movement, has been largely dormant for over a decade, but its rise and decline offer some useful lessons. The ICNRD emerged in 1988 on the initiative of 13 new and restored democracies who sought greater international cooperation but rejected external interference. The second ICNRD conference was held in 1994 under the UN umbrella and led to a recurring UNGA resolution, "Support by the UN system for the efforts of Governments to promote and consolidate new or restored democracies." With rotating hosts in different world regions, ICNRD conferences in the 1990s and early 2000s initially helped to galvanize the UN's broader efforts to support democratic development (see Dumitriu 2003; Hecht 2017; Rich 2017). In 2000, ICNRD conferences became open to the participation of any UN member state, while the more exclusive Community of Democracies, launched in 2000, issued invitations only to states considered to be democratic by its Governing Council. The ICNRD movement enjoyed some dynamism but lost steam in the mid- to late 2000s, in part due to its inclusiveness. After being led by Qatar in 2006–2009 the baton passed in 2009–2012 to Venezuela

---

[22] See https://www.un.org/democracyfund/about-undef.

[23] https://www.un.org/democracyfund/sites/www.un.org.democracyfund/files/contributions_undef_2005-20221104.pdf (last accessed 3/2023).

under President Hugo Chavez, when ICNRD conferences ceased and although the resolution is still on the UNGA provisional agenda, it has not been considered since 2012.

What can be learned? Energy in the early years of the ICNRD movement stemmed from it being an initiative of new or restored democracies themselves and perceptions of the UN system and partners responding to their priorities. For Canada, the ICNRD example suggests the importance of connecting engagement on (democratic) governance in multilateral venues with highly salient current priorities. In the 1990s, new and restored democracies emphasized linkages between cooperation for democracy and challenges of addressing conflicts, social instability, and raising standards of living. New content for the recurring resolution responded to current challenges in years when the movement retained political will, but lack of institutionalization (e.g., a secretariat) partly inhibited its development, as energy focused on the more exclusive Community of Democracies, and alternative regional groupings became more significant to states in regions such as Latin America.[24] Equitable geographical representation was an important feature of the movement's leadership, as well as commitment, credibility, and diplomatic capacity to advance and further the agendas. As self-categorization as a new or restored democracy became less integral to many states' social identities, this framing held reduced relevance for activism on these issues. Today, opportunities for (re-)engagement on inclusive or democratic governance in the UN system appear, for example, in connection with implementation of the 2030 Agenda, climate action, and sustaining peace agendas.

Promising for cooperation related to democratic governance would be to expand the convening functions of global multilateral venues for cross-regional exchanges of good practices, experiences, technical expertise, and democratic innovations. Effectively including a wider range of voices from civil societies has been an ongoing challenge in international policy-making, given the number of potential actors involved and asymmetries of expertise and power (Steffek 2018). With the importance Canada places on civil society, both domestically and internationally, it could be fruitful to explore new avenues for input into global and regional policy-making processes and operations, perhaps using digital technologies. International IDEA is a logical partner in such areas, as it has good connections with

---

[24] Author's interview with Senior IO representative, 10 November 2022, via Zoom.

local civil society actors involved in democracy-related projects through its regional offices. International IDEA has also been active in follow-up to the Summits for Democracy.[25] As power shifts to Asia, Canada could make better use of Vancouver as a natural diplomatic meeting point to facilitate new conversations between representatives of states and societies from the East and West, North and South.

Some discussions among local, national, regional, and global partners have been gaining momentum on topics related to the 2030 Agenda for Sustainable Development and the SDGs. It would seem promising to build on this dynamism in the UN system. Canada's second Voluntary National Review (VNR) of Canada's Implementation of the 2030 Agenda for Sustainable Development is due to be presented to the UN in 2023.[26] On topics related to governance, a large community has mobilized around SDG 16 as a point of orientation. For example, UNDP's Oslo Governance Centre and International IDEA have been engaged in various cross-regional initiatives on SDG 16 (promote peaceful and inclusive societies for sustainable development, provide access to justice for all and build effective, accountable, and inclusive institutions at all levels). According to its 2020 Annual Report, "36% of UNDP's program expenditure was invested in governance in 2020."[27] Beyond SDG 16, there are multistakeholder communities working on broader issues of governance for the SDGs. For example, the OECD and UNDP have issued recommendations on public governance and the SDGs.[28] There has also been a group of "Friends of governance for sustainable development" chaired by the governments of Germany, Morocco, Nigeria, Republic of Korea

---

[25] See, for example, International IDEA's work on monitoring the Summit for Democracy commitments: https://summitfordemocracyresources.eu/commitment-dashboard/ (last accessed 3/2023).

[26] Canada's first VNR in 2018 is available here: https://sustainabledevelopment.un.org/content/documents/20312Canada_ENGLISH_18122_Canadas_Voluntary_National_ReviewENv7.pdf VNRs of all countries can be accessed at: https://hlpf.un.org/countries (last accessed 3/2023).

[27] https://annualreport.undp.org/2020/assets/UNDP-Annual-Report-2020-en.pdf pg. 25.

[28] https://www.oecd.org/gov/sustainable-development-goals-and-public-governance.htm.
  https://publicadministration.un.org/en/Intergovernmental-Support/Committee-of-Experts-on-Public-Administration/Governance-principles.

and Romania.[29] Tapping into synergies with globally salient, expanding frameworks could help both agendas develop new and more effective practices.

Finally, going up a level of abstraction could help infuse democratic ideals with new content. Terminologies like *empowered inclusion, collective agenda formation*, and *collective decision-making* offer possibilities to think about core (democratic) governance principles in new ways (Warren 2017). Disconnecting international conversations from some of the ideological and geopolitical baggage that has burdened democracy in the past decades might offer a chance for it to regain some of its promise. As *sustainable development* has shown, an abstract new term operating in parallel to older concepts could offer a route to exploring bridges between political equality, other democratic ideals, and equality of socioeconomic opportunities and outcomes, as conveyed in the increasingly salient concepts of dignity and leaving no one behind.

Conclusions

This chapter has discussed several potential ideas for Canada's ongoing and future engagement in multilateral democracy cooperation. Large, heterogenous IOs are not a panacea. Nevertheless, efforts in the UN system and regional organizations can complement Canada's bilateral and other cooperation. Democracy has been a basis of division in international society, recently observed atby the 2021 Summit for Democracy and the 2022 Summit of the Americas. Contestation against exclusive approaches by democratic and non-democratic states alike called attention to the salience of additional values, unintended security consequences of isolation, and widespread interest in active participation in less stratified multilateral processes. In a shifting international order, addressing societal inequalities, alongside re-articulating core values such as political equality, might help to revive the next stage of (multilateral) cooperation to support democratic governance.

Of possible ways forward, perhaps most important is the power of Canada's example in communicating with humility that democracy can work and deliver to improve peoples' lives. This entails improving its domestic record on inclusive governance and access to services for all,

[29] https://friendsofgovernance.org/.

as well as other international commitments, including increasing ODA levels.

Ideally, the new Canadian centre for global democracy will have a strong multilateral component. This chapter proposed expanding multilateral platforms for cross-regional exchanges of good practices and democratic innovations among representatives of states and civil societies; updating and reframing terminology used in democracy cooperation; increased recognition of the expertise and contributions of partners in the global South; and connecting democracy cooperation with highly salient current priorities and agendas, such as climate action, sustaining peace, and sustainable development. In inauspicious contexts, some ideological tensions can be mitigated by referring to specific components of democratic governance (e.g., elections, inclusive institutions, fighting corruption), many of which are less contested at the international level. In line with Canada's feminist foreign policy, multilateral democracy cooperation could benefit from reconnecting with ideals of political equality, with attention to equitable socioeconomic and ecological outcomes that are currently salient at the global level.

Protecting human dignity sits at the core of many multilateral organizations because of lessons from the atrocities of World War Two, colonialism, genocides, crimes against humanity, and conflicts. Although related agendas have been contested recently in multilateral diplomacy, the global normative frameworks remain valid and inspirational to many. In cooperation with partners at all levels, Canada can build on its history of constructive multilateral engagement on democratic governance and human rights to help retain the salience of collective lessons learned over time. Inclusive multilateral approaches offer possibilities to bolster the global community's vigilance of states' implementation of their public commitments to global agreements that pursue greater equality and to protect the dignity of all.

Acknowledgements For their helpful comments and critiques on an earlier version, I would like to thank the editors of this volume, Max Cameron, David Carment, and David Gillies, as well as Leonie Holthaus, Miranda Loli, David Moscrop, Jens Steffek, and Victoria Trifonchovska. Special thanks to Massimo Tommasoli for helpful discussions on the topic in 2019. Responsibility for content and any error rests solely with the author.

REFERENCES

Bardall, Gabrielle. 2023. Feminism and International Democracy Assistance (this volume). In *Canada Among Nations*, ed. Maxwell Cameron, David Carment, and David Gillies.

Bridoux, Jeff, Christopher Hobson, and Milja Kurki. 2012. Rethinking Democracy Support. United Nations University Press. http://hdl.handle.net/2160/7877.

Bukovansky, Mlada. 2007. Liberal States, International Order, and Legitimacy: An Appeal for Persuasion Over Prescription. *International Politics* 44: 175–193.

Carment, David, and Yiagadeesen Samy. 2016. Canada's Fragile States Policy: What Have We Accomplished and Where Do We Go from Here? In *Rethinking Canadian Aid*, Second Edition, ed. Stephen Brown, Molly den Heyer, and David R. Black. Chapter XIII. Ottawa: University of Ottawa Press.

Carothers, Thomas. 2016a. Closing Space for International Democracy and Human Rights Support. *Journal of Human Rights Practice* 8: 358–377.

Carothers, Thomas. 2016b. Look Homeward, Democracy Promoter. Carnegie Endowment for International Peace. http://carnegieendowment.org/publications/?fa=62604

Chesterman, Simon. 2004. Building Democracy Through Benevolent Autocracy: Consultation and Accountability in UN Transitional Administrations. Chapter 4 in *The UN Role in Promoting Democracy: Between Ideals and Reality*, ed. Edward Newman and Roland Rich. Tokyo: United Nations University Press.

Clark, Ian. 2005. *Legitimacy in International Society*. Oxford: Oxford University Press.

Claude, Inis L., Jr. 1966. Collective Legitimization as a Political Function of the United Nations. *International Organization* 20 (3): 367–379.

Cooper, Andrew F., and Thomas Legler. 2006. *Intervention Without Intervening? The OAS Defense and Promotion of Democracy in the Americas*. New York: Palgrave Macmillan.

Deng, Yong. 2008. *China's Struggle for Status: The Realignment of International Relations*. Cambridge: Cambridge University Press.

Dumitriu, Petru. 2003. The History and Evolution of the New or Restored Democracies Movement. Paper commissioned for the fifth international conference on new or restored democracies, Mongolia.

Fukuda-Parr, Sakiko, and Thea Smaavik Hegstad. 2019. "Leaving No One Behind" as a Site of Contestation and Reinterpretation. *Journal of Globalization and Development* 0037: 1–10.

Geis, Anna. 2013. The 'Concert of Democracies': Why Some States Are More Equal Than Others. *International Politics* 50 (2): 257–277.

Gillies, David. 2023. Policy and Practice in Canada's International Democracy Support (this volume). In *Canada Among Nations*, ed. Maxwell Cameron, David Carment, and David Gillies.

Hecht, Catherine. 2016. Success After Stalemate? Persistence, Reiteration, and Windows of Opportunity in Multilateral Negotiations. *Journal of International Organizations Studies* 7 (2): 23–38.

Hecht, Catherine. 2017. Advantages and Disadvantages of Inclusive Multilateral Venues: The Rise and Fall of the United Nations General Assembly Resolution on New or Restored Democracies. *International Politics* 54 (6): 714–728.

Hecht, Catherine. 2021. When Democratic Governance Unites and Divides: Social Status and Contestation in the Organization for Security and Cooperation in Europe. *Cooperation and Conflict* 56 (1): 44–64.

Holthaus, Leonie, and Michael Christensen. 2022. The Production of North American and German Democracy Promotion Expertise: A Practice Theoretical Analysis. *International Studies Perspectives* 23: 271–289.

Hurrell, Andrew. 2007. *On Global Order: Power, Values, and the Constitution of International Society*. Oxford: Oxford University Press.

Keck, Margaret E., and Kathryn Sikkink. 1998. *Activists Beyond Borders*: Advocacy Networks in International Politics. Ithaca: Cornell University Press.

Koelble, Thomas A., and Edward Lipuma. 2008. Democratizing Democracy: A Postcolonial Critique of Conventional Approaches to the 'Measurement of Democracy.' *Democratization* 15 (1): 1–28.

Larson, Deborah Welch. 2020. Can China Change the International System? The Role of Moral Leadership. *The Chinese Journal of International Politics* 13 (2): 163–186.

Larson, Deborah Welch, and Alexei Shevchenko. 2014. Russia Says No: Power, Status and Emotions in Foreign Policy. *Communist and Post-Communist Studies* 47 (3–4): 269–279.

Larson, Deborah Welch, and Alexei Shevchenko. 2010. 'Status Seekers:' Chinese and Russian Responses to U.S. Primacy. *International Security* 34 (4): 63–95.

Newman, Edward, and Roland Rich. 2004. *The UN Role in Promoting Democracy: Between Ideals and Reality:* Tokyo: United Nations University Press.

O'Donnell, Guillermo. 1993. On the State, Democratization and some Conceptual Problems: A Latin American View with Glances at some Postcommunist Countries. *World Development* 21 (8): 1355–1369.

Rich, Roland. 2017. *Democracy in Crisis: Why, Where, How to Respond*. Boulder: Lynne Reinner.

Steffek, Jens. 2018. Deliberation and Global Governance. In *The Oxford Handbook of International Political Theory*, ed. Chris Brown and Robyn Eckersley. Oxford: Oxford University Press.

Thomas, Daniel C. 2001. *The Helsinki Effect: International Norms, Human Rights and the Demise of Communism*. Princeton: Princeton University Press.

Tsygankov, Andrei P. 2012. *Russia and the West from Alexander to Putin: Honor in International Relations*. New York: Cambridge University Press.
Viola, Lora Anne. 2020. *The Closure of the International System: How International Institutions Create Political Equalities and Hierarchies*. Cambridge: Cambridge University Press.
Warren, Mark E. 2017. A Problem-Based Approach to Democratic Theory. *American Political Science Review* 111 (1): 39–53.
Young, Iris Marion. 2000. *Inclusion and Democracy*. Oxford: Oxford University Press.
Youngs, Richard. 2016. European Liberal Power as a Two-Way Street. *Carnegie Europe*, May 6. http://carnegieeurope.eu/2016/05/17/european-liberal-power-as-two-way-street/iyco.

CHAPTER 8

Toward Canadian Democracy Protection 2.0 in the Americas?

Kendra D. Carrión-Vivar and Thomas Legler

INTRODUCTION[1]

Recent events have underscored the emergence, persistence, and recurrence of serious threats to democracy across many parts of the Americas. In January 2023, protestors loyal to former president Jair Bolsonaro

---

[1] We are grateful to Max Cameron, David Carment, and David Gillies for their encouraging and constructive feedback. This chapter also benefitted from the valuable information provided by three interviews with senior officials from Global Affairs Canada, whose identity we have intentionally maintained anonymous. The authors would like to thank Paulina Botella and Ximena Villafaña for their research assistance.

K. D. Carrión-Vivar
Mexico City, Mexico
e-mail: kendra.carrion@correo.uia.mx

T. Legler (✉)
Department of International Studies, Universidad Iberoamericana, Mexico City, Mexico
e-mail: thomas.legler@ibero.mx

© The Author(s), under exclusive license to Springer Nature Switzerland AG 2023
M. A. Cameron et al. (eds.), *Democracy and Foreign Policy in an Era of Uncertainty*, Canada and International Affairs, https://doi.org/10.1007/978-3-031-35490-8_8

stormed Brazil's Congress building, many of whom called on the military to topple current president Lula from power. Peru has been wracked by mass protests and political instability in the wake of President Pedro Castillo's attempted self-coup, ouster, and detention by authorities in December 2022. Haiti has been left with little or no functioning government in the midst of rampant gang violence and crime. In Nicaragua and Venezuela, brutal dictatorships continue to repress their opposition. El Salvador's president Nayib Bukele has governed the country since March 2022 under a state of emergency whose official purpose has been to combat criminal gangs, but that has deepened autocratization even further in the process.

Although not to the same extent, even Canada and the United States have been at risk, such as external cyber threats to their electoral systems or the rise of antidemocratic right-wing extremist groups. The recent introduction of the Alberta Sovereignty within a United Canada Act by the government of Premier Danielle Smith potentially threatens federal democratic and constitutional oversight in the province (Snagovsky 2022). This pales however in comparison with the January 6, 2021, attack on the Capitol, just one example of the real democratic erosion that has resulted from Republican illiberalism, and a vivid reminder that even in the United States democracy cannot be taken for granted. At the same time, and as described in the following pages, many of the developments that have put democracy in harm's way across much of the hemisphere of late have been more gradual and subtle.

It is against this ever-evolving backdrop that Canada and a number of other like-minded countries have attempted both bilaterally and through the institutional architecture of the Organization of American States (OAS) and the Inter-American System to promote and defend democracy since the end of the Cold War. During the 1990s and the early 2000s, Canadians developed a vocation for supporting democracy in the Americas. In 1990, as a new member of the Organization of American States, Canada was one of the main advocates for the creation of the Unit for the Promotion of Democracy. Canadian career diplomats and government officials made a name for themselves in the struggle for democracy in such places as the Dominican Republic in 1994 and Peru in 2000–2001. In 2001, as hosts of the Summit of the Americas, Canadian efforts were instrumental in codifying a new hemispheric norm in the Declaration of Quebec City that restricted participation in Inter-American forums and events to member states that were representative democracies. Canada was also an important partner in the coalition that championed the 2001 Inter-American Democratic Charter (IADC).[2]

In recent years, Canadian and collective efforts through the OAS to manage and resolve complex crises in countries such as Nicaragua and Venezuela have been increasingly frustrated. Current adversities in the global, hemispheric, and subregional context have made it more and more difficult for Canada to support democracy effectively in the Americas using its original playbook. Accordingly, it is not surprising that over the past few years, the present Liberal government appears to be undertaking a rethink of how to promote and defend democracy, not only in Latin America and the Caribbean (LAC), but also across the planet.

While still largely rhetorical, in this chapter, we contend that there is evidence to suggest that Canadian foreign policy may be in the process of articulating a new approach to promoting and protecting democracy that is qualitatively distinct from pioneering policies and practices, what we might call version 2.0. As we explain in the following pages, this potential model has four components: the expansion of the notion of democracy protection to extend coverage to everyday civil society defenders of democracy; the greater democratic inclusion of marginalized and vulnerable societal groups; the geopoliticization and securitization of democracy protection, possibly through friend-shoring; and the redefinition of governmental and intergovernmental levers of influence. At the same, it is undeniable that there are still important continuities in terms of both the nature of some of the threats that contemporary democracies face, as well as longstanding Canadian democracy protection policies and practices.

Since Canadian democracy protection 2.0 is still largely at the formative stage, we explore the possible challenges and implications that would be entailed in its implementation across the Americas. While the as yet hypothetical approach appears to make sense from a geopolitical perspective applied at the global level, we raise an important operationalization question with respect to its fit in the current LAC context. Although the prioritization of democratic inclusion dovetails with recent groundswell grassroots pressure across LAC for the greater democratization of social relations, democracy protection linked to geopolitical friend-shoring will not necessarily sit well with the region's second so-called Pink Tide. As we

---

[2] On Canada's role in the establishment of global and regional institutions, see also the chapter by Boehm in this volume.

highlight, these new directions in democracy protection will also continue to encounter some familiar contradictions and dilemmas.

Our analysis is divided into three parts. First, we sketch the shifting global and hemispheric landscape and some of its consequences for Canadian democracy protection in the Americas. Second, we present the characteristics of a possible emerging approach for safeguarding democracy, version 2.0, and contrast it with the original 1.0 model. We also examine the challenges, contradictions, and dilemmas that are entailed in its implementation. Finally, we offer some concluding reflections about the future of Canadian democracy protection in the Western Hemisphere.

The Unpropitious Climate for Defending Democracy in the Americas

Canada's democracy promotion and protection efforts in the Western Hemisphere face an ever-changing and increasingly adverse environment, whose complexity needs to be considered in order to formulate more effective policy. This section discusses evolving democracy-related trends and the challenges they entail for Canadian foreign policy both globally and in the Americas. Specifically, in the following pages, we identify new directions in autocratization, the problems of hemispheric order upheaval and OAS gridlock, recent US policy priorities, and the geopoliticization of the context for safeguarding democracy.

The alarms regarding the state of democracy around the world started ringing in the early years of the twenty-first century when a "democratic recession" (Fukuyama 2006) and the rise of illiberal democracy (Zakaria 1997) were denounced. By 2019, the decline of democratic regime attributes, known as autocratization, had emerged as a global challenge, given the setbacks in a wide variety of countries, including consolidated democracies. These developments opened a new generation of studies that reveal that in addition to more traditional threats such as military coups, contemporary democracies erode gradually and under legal disguise (Lührmann and Lindberg 2019). The newer dangers to democracy are more related to "executive aggrandizement," where "elected executives weaken checks on power one by one, undertaking a series of institutional changes that hamper the power of opposition forces to challenge executive preferences" (Bermeo 2016: 10–11; Diamond 2015). Another trait among contemporary autocrats is the subversion of electoral standards without breaking their democratic façade completely (Levitsky and Way 2010; Lührmann and Lindberg 2019).

Democratic regimes face growing challenges and criticisms. Widespread discontent with political parties, established political elites, economic inequality, and social exclusion has contributed to growing popular dissatisfaction with the state of democracy as well as polarization across a number of countries in the Americas. Brazil, Chile, Colombia, and Ecuador have experienced mass protests in recent years on a scale seldom seen previously. Even Canada felt this democratic dissatisfaction in the form of the so-called freedom convoy protests in early 2022.

Although groundswell popular protest by citizens is healthy for any democracy, the attack on the US Capitol on January 6, 2021, showed that in extreme cases it can also put democratic institutions in jeopardy. Increased levels of disinformation—both through traditional channels and social media—and the contestation of election results in countries with once strong institutions, including the United States and more recently Brazil, have also emerged as potential hazards for democracy. These new threats and their chameleon-like nature pose a formidable challenge for policymakers in terms of how to balance and respect fundamental rights and freedoms while containing attacks on democratic governance.

As other chapters in this volume have highlighted, there has been significant backsliding in global levels of democracy over the past year (see Kinsman and Carment and Palmer). In 2022, the V-Dem Institute identified only 34 liberal democracies, while closed autocracies increased from 25 to 30 in relation to 2020 (Boese et al. 2022). These statistics also reflect the impact of other global contingencies such as the COVID-19 pandemic, during which violations of democratic standards were registered in 144 countries (Kolvani et al. 2021). In fact, some authors refer to the "autocratic impulse" generated by the pandemic both in right-wing as well as left-wing governments all over the world (Erhardt et al. 2022; Manson 2020; Simon 2020). Electoral autocracies—or competitive authoritarian regimes—have replaced democracies as the most common political system around the world, present in 60 countries and covering 70% of the world's population. The decline is especially notorious in the regions of Asia Pacific, Central Asia, Eastern Europe, and Latin America and the Caribbean (Levitsky and Way 2010; Levitsky and Ziblatt 2018; V-Dem Institute 2022; see also Kinsman and Carment and Palmer in this volume).

In a context where transitions to authoritarianism are gradual and thus harder to pinpoint than clear violations of democratic standards such as coups, democracy defenders have fewer clear opportunities to counter actions that subtly erode the system. Contemporary autocrats make use of elusive tactics like censoring or harassing the media, restricting civil society and political parties, or undermining the autonomy of the electoral power in ways that are not necessarily illegal (Lührmann and Lindberg 2019; Kinsman this volume). Moreover, autocrats learn from each other, borrowing tactics from a common playbook perceived to be less risky than abolishing multi-party elections altogether. They also support each other through autocracy promotion; that is, autocratic powers like Russia, China, Iran, and Turkey bolster aspiring autocrats all over the world through material, ideational, and diplomatic cooperation (Vanderhill 2014; Yakouchyk 2018).

There have been important recent transformations in hemispheric order that have made it more difficult to defend democracy multilaterally. The unprecedented regional consensus reached during the 1990s that led to the creation of the Inter-American regime for the defense of democracy, a commonly shared definition of representative democracy, and the adoption of the Inter-American Democratic Charter in 2001 unraveled just a couple of years later with the onset of the so-called Pink Tide.[3] Scoring a series of election victories across Latin America during the first decade of the new millennium, governments of the left, particularly the members of the Bolivarian Alliance of the Peoples of Our America (ALBA), criticized the elitist character of representative democracy, espousing instead alternative notions of plebiscitary and participatory democracy. Under the leadership of Brazil and Venezuela, South American governments formed the Union of South American Nations (UNASUR) in 2008, a regional organization that would soon fashion its own mechanisms for defending democracy, directly challenging the authority of the OAS in this issue-area. The Pink Tide effectively translated into a hemispheric order upheaval that hampered the Inter-American collective defense of democracy at the time. The consensus or critical mass required to invoke the IADC or authorize collective interventions through the OAS could not be reached, especially since the actions of this organization were interpreted by ALBA member states as the

---

[3] On Latin America's original Pink Tide, see Beasley-Murray et al. (2009), Larrabure et al. (2021).

extension of US foreign policy and were thus cataloged as interventionist and colonizing (Legler 2020; Legler and Santa Cruz 2021). The blockage of collective action through the OAS continued even after the end of the original Pink Wave and the emergence through national elections of right-wing governments in important regional and secondary powers such as Brazil and Argentina. Their governments ardently denounced the deterioration of democracy in countries like Venezuela, whose autocratization process deepened after the election of Nicolás Maduro. However, the difficulty in activating the IADC meant that Venezuelan authoritarianism went collectively unpunished. This prompted a group of OAS member states that included Canada to create new mechanisms to broker dialogue and defend democracy in Venezuela through ad hoc and informal minilateral groups, like the Lima Group (Legler 2020).[4]

Along with Venezuela, the contrasting cases of Nicaragua and Honduras raise the question of whether attempts to defend democracy in the Americas depend on the ideological and political affinity of the particular country in crisis. For instance, on the one hand, during the right-wing sway in the region during the previous decade, authoritarian backsliding by the governments of Nicaragua and Venezuela was widely denounced. On the other hand, following the November 2017 presidential election, despite the objections of the OAS election observation mission concerning serious election irregularities and its call for new elections, the anti-Bolivarian and pro-US Honduran government of incumbent president Juan Orlando Hernández was able to prevail (see Di Bonaventura 2021).

More recently, the advent of the second wave of left-wing governments in the region seems both to confirm and refute the potential linkage of the defense of democracy in the hemisphere with questions of ideology. In the case of Nicaragua, both the presidents of Mexico and Argentina, Andrés Manuel López Obrador and Alberto Fernández, have avoided taking a tough stand against Daniel Ortega's autocratic actions that have deepened since 2018, impeding collective efforts within the OAS to invoke the IADC. On the other hand, Chile's millennial head of state, Gabriel Boric, has openly criticized the former revolutionary leader, while in

---

[4] Regarding the surge of ad hoc/informal multilateral organizations, see also the chapter by Boehm in this volume.

Brazil, a re-elected Lula Da Silva, when asked about the Nicaraguan situation, declared that violations of human rights are unacceptable, no matter where they come from (O'Donnell 2022).

There are other nuances among these governments. For instance, in countries like Chile or Colombia, there has been a push for the democratization of social relations, evidenced by initiatives for a new constitution and the inclusion of traditionally marginalized sectors, respectively. Another key difference between both waves is the fact that the second one has been bred within a global trend of nationalist revival and therefore has a noticeably more diminished internationalist vocation than the first one, during which Bolivarian leaders pushed for regional cooperation through the creation of alternative institutions, like the Union of South American Nations (UNASUR), the Community of Latin American and Caribbean States (CELAC), or ALBA. Thus, the treatment of crises like the ones in Venezuela or Nicaragua has been either through bilateral channels, including sanctions, or ad hoc minilateral coalitions that have even included extra-regional partners like the European Union.

These factors are key to understanding the waters in which Canadian policy toward the promotion and defense of democracy in the Americas navigates. This endeavor was never an easy one, particularly due to Latin American suspicions of the defense of democracy as a tool of US intervention. Nowadays, in a region with polarized political positions and in which a variety of democracies, hybrid regimes, and autocracies coexist, the task of collectively defending democracy becomes even tougher. Moreover, as governmental changes around the region reorient the foreign policy of many countries, Canada has lost traditional democracy protection partners, like Argentina and Mexico. The growing difficulty or even stagnation of OAS actions against democracy violations has also called into question the hemispheric commitment with the collective defense of democracy regime.

In fact, there is even evidence that regional multilateral mechanisms to defend democracy have been instrumentalized by aspiring autocrats for their own survival. Nicaragua is a case in point. For years, the Ortega regime selectively invited the OAS to *accompany* (instead of observing) elections, in which the regional organization was excluded from key parts of the processes and did not denounce opaque and controversial elections, particularly the one held in 2011. This instrumentalization of the electoral cooperation mechanism helped strengthen Ortega's position and enabled the perpetuation of the autocratization process that began in

2000 (Carrión-Vivar 2022). Later, during the height of the social unrest that began in 2018, the regime invited the OAS to facilitate dialogue, despite not having any real intentions to reduce its repression against protestors. Thanks to this dialogue process, Ortega was able to gain time and rearticulate official forces, as well as avoid regional condemnation, given the proximity to the OAS General Assembly that year. A similar dynamic occurred once again in 2019, thanks to which Ortega effectively misled the organization's efforts to defend democracy and essentially bought time to consolidate an authoritarian regime in Nicaragua, after which he withdrew the country's membership from the hemispheric forum (Carrión-Vivar 2022).

The complexity and controversy of the state of democracy in hemispheric affairs were closely felt during the 2022 Los Angeles Summit of the Americas (SOA). The Biden administration refrained from inviting Cuba, Venezuela, and Nicaragua, due to their lack of democratic spaces and respect for human rights, which triggered negative reactions from other countries, including Mexico and Bolivia, whose presidents decided to boycott the event (BBC 2022). Conceived in the 1990s as a forum that was intended to unite the whole continent, from Alaska to Tierra del Fuego, the SOA was now unable even to convince some heads of state to attend. Among the absences were Guatemala, Honduras, Uruguay, and El Salvador.

However, this did not impede important pro-democracy initiatives from being launched under the auspices of the Summit. Among them was the Inter-American Action Plan on Democratic Governance (OAS 2022), co-coordinated by the Canadian delegation. The plan reflects new trends in democratic social relations, especially the recognition of civil society and citizen inclusion and participation, a key addition to more traditional emphases on political party systems, electoral cooperation, and hemispheric mechanisms for the defense of democracy.

Recent developments in US policy present new challenges for Canada, not only in the hemisphere but also globally. In what pertains to democracy promotion and protection, the Trump and Biden administrations have held very different stances, with the former maintaining confrontational rhetoric and pushing for regime change in countries like Venezuela. The latter has chosen recently to seek a limited rapprochement toward that country as a means to guarantee its oil supplies against the backdrop of international energy supply disruptions threatened by the war in Ukraine. Whereas Trump sought to engage autocrats like Kim Jong-un from North Korea, under the Biden Doctrine, the global promotion and defense of democracy, in the midst of a perceived existential struggle against autocracies, has become a strategic security priority of the United States (White House 2022). The growing rivalry between the United States and its allies on one side, and China and Russia on the other, adds a geopolitical layer to Inter-American relations not seen since the Cold War. This is especially true in light of Latin America's ties with these two autocratic powers since the beginning of the century, first by the hand of the original Pink Tide governments and later maintained by their successors as strategic partners either in terms of development finance, military cooperation, or as crucial votes in their favor to avoid condemnation in international forums like the United Nations Security Council.

The state of democracy at the global, regional, and subregional levels has direct implications for Canada's strategies to promote and defend democracy in the Americas. Effective foreign policy design is hampered by the difficulty of pinpointing the ideal moment for international actors to take preventive actions before countries in the hemisphere embark on an authoritarian path. Furthermore, policymakers need to be mindful of how aspiring autocrats in the neighborhood are linked and leveraged by extra-regional actors that have geopolitical stakes in the region, which they pursue precisely by supporting and promoting autocracy.

Recent events in Peru suggest that democracy in the Americas can confront both traditional and non-traditional threats simultaneously. On the one side, Pedro Castillo's recent failed attempt to carry out a self-coup in Peru in December 2022 harkens back to similar undemocratic occurrences that occurred in Peru and Guatemala during the 1990s. On the other side, the democratic credibility of Castillo's impromptu successor, acting president Dina Boluarte, has been brought into question by her government's violent crackdown on mass protests by her predecessor's supporters. Accordingly, alongside the persistence of more traditional threats, the shifting problematic presented in this section points to the necessity of updating the instruments for the multilateral defense of democracy. This ought to involve ideally the renewal of the IADC to reflect the new threats mentioned above. However, the withdrawal of Venezuela and Nicaragua from the OAS, and the constant changes in the political landscape of the region that have weakened hemispheric order, suggest that this is not a conducive moment to do so.

Against this backdrop, there are indications that Canada is moving its vision of how to safeguard democracy in the Americas and globally in new directions. As a sign of the times, Canadian policymakers appear to be undertaking a rethink of democracy protection that while not discarding crucial elements of an original version 1.0, could take the shape of a new version 2.0. In the next section, we sketch its key elements, contrasting them with previous preferences for upholding democracy. We then explore the ramifications of a new policy thrust that has yet to be fully operationalized.

Canadian Democracy Protection 2.0

In an increasingly problematic hemispheric and global environment, it would appear that the parameters for a new direction in Canadian democracy promotion and protection have begun to take shape under the current Liberal government. In what follows, and as presented in Table 8.1, we trace four core elements of what might shortly add up to a new Canadian approach to defending democracy: shielding everyday civil society defenders of democracy; the greater democratic inclusion of marginalized and vulnerable societal groups; the geopoliticization and securitization of democracy protection, possibly through friend-shoring; and the redefinition of governmental and intergovernmental levers of influence.

Before presenting the constituent parts of a possible second-generation-style approach to upholding democracy in the Americas, it must be clarified that this does not mean that Canadian authorities no longer pursue the parameters established in the column for Democracy Protection 1.0 as they appear in Table 8.1. Undoubtedly there have been important continuities in Canadian pro-democracy activity. For example, despite emerging priorities, the Canadian government remains one of the key donors for the OAS' Department of Electoral Cooperation and Observation (DECO) (see also Boehm in this volume).

First, in terms of the object of Canadian democracy protection, the notion of what needs to be defended has expanded from a focus on the integrity of democratic regimes to include also the actual defenders of democracy. This makes a lot of sense if we look at how in recent years the governments of Cuba, El Salvador, Nicaragua, Peru, and Venezuela have repressed human rights activists, protestors, journalists, opposition candidates, and students.

Table 8.1 Canadian democracy protection 1.0 vs. 2.0

	Version 1.0	Version 2.0
Object of democracy protection	Democratic constitutional order vs. coups d'état and authoritarian backsliding; focus on serious threats at state and elite level	Defenders of democracy and human rights: activists and journalists; focus on micro-level threats and everyday struggle for democracy in civil society
Object of democracy promotion	Democratic development of democratic institutions: electoral systems, political parties, etc	Democratic inclusion of marginalized societal groups; democratization of social relations
Source of threats to democracy	Internal threats	External threats: Geopoliticization and securitization of democracy protection, friend-shoring
Governmental and intergovernmental levers of influence for Canadian democracy protection	Governmental: Office for Democratic Governance (CIDA); Rights and Democracy. Intergovernmental: OAS, Summits of the Americas, Inter-American Commission on Human Rights	Governmental: Promoting and Protecting Democracy Fund; Centre for Global Democracy? Intergovernmental: Informal minilateral groupings, global multilateral mechanisms

As the state of the art for the hemispheric multilateral defense of democracy at the time, the 2001 IADC's operative clauses focused mainly on addressing serious threats to democratic constitutional orders in the form of coups d'état or authoritarian backsliding by incumbent elected leaders. In other words, the prime purpose of what former OAS secretary-general César Gaviria once referred to as the democratic solidarity paradigm of the Americas was to provide a collective shield against sinister elements who were intent on overturning still fragile democracies by seizing power abruptly in favor of a return to dictatorship. The IADC also provided for the possibility of electoral observation missions, upon the request of the host government, that could report to the Permanent Council whether the conditions for free and fair elections existed, a potential check on leaders' intent on undermining elections in their countries. Although the IADC contains language concerning the importance of civil society and human rights, it does not provide specific clauses for how to defend these.

While undoubtedly Canadian authorities continue to be concerned with how to guard against those who would intentionally promote autocratization, there is evidence that they have amplified the notion of democracy protection to safeguard those on the frontlines in the struggle for democracy. As one Canadian government document put it: "We need to strengthen cooperation between democratic governments and between those governments and the defenders of democracy—journalists, civil society advocates, academics, and others" (Trudeau 2021). The Inter-American Action Plan on Democratic Governance (OAS 2022), which was the fruit of a working group co-chaired by Canada and Panama and adopted at the Los Angeles Summit of the Americas in June 2022, contains multiple references to the protection of these vulnerable groups.

Given the recurring blockage of more traditional efforts to defend democracy multilaterally via the OAS, as we explored in the previous section, this is a potentially meaningful way to contribute toward the struggle for democracy when other means are frustrated. It shifts much of the attention of democracy protection from responding to regime-threatening events at the executive, governmental and constitutional levels to microlevel, every day, and human threats that affect the quality of democracy and human security. It also potentially strengthens a delicate ecosystem for political liberalization in countries where a return to full-scale democratization is still a far-off prospect.

Second, following Table 8.1, beyond countering immediate threats to democracy, there is also a probable enlargement underway with regard to the overall object of democracy promotion (as opposed to democracy protection). Canada's new addition in supporting democracy is advancing the inclusion of hitherto marginalized groups and the strengthening of civil society. Among those explicitly mentioned, the Inter-American Action Plan on Democratic Governance refers to women, girls, LGBTQ2 individuals, indigenous and tribal peoples, persons of African descent, and young people. As one Canadian government source stresses, "Canada's conviction is that for democracy to prosper, it must be inclusive" (Trudeau 2021). In a broad thrust that aims at strengthening the quality of democratic systems, this direction complements and builds on the tradition within Canadian democratic development policy that focused on strengthening political parties, electoral systems, and human rights. Importantly, it is congruent with recent social movement trends across Latin America, in places such as Chile, Colombia, and Ecuador, where mass protests have clamored for a democratization of social relations in favor of groups that have historically been the targets of systemic discrimination and marginalization.

Third, and in line with Table 8.1, with respect to the source of threats to democracy, Canadian democracy protection 2.0 also takes into consideration that democracies are not only subjected to traditional internal threats but also more recent external ones. It reflects a global evolution in threats to democracy, such as the need to safeguard democracy in the digital age. Canadian authorities have repeatedly expressed their concern about cyber threats to the integrity of electoral processes, including the propagation of misinformation and disinformation. Indeed, with this in mind, in 2019, the Trudeau government launched the Plan to Protect Canadian Democracy (Government of Canada 2019b) to shield Canada's own electoral process that year. Echoes of these concerns are found in the aforementioned Inter-American Action Plan on Democratic Governance.

The interest in digital safeguards can be linked with the possible *geopoliticization* and *securitization* of Canadian democracy protection. According to this interpretation, as reinforced by the recent invasion of Ukraine, democracies and dictatorships are pitted against each other in a zero-sum struggle, with the future of the global liberal order at stake. Accordingly, democracy protection possibly assumes growing strategic importance.

Chrystia Freeland (2018, 2022), current finance minister, deputy prime minister, and former foreign minister, is perhaps the staunchest advocate for a geopolitical turn in Canadian democracy protection. In what has become known as the Freeland Doctrine, she recently called for the application of a "friend-shoring approach" to bolster a global alliance of democracies in defense of liberal democracy and the rules-based international order from authoritarian adversaries. Friend-shoring in Freeland's vision entails the strategic strengthening of political, strategic, and economic connections among democracies. Importantly, Freeland calls for the promotion of friend-shoring among LAC, African, and Asian democracies. Although Global Affairs Canada (2022: 5) departmental plans for 2022–2023 specify that democracy and human rights are to be a "core strategic priority," it remains to be seen whether Freeland's ideas will inform a broader reorientation of Canadian foreign policy, as well as policy toward the Americas.

Fourth, it is likely that a move toward Democracy Protection 2.0 would signify a shift in the institutional levers of influence that Canada employs in its pro-democracy efforts. A number of the original governmental and intergovernmental mechanisms at Canada's disposal to advance its interests in this issue-area no longer exist or have undergone modification. For example, the Unit for the Promotion of Democracy at the OAS, originally created in 1990 thanks largely to Canadian initiative, enjoyed a succession of Canadian directors that ended with administrative reforms undertaken under the leadership of Secretary General José Miguel Insulza. It has been superseded by the Department of Electoral Cooperation and Observation. Domestically, the Harper government budget cuts eliminated the Office of Democratic Governance at the Canadian International Development Agency, the Canadian Foundation for the Americas (FOCAL), and the international non-governmental organization Rights and Democracy.

It appears as if the Trudeau government might be attempting to fill this institutional void. In July 2019, it launched a new $10-million Promoting and Protecting Democracy Fund. In December 2021, Trudeau formally announced the creation of a new democracy promotion agency at Biden's Summit for Democracy: The Centre for Global Democracy. However, at the time of writing this chapter, there is little evidence that this latter initiative has taken any tangible steps toward fruition. It is worth recalling that the Harper government also signaled that it would create a new Canadian democracy institute, but that project also never materialized (See also Carment and Palmer in this volume).

With respect to intergovernmental levers, should the OAS and Inter-American institutions such as the Summits of the Americas continue to encounter difficulties in fostering hemispheric cooperation on democracy, it is likely that Canada will need to seek or devise institutional channels outside the Inter-American system. Indeed, as mentioned in the previous section, there are already precedents for this. For example, OAS gridlock prompted Canada and a coalition of like-minded countries to create an informal institutional grouping called the Lima Group in 2017 to pressure for the restoration of democracy in Venezuela. In September 2018, Canada was one of six OAS and Lima Group member states that formally requested that the situation in that country be investigated by the Special Prosecutor of the International Criminal Court for crimes against humanity.

Circumstances at the OAS and in the hemisphere will possibly pressure Canada to continue to put more emphases on minilateralism. It is noteworthy that on the sidelines of the Los Angeles Summit of the Americas in June 2022, Canadian government officials convened a roundtable discussion with "some of its closest partners": Barbados, Belize, Chile, Ecuador, and Jamaica (Trudeau 2022b). "Strong and resilient democracies" were among the issues they addressed. Canada also signed a joint declaration at the summit with a new grouping called the Alliance for Development in Democracy, comprised of Costa Rica, the Dominican Republic, and Panama (later joined by Ecuador), in order "to establish a strategic dialogue to ensure continued collaboration on advancing inclusive economic growth and strengthening democracy in the hemisphere" (Global Affairs Canada 2022).

Finally, it is worth noting that Canada also has the potential to influence LAC developments more indirectly via the diversification of the global multilateral mechanisms through which it attempts to promote a democracy agenda. In this regard, 2022 was a particularly active year for Canadian leadership in terms of chairing or coordinating a number of these mechanisms: the G7 Rapid Response Mechanism; the Freedom Online Coalition; the Open Government Partnership (OGP) Steering Committee; the Media Freedom Coalition; International IDEA; and the Community of Democracies.

As an approach that appears still largely rhetorical and at the conceptual stage, it is important to consider some of the implications of putting Canadian democracy protection 2.0 into action in the Americas. We present some reflections on this in the next section.

Implications of Canada's Possible Adoption of Democracy Protection 2.0

Beyond the declaratory, many of the specifics of how to operationalize Democracy Protection 2.0 across the hemisphere remain unclear. Moreover, as we highlight below, Canadian efforts must contend with the political realities of a newly arrived second Pink Tide in the region, as well as the reputational challenges posed by various ongoing contradictions and tensions in Canadian policy and diplomatic action.

It is not certain what real resources the Canadian government is prepared to invest in the emerging priorities outlined in the previous section, and whether that funding will be targeted in a strategic, coherent, and doctrinal way, or an ad hoc manner. At the Los Angeles Summit of the Americas, Trudeau announced a modest contribution of $17.3 million for an eclectic set of projects supporting democratic governance (Trudeau 2022a). Already, the Inter-American human rights system, made up of the Inter-American Human Rights Commission and Court, has been historically hampered in its ability to provide the types of protection envisioned due to its human resource and budgetary limitations.

With respect to the possible geopolitical turn in Canadian democracy protection policy, LAC governments may not necessarily share the same zero-sum perception or the same compulsion to choose sides with respect to the aforementioned global democracy-authoritarianism divide. Any attempts to promote friend-shoring and democratic alignment in the hemisphere are likely to run up against a strong LAC predilection for autonomy, solidarity, and diversification. As indicated above, this penchant was evident during the first decade of the new millennium, when Latin American and South American governments sought to promote autonomous regional governance vis-à-vis the United States, and to a lesser but significant extent, Canada, via the creation of CELAC and UNASUR. It was also present in the pressure across governments of different ideological stripes for the renewal of Cuban participation in the OAS and Inter-American System, despite that country's authoritarian regime. It should not be forgotten that China is now the main trading partner for a number of South America's larger economies and is that region's largest trading partner. In the face of the growing superpower confrontation among the United States, China, and Russia, a group of intellectuals and ex-functionaries have called for LAC countries to adopt strategic postures of active non-alignment (Fortin et al. 2023).

The attempt to move Canadian democracy protection in novel directions also coincides with the rise electorally over the past two years of a second wave of center-left governments to hold power across most of LAC. Although some of its constituents, like the government of President Boric of Chile, are critical of the situation in Nicaragua and Venezuela, others will be more inclined to advocate the rights of sovereignty and self-determination against any US or Canadian efforts to promote some form of pro-democracy intervention in the region. Mexico, formerly one of Canada's most reliable partners in the collective defense of democracy, has become under President López Obrador precisely one of those governments that advocates against multilateral democracy protection and in favor of non-intervention and self-determination.

It is also foreseeable that under the leadership of the new Lula government, Brazil and its partners will promote some renewed version of regional autonomy in South America, including importantly the right for South Americans to manage or solve South American problems, including political crises, without the involvement of the United States or Canada. This could bring a renewal of the contested multilateralism that occurred between the OAS on one side, and CELAC and UNASUR on the other during the years of the first Pink Tide. It is conceivable that UNASUR will be resurrected in some form and once again challenge the traditional role and authority of the OAS as the reinforced or hub institution for regional democracy protection. However, the prioritization of Brazil's international and regional agenda remains to be seen, especially given the immediate need for the country's authorities to focus on matters at home in the wake of the Brasilia riots that erupted two weeks after Lula's inauguration.

Canadian efforts must therefore contend with the likelihood that the OAS and the Summit of the Americas process will continue to play a reduced and contested role in the coming years. Consequently, if friend-shoring is to be operationalized as a mainstay of Canadian democracy promotion and protection in the Americas, it will have to be implemented more through flexible and informal minilateral arrangements than via the OAS and the Inter-American system. Moreover, it is more feasible for Canada to promote lower-key economic nearshoring with democratic economic partners than more overt political friend-shoring in the hemisphere. This appears to have been the tone struck at the January 2023 North American Leaders Summit, among three elected governments that had few prospects for significant political cooperation on the democracy front but recognized the potential of strengthening regional supply chains.

These challenges are on top of recurring, persistent and unresolved contradictions, tensions, and dilemmas in Canadian democracy promotion. As observers have noted, Canada's ability to articulate and apply a coherent, principled policy on democracy protection in the Americas is made difficult by its commercial interests in the hemisphere and the weight of its bilateral relations with its powerful neighbor, the United States (Burron 2016; Wylie 2021). For instance, Canada's reputation as a champion of democracy has been tarnished by the controversy surrounding the operations of various Canadian mining companies in the hemisphere. A recent report uncovered evidence of serious human rights violations by some of these companies over a fifteen-year span (see Justice and Corporate Accountability Project 2017; Wylie 2021).

There is also a question of coherence with respect to the measures that the Canadian government has applied against various democratic problem cases across LAC. For instance, whereas Canada has traditionally adopted a policy of constructive engagement vis-à-vis authoritarian Cuba since the 1960s, it has implemented a series of sanctions in recent years against the governments of Nicaragua and Venezuela due to their abysmal democracy and human rights records. In light of the harsh crackdown of Cuban authorities against protests on that island in July 2021, it is not clear why successive Canadian governments have been inclined to continue to use a soft or "carrots" approach to promote political change in the former, while applying "sticks" in the latter.

Another related anomaly has to do with the posture of the Lima Group toward Cuba, of which Canada was a prominent member. Although the Lima Group was originally formed in 2017 to push for the restoration of democracy in Venezuela, in the declaration that Canada and other members of this grouping emitted in their May 3, 2019, meeting, they recommended that all necessary actions be undertaken to include Cuba in the quest for a solution to the Venezuela crisis (Government of Canada 2019a). Although Cubans had previously distinguished themselves for their contributions to the peace process in Colombia, it is clearly contradictory at some level that an autocracy like Cuba be recruited to help find a democratic solution to the political crises in authoritarian Venezuela.

Whereas the above-mentioned left-wing governments have been targeted for criticism or sanctions, other right-wing governments in Central America that have also recently committed serious transgressions against democracy, such as El Salvador, Guatemala, and Honduras, have elicited only modest criticism from Canadian authorities. Since taking office in June 2019, President Nayib Bukele has systematically dismantled horizontal democratic checks and balances in El Salvador, governing the country via a state of emergency over the past year. In 2019, the then Guatemalan government of Jimmy Morales ejected the U.N. International Commission against Impunity in Guatemala (CICIG). In Honduras, despite the critical report of the OAS' own election observation mission about serious electoral irregularities, incumbent president Juan Orlando Hernández won reelection in the November 2017 elections. Although Canadian government officials conveyed their concerns discretely behind the scenes and via low-key channels in these cases, it remains unclear why governments of the right who put democracy at risk have received different responses than those of the left. Undoubtedly, these discrepancies have provided critics of the Canadian government with ammunition to argue that it does not treat all the transgressors of democracy equally.

Conclusion

We have argued on the basis of a series of clues that Canadian policymakers are possibly on the cusp of introducing a new approach to safeguarding democracy in the Americas, what we have called Canadian democracy protection 2.0. As we have shown, it moves beyond the original version 1.0 in four important ways: the object of democracy protection; the focus of democracy promotion; the source of threats (internal versus external); and, the levers of influence it utilizes. Nonetheless, it will not necessarily replace original pro-democracy practices and emphases; rather, 2.0 promises a high level of complementarity, continuity, and most of all, adaptability. In the face of the fast-changing dynamics in the Americas and the world, it is imperative that Canada find plausible paths of action amid a resurgence of nationalism, populism, and the frequent impasse in multilateral forums like the OAS.

Rather than signaling a weakening in its strategies to promote and defend democracy, Canada's expansion of the notion of what needs to be defended, with the inclusion of civil society defenders and marginalized and vulnerable societal groups, shows that it is not willing to compromise its standards, but rather, to address a difficult context in creative and meaningful ways. The complexity of the current juncture, filled with what our sources have called "grey zones" in authoritarian backsliding, calls for the creativity and resourcefulness of foreign policy decision-makers. In terms of our hemisphere, this translates into Canada trying to defend democracy through novel and pragmatic forms of cooperation in other important areas with old and new partners, hoping for positive spillovers that enhance governance in the continent. Interesting examples of this strategy include the joint initiatives for gender equality and the inclusion of indigenous populations with Mexico, and the establishment of a free trade agreement with Ecuador, intended to foster trust and improve the prospects for democratic governance in this South American country.

In terms of the possible *geopoliticization* and *securitization* of Canadian democracy protection, beyond friend-shoring, this new approach shows Ottawa's concern with what have become mainstream threats to democracy in the digital era, including misinformation, cyberattacks, and the contestation of electoral processes in both consolidating and consolidated democracies. Moreover, according to our diplomatic sources, Canadian officials are receptive to working with governments of different ideological stripes in the hemisphere who are committed to democracy. This will dissipate possible tensions with some of the Pink Tide 2.0 countries and open possibilities for cooperation with those among its elected leaders who are also pushing for more inclusion and horizontal societal relations.

In what pertains to the OAS, Canada remains committed to supporting the Department for Electoral Cooperation and Observation (DECO), an entity whose technical expertise and credibility remain a pillar of the organization. Moreover, appreciating the difficulty of mobilizing collective action for democracy through the IADC, Canada maintains active channels of dialogue with other member states with the aim of finding solutions to pressing democratic crises such as those of Venezuela and Nicaragua. At the same time, as we mentioned previously, frequent OAS gridlock presents an imperative for Canada and its partners to devise new informal and minilateral mechanisms to address threats to democracy.

From an optimistic viewpoint, democracy protection 2.0 could offer the possibility of building productive relationships and partnerships in the continent that go beyond traditional trade and mining interests. It remains to be seen what the actual gap between rhetoric and practice will be in terms of safeguarding democracy, both in the Americas and worldwide.

References

BBC. 2022. Lo que las ausencias en la Cumbre de las Américas revelan sobre el peso de EE.UU. y la democracia en la región. *BBC News Mundo*, June 8. https://www.bbc.com/mundo/noticias-america-latina-61727420.

Beasley-Murray, Jon, Maxwell A. Cameron, and Eric Hershberg. 2009. Latin America's Left Turns: An Introduction. *Third World Quarterly* 30 (2): 319–330. https://doi.org/10.1080/01436590902770322.

Bermeo, Nancy. 2016. On Democratic Backsliding. *Journal of Democracy* 27 (1): 5–19. https://doi.org/10.1353/jod.2016.0012.

Boese, Vanessa A., Nazifa Alizada, Martin Lundstedt, Kelly Morrison, Natalia Natsika, Yuko Sato, Hugo Tai, and Staffan I. Lindberg. 2022. Autocratization Changing Nature? Democracy Report 2022. *Varieties of Democracy Institute (V-Dem)*. Last Modified March 1, 2022. https://doi.org/10.2139/ssrn.4052548.

Burron, Neil A., and The New Democracy. Wars. 2016. *The Politics of North American Democracy Promotion in the Americas*. London: Routledge.
Carrión-Vivar, Kendra Dominique. 2022. *El rol de la OEA en el proceso de autocratización de Nicaragua*. Thesis to obtain the degree of Ph.D. in Social and Political Sciences. Universidad Iberoamericana.
Di Bonaventura, Leonardo. 2021. The Collective Promotion of Democracy and Authoritarian Backsliding: The Organization of American States in Venezuela, Nicaragua, and Honduras. *The Latin Americanist* 65 (2): 233–263. https://doi.org/10.1353/tla.2021.0017.
Diamond, Larry. 2015. Facing Up to the Democratic Recession. *Journal of Democracy* 26 (1): 141–155. https://doi.org/10.1353/jod.2015.0009.
Erhardt, Julia, Maximilian Filsinger, and Markus Freitag. 2022. Leaving Democracy? Pandemic Threat, Emotional Accounts and Regime Support in Comparative Perspective. *West European Politics* 46 (3): 477–499. https://doi.org/10.1080/01402382.2022.2097409.
Fortin, C., J. Heine, and C. Ominami, eds. 2023. *Latin American Foreign Policies in the New World Order: The Active Non-Alignment Option*. London: Anthem Press.
Freeland, Chrystia. 2018. Diplomat of the Year Chrystia Freeland: Read the Transcript. *Foreign Policy*, June 14, 2018. https://foreignpolicy.com/2018/06/14/2018-diplomat-of-the-year-chrystia-freeland-read-the-transcript/
Freeland, Chrystia. 2022. How Democracies Can Shape a Global Economy. Remarks by the Deputy Prime Minister at the Brookings Institution in Washington, D.C. *Government of Canada*. Last Modified October 11, 2022. https://deputypm.canada.ca/en/news/speeches/2022/10/11/remarks-deputy-prime-minister-brookings-institution-washington-dc.
Fukuyama, Francis. 2006. There are No Shortcuts to "The End of History." *New Perspectives Quarterly* 23 (2): 34–38. https://doi.org/10.1111/j.1540-5842.2006.00804.x.
Government of Canada. 2019a. *Lima Group Declaration*, May 3. https://www.international.gc.ca/world-monde/international_relations-relations_internationales/latin_america-amerique_latine/2019a-05-03-lima_group-groupe_lima.aspx?lang=eng.
Government of Canada. 2019b. *Plan to Protect Canada's Democracy*. Canada. Last Modified September 1, 2021. https://www.canada.ca/en/democratic-institutions/services/protecting-democracy.html.
Government of Canada. 2022. *2022–2023 Departmental Plan*. Ottawa: Global Affairs Canada. Accessed January 2023. https://www.international.gc.ca/transparency-transparence/departmental-plan-ministeriel/2022-2023.aspx?lang=eng.

Justice and Corporate Responsibility Project. 2017. *The "Canada Brand": Violence and Canadian Mining Companies in Latin America*. Osgoode Legal Studies Research Paper No. 17/2017. Toronto: Osgoode Hall Law School.

Kolvani, Palina, Martin Lundstedt, Amanda B. Edgell, and Jean Lachapelle. 2021. Pandemic Backsliding: A Year of Violations and Advances in Response to Covid-19. *V-Dem Institute Policy Brief* 6 (32): 1–6. https://www.v-dem.net/media/publications/pb_32.pdf.

Larrabure, Manuel, Charmain Levy, Maxwell A. Cameron, Joe Foweraker, Lena Lavinas, and Susan Jane Spronk. 2021. Roundtable: The Latin American State, Pink Tide, and Future Challenges. *Globalizations* 20 (1): 115–131. https://doi.org/10.1080/14747731.2021.1925813.

Legler, Thomas, and Arturo Santa Cruz. 2021. Two Decades of Hemispheric Order Upheaval in the Americas. In *Global Politics and the International System: Narratives from Mexico*, 51–71. Instituto Matías Romero: Ciudad de México.

Legler, Thomas. 2020. A Story within a Story: Venezuela's Crisis, Regional Actors, and Western Hemispheric Order Upheaval. *European Review of Latin American and Caribbean Studies* 109: 135–156.

Levitsky, Steven, and Daniel Ziblatt. 2018. *How Democracies Die*. New York: Crown.

Levitsky, Steven, and Lucas A. Way. 2010. *Competitive. Authoritarianism; Hybrid Regimes after the Cold War*. Cambridge University Press: New York. https://doi.org/10.1017/CBO9780511781353.

Lührmann, Anna, and Staff I. Lindberg. 2019. A Third Wave of Autocratization is Here: What is New About It? *Democratization* 26 (7): 1095–1113. https://doi.org/10.1080/13510347.2019.1582029.

Manson, Joseph H. 2020. Right-wing Authoritarianism, Left-wing Authoritarianism, and Pandemic-mitigation Authoritarianism. *Personality and Individual Differences.* 167 (1): 1–6. https://doi.org/10.1016/j.paid.2020.110251.

O'Donnell, María. 2022. Celso Amorim: Las violaciones a los derechos humanos son inaceptables, vengan de donde vengan. *CNN en Español*, September 17, 2022. https://cnnespanol.cnn.com/video/lula-da-silva-der echos-humanos-nicaragua-celso-amorim-conecta2/.

OAS. 2022. *Inter-American Action Plan on Democratic Governance*. Los Angeles: California. Ninth Summit of the Americas. OEA/Ser.E CA-IX/doc.5/22, 8–10 June, 2022. http://summit-americas.org/documentos_ofic iales_ixsummit/CMBRS02295e02.pdf.

Simon, S. 2020. Subtle Connections: Pandemic and the Authoritarian Impulse. *Survival* 62 (3): 103–111.

Snagovsky, Feo. 2022. Troubling Trends in Canadian Democracy. *Policy Options Politiques*, December 2, 2022. https://policyoptions.irpp.org/magazines/dec ember-2022/threats-canadian-democracy/.

Trudeau, Justin. 2021. *Summit for Democracy 2021 submission and commitments: Canada. Government of Canada.* Last modified 9 December 2021. https://pm.gc.ca/en/news/backgrounders/2021/12/09/summit-democracy-2021-submission-and-commitments-canada.

Trudeau, Justin. 2022a. *Canada's New Investments and Assistance in Latin America and the Caribbean.* June 10. https://pm.gc.ca/en/news/backgrounders/2022a/06/10/canadas-new-investments-and-assistance-latin-america-and-caribbean.

Trudeau, Justin. 2022b. *Prime Minister Justin Trudeau Hosts Leaders Roundtable on Key Regional Issues at the Summit of the Americas.* June 9. https://pm.gc.ca/en/news/readouts/2022b/06/09/prime-minister-justin-trudeau-hosts-leaders-roundtable-key-regional-issues.

Vanderhill, Rachel. 2014. Promoting Democracy and Promoting Authoritarianism: Comparing the Cases of Belarus and Slovakia. *Europe-Asia Studies* 66 (2): 255–283. https://doi.org/10.1080/09668136.2014.882621.

White House. 2022. National Security Strategy. Washington, D.C., October 12. https://www.whitehouse.gov/wpcontent/uploads/2022/10/Biden-Harris-Administrations-National-Security-Strategy-10.2022.pdf.

Wylie, Lana. 2021. Canada and Latin America. In *The Palgrave Handbook of Canada in International Affairs*, ed. Robert W. Murray and Paul Gecelovsky, 705–728. Switzerland: Springer Nature Switzerland AG.

Yakouchyk, Katsiaryna. 2018. Beyond Autocracy Promotion: A Review. *Political Studies Review* 17 (2): 147–160. https://doi.org/10.1177/1478929918774976.

Zakaria, Fareed. 1997. The Rise of Illiberal Democracy. *Foreign Affairs* 76 (6): 22–43. https://doi.org/10.2307/20048274.

CHAPTER 9

Feminism and International Democracy Assistance

Gabrielle Bardall

INTRODUCTION

Democracy-support advocates have long held that strengthening women's political participation and protecting gender equality is an important way to build democracy and counter authoritarianism. The rise of autocratic backlash to feminism and autocrats' weaponization of women's rights (Bardall 2019; Bjarnegard and Zetterberg 2022; Butler 2021, Chenoweth and Marks 2022) make a compelling case for the urgency of defending women's rights as part of the broader project of defending democracy.

Women's rights and political participation have been an integral part of Canadian international development policy for nearly half a century. As early as 1976, the former Canadian International Development Agency (CIDA) was recognized as one of the world leaders in women's development programming. By 1995, the year of the Beijing Conference,

G. Bardall (✉)
GSPIA, Herizon Democracy, University of Ottawa, Ottawa, ON, Canada
e-mail: gbardall@herizondemocracy.org
URL: https://www.herizondemocracy.org

© The Author(s), under exclusive license to Springer Nature Switzerland AG 2023
M. A. Cameron et al. (eds.), *Democracy and Foreign Policy in an Era of Uncertainty*, Canada and International Affairs, https://doi.org/10.1007/978-3-031-35490-8_9

Canada's Federal Plan for Gender Equality (Status of Women Canada 1995) explicitly made the connection between gender equality as a driver of the quality of democracy in Canada. Women's rights, gender equality and now, feminism are integral to Canada's approach to democracy assistance.

Yet, the relationship between gender and democracy is rarely problematized in the aid community in Canada or elsewhere. The objectives of democracy assistance as we know it today are straightforward: to support and promote democratic processes and institutions, enhance human rights protections and build the capacity of local actors to participate in democratic governance and hold their leaders accountable. These objectives are based on the conviction that true democracy is inclusive, non-discriminatory and representative and the recognition that women's rights are human rights. Thus, it has long felt safe to assume that as democracy assistance objectives are progressively achieved, gender equality and empowerment must advance in lockstep.

However, the reality of democratization has proven to be much more complex. From Honduras to Zimbabwe, Myanmar to Tunisia, women's movements have been sidelined after democratic transitions take place and elected governments roll back women's rights. Eighty-five percent of democracies in the world (and 91% of non-democracies) are led by men and we are still nearly a century away from seeing gender parity in the world's parliaments. Autocratic regimes regularly employ gender-washing as a strategy to masquerade as democrats while brutally repressing dissident feminist movements and women in the opposition.

In light of this, should Western democracies like Canada adopt explicitly feminist approaches to democracy assistance to compensate for injustice or to deepen the quality of democracy? If so, what exactly *is* a feminist approach to democracy assistance?

This chapter unpacks these questions. As Canada looks to deepen its engagement for democracy support under the Feminist International Assistance Policy (FIAP), this is a moment to look back on how a feminist framework has contributed (or detracted) from democracy aid. It is also the right time to consider pressing questions about the relationship between feminism and democracy and set a clear roadmap to feminist democracy objectives.

The chapter draws on interviews with nearly a dozen experts, ranging from Parliamentarians to Canadian and American practitioners in democracy support and/or women's equality work as well as academics and civil servants. It is constructed in two parts. Part I looks at FIAP's impact on democracy assistance over the past five years since it was introduced. I look at the implications of the feminist conceptual framework through a review of policy documents and comparative global commitments to democracy by like-minded states at the 2022 Summit for Democracy. I also consider how feminism has played out in practice, through an analysis of democracy assistance data from the Global Affairs Canada project finder database.

Part II looks at the way forward. It explains the conceptual gaps and conflicts between feminism and democratization theory and their implications for the way international democracy assistance is provided. I conclude by offering a number of conceptual and practical recommendations for bringing feminism and democratization in closer alignment.

Part I. Taking Stock of Feminism & Democracy Support to Date

Development practitioners and scholars are continually evolving in their approach to gender issues. The "Women in Development" (WID) approach of the 1970s and 1980s was criticized for being too narrowly focused on women as a homogeneous group and for failing to address underlying gender inequalities and power dynamics that perpetuate marginalization. WID gave way to "Gender and Development" (GAD) in the 1980s and 1990s, recognizing that inequality is embedded in social, economic and political systems and structures. GAD introduced widely-used approaches like gender mainstreaming into international development. The current trend in development practice and scholarship is a shift toward a more feminist approach to development. This aims to challenge and transform unequal power relations and eliminate the patriarchal and gendered structures that perpetuate inequality and oppression. Over a dozen countries in the world have adopted (or announced their intent to develop) Feminist Foreign Policies.

Following these trends in international development thinking, the importance of gender in Canada's international democracy assistance has consistently grown and evolved in the past decades. The following analysis considers what this shift looks like both conceptually and in practice under Canada's FIAP. Conceptually, the recent introduction of a feminist framework is a gradual deepening of engagement on gender issues, rather than a transformation in how Canada approaches democracy support. In practice, the shift to a feminist policy has coincided with a shrinking of aid in the traditional core areas of democracy and governance assistance, a major increase in funds for feminist movements without explicit connection to democratic institutions and processes, and the implementation of democracy and governance (DG) programs through international organizations.

From Gender & Development to Feminism in Democracy Assistance Policy: Concepts Are Gradually Edging Forward

The connection between democracy support and women's rights dates to Canada's 1995 Federal Plan for Gender Equality. The plan emphasized sustaining and advancing women's "equitable share of power and leadership in decision-making processes" through a series of recommendations primarily targeting recruitment, employment and training in the public service. While focusing on women's descriptive representation (i.e., numerical equity), it laid the groundwork for addressing gender discrimination within the institutions of Canadian democracy (para. 345). The 1995 Plan prioritized increasing women's political participation in decision-making processes as a goal for Canadian international development assistance (para. 383).

Gender equality and women's rights have remained cross-cutting themes throughout Canada's international democracy support programming ever since. A decade into the Plan, CIDA employed a three-prong framework for promoting gender equality in governance: promoting women's equal participation in decision-making at all levels; fighting gender-specific human rights violations such as sexual violence; and building the capacity of partners to promote gender equality.

The FIAP deepens and modestly extends this framework for gender in democracy assistance. FIAP's Action Area 5 on Inclusive Governance reiterates the three earlier thematic agents of change and adds a fourth: rule of law/access to justice (Global Affairs Canada 2017). First, although FIAP's approach to women's political participation remains rooted in overcoming barriers to women's descriptive representation, it makes some important steps forward. Specifically, it underlines the barriers that exist for women both in attaining leadership positions as well as in exerting real influence when they hold those roles, including the existence of gender-based political violence. In terms of human rights, FIAP deepens the pre-existing human rights component by adding intersectionality as a lens for interpreting discrimination. The third pillar, creating an enabling environment for civil society, is not elaborated in the policy documents but (as we shall see) occupies a significant focus in implementation.

FIAP's main addition to the framework for gender in international democracy assistance is in the elaboration of a fourth pillar: rule of law and access to justice. "Rule of law" in this context refers to legal reform on areas with notable gendered impact, such as marriage and divorce law, inheritance, property and land ownership. Access to justice includes equal protection by state institutions and ensuring that judicial actors hold perpetrators to account for acts of sexual violence.

An important—and, as I will discuss, sometimes challenging—element of FIAP's theory of change is that it views women's leadership and political participation as both a driver and an outcome of strong democracy. Action Area 5 asserts that women's presence in government leads to better decision-making and improved quality of life. It directs Canada to support women politicians to implement gender-sensitive reform and legislation as a means to advance the interests of other marginalized groups (including women). In terms of the empowering outcomes of inclusive governance, FIAP points to ending legal discrimination, increasing decision-making over resources and prosecuting gender-based and sexual violence.

In sum, consistent with other general analyses of FIAP (Tiessen 2019; Parisi 2020) and despite FIAP's rhetoric innovation, FIAP's stated framework is an extension of a long-standing Canadian approach to gender and democracy. Although it alludes to transformative feminisms, it is firmly anchored in the traditions of liberal feminism and procedural democracy. Liberal feminism emphasizes individual rights and freedoms and views gender equality as a matter of equal treatment under the law. It links gender equality to economic growth ("Feminist Neoliberalism") (Parisi 2020). Procedural definitions of democracy focus on the processes of democracy, and the mechanics of how decisions are made and power is exercised. Canada is not unique in this: liberal feminism and procedural democracy are the dominant theories in today's international democracy assistance practice. FIAP casts an aura of transformative feminism in its allusions to intersectionality and socio-economic inequality, however in practice, it avoids explicitly targeting transformative feminist goals or more substantive definitions of democracy.

Feminist Democracy Assistance in Practice, 2017–2022

Under FIAP, Canada committed to ensuring that no less than 95 percent of its bilateral international development assistance targets or integrates gender equality. While the overall value of both democracy assistance funding and of gender equality funding has been critiqued as insufficient (Novovic 2022), the changing nature of democracy assistance spending is noteworthy, as are the perspectives of those implementing democracy programs.

To interpret patterns and perspectives on Canada's democracy assistance spending before and after the introduction of FIAP, interviews were undertaken with Canadian and international practitioners that have engaged on GAC programs under FIAP.[1] In addition, I conducted a limited analysis of data available on the Global Affairs Canada (GAC) project browser (GAC 2023).

The project browser records 602 projects with at least some thematic relevance to democracy and governance (DG) support between 1999 and February 2023, worth a total of $4.76 billion in maximum contributions. Of these, I identify 199 projects (worth $689 million in maximum contributions) as "core" democracy and governance assistance programs, based on the thematic sectors they focus(ed) on and whether or not the DG sector was the primary area of focus. Specifically, I looked at only those projects with cumulatively 50% or more focus on three sectors of GAC's classification scheme: (i) democratic participation and civil society, (ii) elections and (iii) legislatures and political parties.[2] One hundred and fifty-eight projects meeting these criteria were undertaken prior to FIAP

---

[1] It was beyond the limited resources of this modest assignment to interview the most important stakeholders: the beneficiaries in the countries where Canada's democracy assistance is implemented. A more inclusive, funded research initiative would be valuable.

[2] DG is a broad area with many subfields ranging from judicial strengthening to decentralization programs to independent media and anti-corruption. For the purposes of this brief review, I chose to limit the sample to these three key areas.

(1999-mid 2017,[3] totaling $579 million in maximum contributions) and 41 under FIAP (totaling $110 million in maximum contributions as of February 2023) (hereafter "core DG projects").

Overall international assistance in the "Government and Civil Society" sector has been growing steadily since 2018 and has been a consistent priority area for Canadian aid (8–10% of overall ODA between 2018 and 2021) (Government of Canada 2022). However, within that space, the data indicate a significant decrease in spending on core DG projects in the three areas of analysis since the introduction of FIAP, from an average $34.1 million/year prior to 2017 to $18.3 million/year thereafter. This decline is part of a steady decrease in funding for the three core DG areas since the change of government in 2015, with a partial recovery over the past 2 years. The introduction of the FIAP does not appear to impact this trend. The 2015–2022 period is the second major decline-and-rebound cycle in just over a decade: core DG funding also fell precipitously in 2010, recovering to its near peak by 2015 as discussed elsewhere in this volume.

Under FIAP, Canada has prioritized implementing DG projects via the United Nations and regional organizations[4] and pulled back from working with Canadian organizations. These international organisations (IOs) are the only category of implementers to see an increase in annual new program values for core DG programs under FIAP (+28% compared to pre-FIAP levels). Although Canadian implementers continue to receive a similar proportion of funds for Canada's core DG programs (42% annually) pre- and post-FIAP, in real numbers, Canadian democracy assistance organizations have borne the brunt of the decreased spending. Canadian democracy assistance organizations have lost nearly half their annual average new program values since the introduction of FIAP (–$6.7 million in average annual program value, or –48%). Apart from IOs, all other categories of implementers also saw declines in core DG program budgets under FIAP. US-based democracy organizations experienced the second

---

[3] FIAP was announced on June 9, 2017. I classify programs with start dates beginning August 29, 2017, as FIAP programs, assuming some lag time between initial negotiation and project launch. In reality, this lag time may have been significantly longer. Likewise, any re-programming and add-on funds to programs signed prior to FIAP would have been designed according to the feminist principles but not captured by the database. Thus, the August 2017 cut-off date should be viewed as a soft and data presented here are indicative but imperfect.

[4] Specifically, the Organisation of American States, OAS.

biggest decline (−$3 million, or −78% from pre-FIAP values). Direct bilateral support to foreign governments and core DG programs financed via Canada's embassies and high commissions zeroed out (Fig. 9.1).

To analyze program themes and content, I performed a thematic analysis of 127 anticipated outcomes associated with the 41 core DG programs funded under FIAP. Strengthening women's participation in

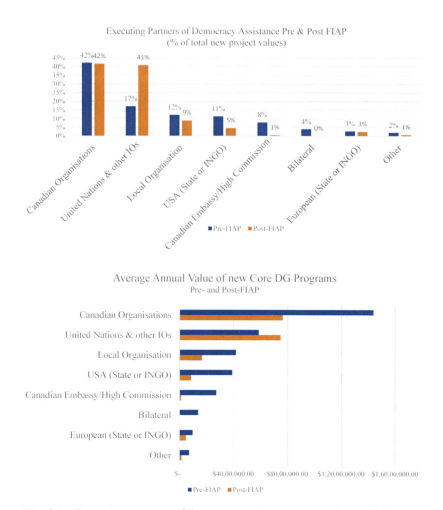

Fig. 9.1 Executing partners of democracy assistance pre- and post-FIAP

decision-making writ-large is the most frequently targeted outcome, reflected in 19% of outcomes. Aiding specific categories of women is minimally reflected in other outcomes: supporting women legislators (4%), supporting women candidates (0.8%) and supporting women voters (0.8%). Civil society organisation (CSO) capacity building (11%) and strengthening CSO networking (4%) are significant themes; some CSO outcomes are specific to women's CSOs while others do not specify. Support to institutions and processes is the next most significant focus, with 13% of outcomes targeting responsive institutions and policy, and 7% providing technical elections support.

Thematic analysis offers a top-level view into the language of feminism in core DG program outcomes. Fifty-five percent of outcomes are specific to women or gender. Only 3 of the 41 projects use the word "feminist" or "feminism" in their outcomes; no outcomes use the verbs "transform" or "challenge" or the nouns "power" or "patriarchy." Terms commonly associated with intersectionality appear infrequently. Four outcomes (3%) mention youth and four mention "marginalized groups/populations" (none in the context of multiple or compound marginalization). Only one outcome each refers specifically to intersectionality, LGBTQI issues, or ethnicity (<0.01%). Race/racism, (dis)ability, indigeneity, (de)colonialism, transgender, sexism and classism are not mentioned in any outcomes under the 41 core DG projects (Fig. 9.2).

The takeaways from this should be carefully nuanced. First, this brief analysis only looks at a very specific area of democracy aid (core DG projects), which has declined in the context of growing support for Government and Civil Society sector assistance overall. This suggests that Canada's democracy assistance is shifting to other subfields. It is also highly likely that feminist DG outcomes are being achieved elsewhere in the landscape of Canadian aid that is not captured in GAC's coding or that have not been appropriately linked with DG outcomes. Specifically, Canada's $300-million multi-year investment in the Equality Fund (announced in 2019) dwarfs the $101 million invested in core DG projects since mid-2017. "Shifting power" by supporting women's movements in Canada and in the world is one of the Equality Fund's three core themes. As discussed below, the degree to which support to feminist

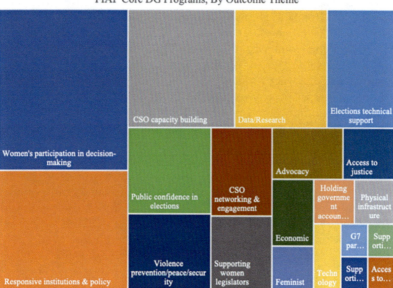

Fig. 9.2 FIAP core DG programs, by outcome theme

movements shifts power within the formal institutions and processes of democratic governance is key.[5]

Beyond these caveats, this analysis depicts important though nascent and inconsistent progress. While these outcomes might appear disappointing to feminist readers, FIAP has spurred democracy assistance implementers to pause and think about gendered impacts of democracy interventions and question assumptions about how they do business. As one firsthand account noted, prior to FIAP, use of the word "feminism" was openly opposed in some US-based democracy assistance organizations, where today exposure to FIAP has helped in normalizing and accepting the concept. Although, as another, American interviewee stated, "we are still building democracies for men," FIAP DG implementers are spurred to think about how to challenge the status quo of power relations

---

[5] An Equality Fund senior staff member was interviewed in the course of this research; however, it was beyond the scope of this project to conduct an equally detailed analysis of project content and spending through the Equality Fund.

through their programs, rather than passively reinforce it. Other international aid agencies are taking note and striving to follow suit. One of the key challenges of FIAP is holding implementers accountable to deepening this nascent change, in particular regarding the language of power and intersectionality.

Lastly, under FIAP Canada appears to be implementing DG goals via "upwards" funding (i.e., implementing via international organizations) and "downward" funding (via global grassroots organizations supported through the Equality Fund). Both trends bear further reflection. While GAC has prioritized working with international organizations for core DG activities under FIAP, Canada has committed to expanding the availability of Canadian expertise and assistance for democracy and governance assistance (Prime Minister of Canada 2021). Time will tell how this plays out.

Finally, supporting grassroots feminist movements is a powerful feminist approach, however, there is an apparent disconnect with the institutional and procedural outcomes of core DG work. There is work to be done to bring these fields closer together: just as the outcomes to date of core DG work may be discouraging for feminists, this apparent institutionalist gap in the feminist space is likely to disappoint democracy assistance actors. Constructing a coherent, feminist approach to democracy assistance is needed to move forward in lockstep.

Part II. Toward a Framework for Feminist Democracy Assistance

At the outset of this chapter, I asked whether or not a feminist framework was a useful approach for addressing inequality in governance, deepening the quality of democracy and combatting authoritarianism. Despite the conceptual gaps and uneven practical applications described above, feminism is indeed a singularly powerful framework for advancing increasingly inclusive and robust democracy. It is powerful because it compels democracy assistance actors and scholars to double back and re-evaluate how to define goals and measure success in a way few, if any, major approaches to development assistance have achieved. This is necessary if the field of practice is to rise to meet the manifold challenges facing democracy worldwide.

Based on the analysis above, this section looks at three areas that must be addressed to constructively align feminism and democracy assistance.

First, actors need to converge on the brand of feminism that democracy assistance will pursue. I argue that feminist institutionalism is a logical if still contentious objective. Second, democracy programs and feminist movements must find common ground around institutions and processes. Specifically, (a) political gender equality should not be a second-tier priority for democracy actors during political transitions and (b) feminist movements will strengthen the quality of democracy by deepening links with state institutions and processes. Third, democracy support must eliminate gender essentialism and ensure that they sustainably widen political space and level the playing field across multiple axes of diversity, intersectionality and pluralism.

Little "l" Liberal Feminism: Growing Contradictions for Democracy Support

Under FIAP, the language of Canada's democracy assistance framework (like other bilateral and UN frameworks) reflects transformative ambitions and values the lens of intersectionality. However, no coherent policy roadmap exists for a transformative and intersectional feminist approach to democracy support, in Canada or elsewhere. In its absence, a multitude of conceptual conflicts arises within the reigning "little l" liberal feminist approach.

In its defense, the pragmatism and gradualism of the liberal feminist approach have been advantages to building links with democracy assistance. As insufficient and problematic as the "add women and stir" approach may be, even this most basic goal was not a given within the democracy assistance community for much of modern history. The little "l" feminist emphasis on increasing the sheer number of women in elected bodies worldwide and empowering individual women has achieved major advances in the past two decades although huge gaps remain. Liberal feminist frameworks have provided simple and clear benchmarks for measuring progress for democracy assistance actors who were often uninitiated at best, or resistant to gender work at worse. As described by one interviewee, liberal feminism opened a door to normalizing the "F[eminist] Word" for democracy practitioners and the general public, where more progressive feminisms were viewed as alienating. It has made necessary but insufficient contributions to achieving political gender equality.

However, as policies like FIAP push toward more transformative feminist goals, Western democracy assistance's anchor in liberal feminism is increasingly problematic. Critics of liberal feminism argue that the focus on individuals masks the ways in which social structures, institutions and political processes disadvantage women. While liberal feminism may liberate individual women, women remain dependent on a patriarchal state. Indeed, critics argue that liberalism's "add women and stir" approach to democracy is fundamentally incompatible with feminism because it offers women a "piece of the pie as currently and poisonously baked" (Robin 1996). Postcolonial and black feminists further spurn liberal feminism for propagating the "white savior complex" instead of recognizing the diverse power dynamics at play with multiple, overlapping sources of oppression (Simien 2008; Choquette 2020). In other words, liberal feminism is inherently incapable of transforming power relations or of incorporating intersectionality. Continued use of transformational language in rhetoric but liberal approaches in practice is problematic.

Feminist institutionalism offers an obvious next step but is yet to be consistently accepted and applied within democracy assistance. Feminist institutionalism aims to transform power relations by working within existing institutions and power structures to reduce inequality and increase women's rights and representation through the lens of intersectionality (Mackay et al. 2010; Mackay and Waylen 2009). Common feminist institutionalist strategies include the use of gender quotas, women's caucuses, designing gender-sensitive parliaments, advocating on political party candidate selection, gender-sensitive electoral security planning and gender-sensitive political finance reform. Some of these—like the most widely identified feminist institutionalist approach (gender quotas)—continue to face substantial resistance. Others are increasingly common activities in democracy assistance projects but are yet to be viewed as central parts of an overall democracy strategy.

Bridging the Divide Between Women's Movements and Institutions

The contribution of feminist and women's movements to advancing rights and democracy is well-documented from the 1990s through today (Basu 2018; Beckwith 2000; Hawkesworth 2018; Nelson et al. 1994). However, while feminist movements consistently advance democracy movements, democratization processes do not always result in a better situation for women (Caprioli and Douglass 2008; Lovenduski 2019; Dahlerup 2018). Feminist mobilizations are influential in provoking or facilitating transitions from conflict or authoritarian rule to democracy, but they often fail to transform patriarchal political power structures, even under democracy (Phillips 1991; Mansbridge 1998; Inglehart et al. 2003; Cornwall and Goetz 2005; Beer 2009; Erny 2014; Bardall and Meyers 2018). Authors Viterna and Fallon sum up this unfortunate reality: "Most scholars conclude that democratization has done little to improve women's political influence within the state, even where women were active in the transition" (Viterna and Fallon. 2008, p. 669). Thus, the question democracy assistance actors need to answer isn't simply about how feminist movements successfully support democracy, but *how do feminist movements successfully support feminist democracy?*

Democracy assistance providers should focus on two critical junctures to ensure sustainable feminist outcomes in democracy. First, political transitions offer a short but crucial window for establishing greater rights and equality, especially for constitutional protections and strong gender quotas. When this opportunity is missed, it can be difficult if not impossible to re-coup (Waylen 2007). However, gender equality is often set aside as a second-tier priority to the pressing imperatives of conflict resolution and transition. In so doing, emerging democracies cripple themselves before they are even launched and often reproduce oppressive, conflict-prone power structures. A feminist approach to democratization would view political transition as incomplete so long as gender equality is not fully addressed. The Women, Peace and Security Agenda provides guidelines to apply through political transition and—critically—beyond the negotiating table and into democratization processes and institutions.

Second, it is necessary to build more bridges between support to feminist movements and support to the institutions and processes of democracy. As suggested in the interviews, providing aid to feminist advocacy without ensuring that state institutions are equipped to receive and respond to feminist demands, can backfire and create unrealistic expectations or antagonism. Other interviewees pointed to a common paradox: "whenever a feminist leader joins a political party and gets elected to office, she is immediately viewed as a 'sell out' and becomes the enemy of the feminist movement." This is clearly at odds with the ultimate goal of a feminist vision of democracy, i.e., where state institutions and power structures reflect people of all genders and address multiple, intersecting forms of inequality.

Aid providers should be aware of these risks and design programs accordingly. Just as support to core democracy programs should be firmly anchored in feminist goals, aid to feminist movements should always target building stronger democratic institutions. If, indeed, the feminist institutionalist approach is the way forward for the field of democracy assistance, then support to feminist movements should prioritize getting feminist leaders elected to office, transforming democratic processes and building strong feminist constituencies to hold institutions accountable. The state should be viewed as the ultimate prize, not as the adversary.

No Place for Essentialism in Democracy Support

As others have flagged since its inception (Tiessen, 2015; Morton et al. 2020; Cadesky 2020), FIAP's conceptual frame essentializes and instrumentalizes women's role in development. In the case of democracy, FIAP views women's participation as both the drivers of democratic quality and as the outcome of greater democracy. The policy is grounded in the assumption that women-as-a-whole will naturally advance policy for the greater good, especially for diverse and marginalized groups.

Such essentialist views have been widely abandoned and are inconsistent with today's understanding of women's diversity (Childs and Krook 2008). Importantly for democracy actors, essentialist perspectives are anti-strategic. Autocrats worldwide leverage these seemingly benign stereotypes about women in politics to undermine democracies. As such, uncritical and/or latent sexist stereotypes pose a national security threat.

Single-party and hybrid authoritarian states regularly genderwash their regimes to gain democratic cred, to meet their development goals and to retain favorable trade and diplomatic relations with the West. Indeed, Western insistence on increasing women's representation in dominant party states can kill two birds with one stone for autocrats seeking to boost their relations with Western democracies while sidelining opposition and consolidating their control at home.

While advancing descriptive representation is always an important and necessary step, democracy assistance providers cannot turn a blind eye to this kind of manipulation and must adapt assistance approaches accordingly. First, this means taking a more nuanced view of gender. Specifically, democracy support programs would do well to place greater emphasis on political pluralism and socio-economic diversity in measuring Equality–Diversity–Inclusion (EDI) outcomes.

Diversity and intersectionality in terms of identities such as race, sexual orientation, gender identity, religion and ability are incontestable. They have long been the primary focus for feminists advocating for breaking down views of women as a homogeneous group. However, in terms of democracy and politics, political pluralism and economics are equally salient. Consider the context of gender and party magnitude: opposition parties in transitional democracies are often fragmented, underfunded and poorly organized compared to incumbent parties. Competition between multiple opposition parties is fierce and women's voices are more likely to be crowded out as male aspirants and candidates vie for a severely limited political space. In contrast, ruling parties in dominant party states are much more likely to have the resources and political incentive to support more diverse candidates. As research on electoral system design suggests, "If parties can nominate more than one person they will be more likely to nominate a balanced slate than if they are only able to nominate one person per district. If only one candidate is to be nominated, it will often be the male incumbent, and challenging him with a woman candidate can create tensions within the party. Also, if faced with the decision between a man and a woman, parties will often choose the man, as he is seen as the most broadly accepted candidate" (Larserud and Taphorn 2007). These same principles apply to opposition and ruling party dynamics in dominant party states.

Socio-economics are also critical criteria. Worldwide, access to political power is determined by access to wealth and influence networks, which are traditionally male-dominated. Women who successfully enter this space must find ways to accede to these high entry thresholds and moneyed networks. Because of this, politics remains an elite space for people of all genders. A feminist approach would seek to reverse this equation by targeting the cost of politics and making political fundraising more broadly accessible.

Finally, as others have argued, adapting a feminist approach means shifting emphasis away from individual women and toward values of equality and social justice. Simply put, people of all genders can be feminists, just as women can uphold oppressive patriarchal power structures. The shift to a feminist framework implies prioritizing values including peace between and within nations, environmental integrity, government accountability and representativity, the protection of human rights and the disruption of colonial, racist, patriarchal and male-dominated power structures, alongside the goal of gender equality (Thompson et al. 2021).

In practice, integrating this perspective would relieve an inconsistency identified by several interviewees about needing to design GAC programs that are about "all women, all the time" (sometimes in conflict with other identified priorities) in order to meet the G3 classification and succeed in winning program funding. Under this understanding of feminism, the G3 classification would be based on the impact of programs in transforming or disrupting oppressive power structures and advancing feminist values.

Conclusion

The introduction of feminism to the field of democracy assistance has the potential to be one of the most significant and constructive renewals since the inception of this form of foreign aid if we are willing to rise to the challenge. In this chapter, we have reviewed the first years of Canada's feminist international development policy insofar as it has played out for international democracy assistance.

Despite the use of feminist language, FIAP's conceptual framework is still linked to more traditional gender and democracy approaches. Supporting feminist movements is a highlight of FIAP but has few visible links with institutional democracy assistance. Although ODA for Government and Civil Society programs has increased in recent years, there appears to be a decline in support for key institutions and processes of democracy (the "core DG" fields of this analysis). The data analysis suggests a firm reliance on UN and regional organizations, decreasing support for Canadian implementing organizations, and an increase in funding to women's movements but without explicit links to democratic institutions or processes. Also, contrary to conventional assumptions, it suggests a decreased reliance for program delivery through US-based organizations in these specific subfields. The missing connection between feminism and democratic institutions is especially of concern.

Despite these mixed outcomes, the introduction of FIAP opens the door of opportunity to an exciting renewal in the practice of democracy assistance. Key elements of this include (a) shifting from liberal to institutional feminism as a conceptual framework, (b) identifying mutually reinforcing connections between feminist and democracy support practices and goals and (c) moving away from essentialism and "women first" approach toward intersectionality and diversity (including socio-economic and political pluralism) and feminist values (not only female bodies).

Based on these findings, a path forward for feminist democracy assistance begins to emerge. Establishing objectives for feminist democratization will flip the table on our current ways of measuring. Understanding that women's presence in decision-making is necessary but insufficient to inclusive democracy, a feminist approach to democratization would revise how we interpret current benchmarks such as the proportion of women elected to institutions, registered to vote or participating in feminist movements. Instead of seeing these as the final goals, they should be seen as intermediary steps toward broader democratization objectives of social equality and justice.

The goal of feminist democracy assistance can be defined as promoting and supporting the development and consolidation of transparent and accountable governance systems that disrupt historically oppressive power structures and advance peace, equality, human rights and environmental integrity through equitable democratic representation. Specific outcomes can be built upon this goal and may include:

- Redefining measurements of democracy and political gender equality to employ intersectional standards that emphasize political pluralism and socio-economic diversity;
- Achieving and going beyond descriptive representation and emphasizing the substantive contributions of diversity in public life;
- Ensuring the Women, Peace and Security Agenda is applied beyond the negotiation phase and throughout democratic consolidation;
- Ending the double standard for electoral standards in democratization processes that views the enforcement of laws defending women's participation and security in the exercise of their civil and political rights as secondary;
- Ending impunity for violence against women in politics, which undermines democracy and advances authoritarian agendas;
- Leveling the financial playing field in access to politics;
- Accompanying change and understanding shifts in the drivers of political participation between generations and over policy lifespans; and
- Looking inward and holding democracy assistance providers accountable to feminist goals internally as well as externally.

Setting clear goals and targets will steer the course forward and help bring together disparate actors around a common cause. Current shortcomings in practice and policy should be viewed with a big-picture perspective: we are only beginning to explore and experiment with an ambitious and transformative new chapter in how we live our values. Democracy is a moving target with continually expanding horizons, as the arc of justice continues to bend. Integrating a feminist perspective helps shape an ever-greater concept of democracy and will advance Canada among nations.

References

Bardall, G., and E. Meyers. 2018. *Violence against Women in Politics: A Barrier to Peace and Security*. Policy Brief, Washington DC: U.S. Civil Society Working Group on Women, Peace, and Security.

Bardall, Gabrielle. 2019. "Autocrats use feminism to undermine democracy." *Policy Options*, October 30.

Basu, Amrita. 2018. *The Challenge of Local Feminisms: Women's Movements in Global Perspective*. Routledge.

Beckwith, Karen. 2000. Beyond Compare? Women's Movements in Comparative Perspective. *European Journal of Political Research* 37 (4): 431–468.

Beer, Caroline. 2009. Democracy and Gender Equality. *Studies in Comparative International Development* 44: 212–227.

Bjarnegard, Elin, and Par Zetterberg. 2022. How Autocrats Weaponize Women's Rights. *Journal of Democracy* 33 (2): 60–75.

Butler, Judith. 2021. "Why is the Idea of 'gender' Provoking Backlash the World Over?" *The Guardian*, October 23.

Cadesky, Jessica. 2020. Built on Shaky Ground: Reflections on Canada's Feminist International Assistance Policy. *International Journal* 75 (3): 298–312.

Caprioli, M., and K.L. Douglass. 2008. Nation Building and Women: The Effect of Intervention on Women's Agency. *Foreign Policy Analysis* 4 (1): 45–65.

Chenoweth, Erica, and Zoe Marks. 2022. "Revenge of the Patriarchs: Why Autocrats Fear Women." *Foreign Affairs*, February 8.

Childs, Sarah, and M.L. Krook. 2008. Critical Mass Theory and Women's Political Representation. *Political Studies* 56: 725–736.

Choquette, Éléna. 2020. "Canadian Liberalism and Gender Equality: Between Oppression and Emancipation." In *The Palgrave Handbook of Gender, Sexuality, and Canadian Politics*, edited by M Tremblay and J Everitt. Palgrave Macmillan.

Cornwall, P., and A.M. Goetz. 2005. Democratizing Democracy: Feminist Perspectives. *Democratisation* 12 (5): 783–800.

Dahlerup, Drude. 2018. *Has Democracy Failed Women?* MA: Cambridge and Malden.
Erny, Matthias. 2014. "Gender and democratization." *European Scientific Journal* (Special Issue 2): 198–213.
GAC. 2023. *Project Browser.* Accessed Feb 13, 2023. https://w05.international.gc.ca/projectbrowser-banqueprojets/ .
Global Affairs Canada. 2017. *Canada's Feminist International Assistance Policy* . Accessed 12 16, 2021. https://www.international.gc.ca/world-monde/issues_development-enjeux_developpement/priorities-priorites/policy-politique.aspx?lang=eng#5.5.
Hawkesworth, Mary E. 2018. *Globalization and Feminist Activism.* Rowman & Littlefield.
Inglehart, R., P. Norris, and C. Welzel. 2003. "Gender equality and democracy." *Human Values and Social Change*, 91–115. Brill.
Larserud, Stina, and Rita Taphorn. 2007. *Designing for Equality Best-Fit, Medium-Fit and Non-favourable Combinations of Electoral Systems and Gender Quotas.* Stockholm: International IDEA.
Lovenduski, Joni. 2019. "London School of Economics, Politics & Policy." *Democracy's Failure to Deliver Equality for Women Results from Fundamental Biases of Design.* April 1. Accessed 1 13, 2023. https://blogs.lse.ac.uk/politicsandpolicy/feminist-reflections-on-representative-democracy/.
Mackay, F., and G. Waylen. 2009. Feminist Institutionalism. *Politics & Gender* 5 (2): 237–237.
Mackay, Fiona, Meryl Kenny, and Louise Chappell. 2010. New Institutionalism Through a Gender Lens: Towards a Feminist Institutionalism? *International Political Science Review* 31 (5): 573–588.
Mansbridge, J. 1998. "Feminism and Democracy." In *Feminism and Politics*, edited by Anne Phillips, 142–158. Oxford University Press.
Morton, S.E., J. Muchiri, and L. Swiss. 2020. Which Feminism(s)? For Whom? Intersectionality in Canada's Feminist International Assistance Policy. *International Journal* 75 (3): 329–348.
Nelson, B. J., N. Chowdhury, and N. Caudhurī. 1994. *Women and Politics Worldwide.* Yale University Press.
Novovic, Gloria. 2022. "Canada's International Assistance: Underfunded Feminist Ambitions." *The Reality of Aid Network.* March 14. Accessed Jan 4, 2023. https://realityofaid.org/canadas-international-assistance-underfunded-feminist-ambitions/.
Parisi, Laura. 2020. Canada's New Feminist International Assistance Policy: Business as Usual? *Foreign Policy Analysis* 16 (2): 163–180.
Phillips, A. 1991. *Engendering Democracy.* Penn State Press.

Prime Minister of Canada. 2021. *Summit for Democracy 2021 Submission and Commitments: Canada* . Dec 9. Accessed Jan 16, 2023. https://pm.gc. ca/en/news/backgrounders/2021/12/09/summit-democracy-2021-submis sion-and-commitments-canada.

Robin, Morgan. 1996. Light Bulbs, Radishes and the Politics of the 21st Century. In *Radically Speaking: Feminism Reclaimed*, ed. Diane Bell and Renate Klein, 5–8. Chicago: Spinifex Press.

Simien, Evelyn M. 2008. Black Feminist Theory Charting a Course for Black Women's Studies in Political Science. *Women & Politics* 26 (2): 81–93.

Status of Women Canada. 1995. *Setting the Stage for the Next Century: The Federal Plan for Gender Equality.* https://publications.gc.ca/collections/Col lection/SW21-15-1995E.pdf. Ottawa, ON.

Thompson, Lyric, Ahmed Spogmay, and Tanya Khokhar. 2021. "Defining a Feminist Foreign Policy: A 2021 Update." Accessed 1 13, 2023. https:// www.icrw.org/publications/defining-feminist-foreign-policy/#:~:text=%E2% 80%9CFeminist%20foreign%20policy%20is%20the,all%3B%20seeks%20to%0d isrupt%20colonial%2C.

Tiessen, Rebecca. 2015. Gender Essentialism in Canadian Foreign Aid Commitments to Women, Peace, and Security. *International Journal* 70 (1): 84–100.

Tiessen, Rebecca. 2019. *What's New about Canada's Feminist International Assistance Policy: The Problem and Possibilities of 'More of the Same'.* joint Policy Paper from The School of Public Policy and the Canadian Global Affairs Institute, Calgary: University of Calgary, School of Public Policy & CGAI.

Viterna, Jocelyn, and Kathleen M. Fallon. 2008. Democratization, Women's Movements, and Gender-Equitable States: A Framework for Comparison. *American Sociological Review* 73 (4): 668–689.

Waylen, G. 2007. *Engendering Transitions: Women's Mobilization, Institutions and Gender Outcomes.* Oxford University Press.

CHAPTER 10

Quiet Helpful Fixer or Boisterous Norm Advocate? Canada as a Mediator

Peter Jones

INTRODUCTION

The field of international mediation is witnessing a significant debate over the proper role of a mediator. Where once it was held that the primary quality of a mediator, and particularly a middle-power one, was an ability to quietly convene those in conflict and help them to find a way forward,

Executive Director of the Ottawa Dialogue, an organization which runs Track 1.5 and Track 2 dialogues around the world and Professor in the Graduate School of Public and International Affairs at the University of Ottawa. The author wishes to thank the editors and reviewers of this volume, Patricia Fortier, Gordon Venner and several others (who commented on the basis of anonymity) for their feedback on drafts of this paper. The author is solely responsible for the contents of this paper.

P. Jones (✉)
Graduate School of Public and International Affairs, University of Ottawa, Ottawa, ON, Canada

© The Author(s), under exclusive license to Springer Nature Switzerland AG 2023
M. A. Cameron et al. (eds.), *Democracy and Foreign Policy in an Era of Uncertainty*, Canada and International Affairs, https://doi.org/10.1007/978-3-031-35490-8_10

there is now an increasing strain of thought that a mediator has a responsibility to promote certain norms as an intrinsic part of the solution to a conflict. Many of these norms are ones that Canada firmly champions on the world stage. While popular in many quarters, not everyone entirely supports this direction in mediation. At the level of those involved in the conflict, those in power—who are usually elite and male—take the view that outside "interference" with their society is not acceptable. It is easy to dismiss their criticism with a simple, "Well, they would feel that way, wouldn't they?" but the deeper question is whether outsiders have the right to require that their beliefs—usually Western and liberal—should be the foundation of the settlement of someone else's dispute.

Beyond this philosophical level, there are two issues. First is the question of whether this "norm" imperative can be pursued in situations where its requirements are perceived as alien, or whether the attempt to do so may be self-serving for the norm advocates and actually apt to do more harm than good on the ground. Second, there lies the question of whether those who seek to position themselves as mediators should approach that task through the "lens" of a particular agenda—be it the current norm advocacy agenda of the Liberal government, or the agenda espoused by the previous Conservative government of promoting such things as Judeo-Christian values as being at the heart of Canada's approach to the world. In short, there is the question of whether a country which seeks to act as a mediator should approach that task primarily through a particular framework, which will affect how it goes about the business of mediation or should be prepared to prioritize the mechanics of mediation itself, even where doing so might take it to places with which its broader beliefs and policies are not entirely comfortable.

If Canada is to play a greater role in mediation, which there is evidence that some in the foreign policy establishment believe it should, ways will have to be found to deal with these issues. This paper will review the evidence that mediation seems to be a subject of quietly growing interest for some in Canada's foreign policy community. The paper will then examine the growing debate over whether and how the advocacy of norms should lie at the heart of mediation efforts. Finally, the paper will discuss what this situation may mean for Canada should it choose to try to make mediation a larger part of its foreign policy toolkit. It should be noted that, while much of this paper will discuss the issues in terms of the norms which are held by the present Government, the broader issue is a bipartisan one—are Canadian Governments, whether Liberal or Conservative, prepared to mediate when this requires them to act in ways which their policy, and even their value frameworks find objectionable and are they prepared to achieve a bipartisan consensus on this?

Canada and Mediation: A Quietly Growing Interest?

While many Canadians may believe that this country has been at the forefront of international conflict mediation for many decades, the reality is less clear. Individual Canadians have played important roles in the field, but Canada's official involvement has been largely ad hoc. There has not been a systematic engagement, in the way that some countries, such as the Scandinavians and others have made mediation an intrinsic part of their approach to foreign policy. Rather, Canadian officials have been deployed into mediations in a rather random way. Historically, there has been no buy-in at the political level for efforts to systematically develop a capacity to play a significant role in the field (Jones 2013; Hoffman 2013).

The election of the Liberal Government in 2015 seemed to herald the possibility that this might change. The official platform of the Liberals included a reference to mediation as a priority, albeit to the support of others doing the task rather than it being a specifically Canadian role. This was part of a general push to "re-capture" Canada's supposedly traditional place as a leading force in the peacemaking field. The Mandate Letter of PM Trudeau's the first foreign minister instructed him to "increase Canada's support for United Nations peace operations and its mediation, conflict-prevention and post-conflict reconstruction efforts" (Mandate Letter, November 12, 2015). Although some officials at the time interpreted this as a possible opening to create a more thoroughgoing Canadian capacity for involvement in mediations, and developed proposals for Canada to be more active, there was little political appetite for an expansive interpretation (Jones 2019).

If Canada's desire to see its own officials involved in messy mediation situations was lukewarm, it has been willing to spend significant money to encourage and support others to do so. These have included the UN, NGOs and other specialist groups who have been supported in order to help build mediation capacity in various conflict zones. The "Stabilization and Reconstruction Task Force" (START) was re-named as the Peace and Stabilization Operations Programme (PSOPS) in August 2016. At the same time, it was given instructions to more fully implement the present Government's agenda around a set of norm-based imperatives which recast Canadian foreign policy as being more fully harnessed to the advocacy of a set of objectives, such as Canada's "Feminist Foreign Policy". The Prime Minister and his Ministers have repeatedly made the point that Canada's approach to conflict and peacebuilding has these issues at its heart. This was done recently, for example, in the speech made by Minister Joly to the 2022 United Nations General Assembly debate (Joly, UNGA speech, 2022). This approach is reflected in programming. On its website, for example, PSOPS states that:

> Women and girls play vital roles in establishing and maintaining peace. Given their important role, PSOPs supports enhancing women's active participation in conflict prevention, stabilization and peacebuilding initiatives, and actively advocates for early and meaningful participation of women in peace and security efforts … PSOPs manages the distribution of over $100 million per year in grants and contributions toward the ultimate goal of increased peace, security and stability for people, particularly women and girls, in fragile and conflict-affected states and situations … Projects undertaken by PSOPs are inclusive and gender-responsive … (PSOPS website)

In short, the current government has, publicly at least, made the norm-based imperatives of its foreign policy agenda the "lens" through which conflicts are analyzed and peacebuilding policy is developed. This is nothing new. Previous Liberal governments have done the same thing through different lenses in the past (Responsibility to Protect, Landmines) and the Conservative governments have done the same thing through their favoured lenses (support for Israel and the promotion of "Judeo-Christian" values as a foreign policy objective). In both cases, governments believed that Canada's policies towards, and involvement in, conflict situations should be predicated on support for values, frameworks or causes in which they believed.

Over the years, however, other international actors have quietly questioned Canada as to whether it is prepared to shoulder a greater extent of the burden of actually mediating conflicts and have pressed Ottawa to play a greater role (interviews with foreign diplomats in Ottawa and elsewhere). Apparently, not having given up on hopes that Canada would take on a more significant role in this field, work has recently been going on at the level of officials within GAC over the past 18 months to see if ways cannot be found to quietly develop a more systematic role for Canada in mediation, beyond the funding that PSOPS provides to others who are involved in the field. This has included the creation of an internal advisory group on mediation and other efforts to consider ways Canada could play a more active role, such as the appointment of a mediation "champion" within GAC at the Assistant Deputy Minister level (interviews).

News did break recently that Canada has quietly facilitated a process of dialogue involving the Government of Cameroon and various groups involved in the fighting in that country, leading Ottawa to announce that it had been asked to formally serve as mediator. This may have been the first sign that the desire of some in GAC to be more active in mediation was being implemented. However, the announcement that agreement had been reached to initiate a Canadian mediated peace process was quickly met by the Government of Cameroon announcing that no such agreement had been reached (Global Affairs Canada 2023; York and Njie 2023; York 2023). This may be indicative of high-level splits within the Cameroon Government. As of the time of writing, Canada has said that it sticks by its original announcement and will continue to work with interested parties as mediator (Robertson 2023; interviews). Whatever the reality may be, the incident serves as a reminder of the complexities and frustrations of a mediation process and the need for all involved to demonstrate great patience, and not a little reticence when it comes to publicity.

The State of the Field: Mediation or Advocacy (or Advocacy as Mediation)?

Beyond the specifics of the Cameroon case, the apparent determination of PSOPS to insist that its grantees are working within the framework of the advocacy of certain norms is reflective of their approach to a long-standing debate in the field. The peacebuilding space, at both official levels and the space involving NGO actors, has been grappling with the question of the proper role of norm advocacy for some years. This is an evolution of the field, the early years of which were marked by a belief that mediators should be largely focused on assisting the parties to achieve such things as official ceasefires and other such agreements. This usually meant helping elites from the conflicting parties to hold quiet, initially deniable dialogues with the hope of developing ways to manage and even resolve their conflicts (Mitchell 2001; Kelman 2002; Fisher 2002).

With the publication of such documents as the UN Secretary General's *Agenda for Peace* in 1992, it is increasingly argued by many in the field that a deeply transformative peace should be the goal, one which addresses unless underlying social, political and economic factors which caused the conflict (Boutros-Ghali 1992). Part of this effort has come to involve a strong imperative that voices not generally involved in official negotiations should have a place at the table to raise their issues, often regarding inequality and the lack of justice in their societies (Babbitt 2009a, b). Beyond this, there is now a strong sense in some quarters that the role of mediators, both official and non-official, should include the promotion of "norms" as part of the process; that mediators must use their agency and influence to promote the adoption of these norms as part of any peace agreement (Hellmuller et al. 2020). The United Nations has officially stated that this approach must be part of any mediation process it is involved with (United Nations *Guidance* 2012). These norms include a strong sense that peace negotiations must be more inclusive of voices not usually represented in elite-level negotiations; that human rights and other such "norms" must be included and promoted in peace negotiations and agreements; and that negotiations must be "owned" by local actors, rather than imposed or driven from the outside. Taken together, these drives are known in some quarters as the "inclusion" agenda—the imperative of the inclusion of those not generally present in negotiations, and the inclusion of international norms in the mediation process. While this agenda is not universally agreed, debate over it is one of the key discussions in the mediation and peacebuilding field today (Vuković 2021; Paffenholtz and Zartman 2019; Donias and McCandless 2017).

The promoters of this agenda believe strongly that peace agreements, and the mediations which lead to them, must seek not merely to allow elites, who often benefit from the conflict, to manage their conflicts while remaining in power. They must do nothing less than transform the underlying causes of the conflict and improve the lives of the common people most affected by conflict (Papagianni and Federman 2022; Gamaghelyan 2021; Lederach 2005). This "moral imperative" to make peace agreements more just and inclusive is supported by arguments that peace agreements which fail to do so are more likely to be short-lived, whereas agreements which do tackle these issues may be more difficult to achieve but will lead to agreements more likely to be enduring (Koppell 2022; Krause et al. 2018). "Inclusion" has thus become a central issue in the field and several institutes and other organizations have been created to study and promote the agenda, such as the "Institute for Inclusive Security" (website), "Inclusive Security" (website), "Inclusive Peace" (website) and others. By contrast, sceptics of this agenda include many who support these ideas in principle, but note that experience tends to show that the application of such norms in actual conflict situations is fraught with dangers and difficulties. These range from problems when the norms are applied without due regard for local sensitivities and become themselves a cause of difference and conflict (Zahar 2012), to problems when local elites say they agree with inclusion and other norms, but then use their power to corrupt the process. This results in agreements which claim to espouse these ideas but are really exercises in taking them on board superficially while manipulating them into sham agreements which actually change little (Mendes 2020; Palmiano Federer, forthcoming).

At one level, the criticisms of the inclusion agenda argue that it is such a broad concept that, beyond attractive declaratory claims, it is difficult to prove that it either works or makes a real difference on the ground (Hirblinger and Landau 2020). After an extensive review of peace processes which did and did not include representation by women's groups Dayal and Christien (2020) concluded that there is no correlation between the presence of women's groups in a peace process and the eventual incorporation of gender provisions into peace agreements. Others respond that the inclusion of women's groups in peace processes, where it has been done, has usually come in the form of such groups being invited to attend consultations with the (male and elite) negotiators in order to offer the appearance of "legitimacy" to agreements already reached, rather than having a real seat at the negotiation table (Papagianni and Federman 2022; Enloe 2013; Hudson et al. 2008–2009). More broadly, critics of the inclusion agenda charge that it has resulted in the creation of an international group of experts and consultants, at both the official and unofficial levels, who have become a self-referential elite, descending on conflicts to superficially intervene in the service of promoting their agenda, but without really understanding the lives of the people affected by the conflict (Palmiano Federer 2021; Autesserre 2014; Hara 2003). The proponents of the inclusion agenda strongly disagree with these points. They argue that it is the only way for a mediation process to break the monopoly of power of those who caused the conflict and benefit from it and that real peace cannot be achieved until this is done. (Papagianni and Federman 2022; Gamaghelyan 2021).

Looking Forward: A Role for Canada as a Mediator?

The debate in the field notwithstanding, the current government of Canada has publicly adopted the "inclusion agenda" as the basis of its policies on peacebuilding and intervention in conflicts. As noted above, PSOPS, GAC's policy lead on conflict intervention, has placed this agenda at the heart of decision-making on support for mediation and peacebuilding. More broadly, Canada has been quick to loudly sanction and ban those governments, organizations and individuals who it holds to be violating these norms in a variety of settings around the world as a show of its disapproval of their actions and its support for this agenda. If there is work going on behind the scenes to find ways to increase Canada's role in the mediation field, the adoption of the inclusion agenda as the framework through which Canada assesses its involvement in peacebuilding has implications for what Ottawa may be prepared to attempt.

In particular, if Canadian officials wish to open up a policy space for Canada to officially take upon itself a more active role in mediation, while also basing its approach to peacebuilding firmly on advocacy on behalf of the inclusion agenda, that agenda may constrain what kinds of situations Canadian official mediators can get involved in and what they can support. More traditional official mediation often involves quietly talking to, and even working closely with, those local elites who are generally opposed to the imperatives of the inclusion agenda. It can involve helping them find ways to "cut deals" which may reduce the fighting but are unlikely to have the interests of the inclusion agenda at their heart if these challenge the supremacy of the elites at the table.

As the experience of countries which make this mediation role a key part of their foreign policies shows, inviting to one's own country people who are otherwise banned or sanctioned for having violated norms is not without controversy. Norway, for example, came in for strong criticism in 2022 from human rights, women's and other groups for having invited to Oslo leaders of the Taliban in Afghanistan, and thereby, in the view of the critics, legitimized their takeover of the country (or at least recognized it). Norway's response that the meetings were to discuss the delivery of aid to the people of Afghanistan, that no progress could be made on this vital humanitarian matter without talking to those in power, and that Norway explicitly did not recognize the Taliban government, did not cut much ice with vocal opponents. This incident exposes the difficulties and dangers inherent in playing this role (Fazl-E-Haider 2022; Keyton 2022; Shams and Shaifullah 2022).

A key question about whether Canada is willing to take on a more active role as a mediator is thus whether Ottawa is prepared to accept this kind of criticism, particularly when it involves talking to those who its foreign policy agenda of the moment has placed beyond the pale, and even caused Ottawa to place sanctions on. Of course, not all such meetings need to be as public as the Oslo meeting was; it is possible to invite those who are leading groups or governments whose policies one disagrees with for secret talks. But these run the risk of eventually being made public, sometimes in uncontrolled and unpredictable ways, leading to charges of hypocrisy. One can also hold such meetings outside of Canada, though the ability of the government to claim that it is a player in the field may be compromised if Ottawa refuses to hold any meetings here. Moreover, even if they are held in third locations, the fact that the Canadian Government was actively hosting and/or assisting a process of dialogue involving those who it has sanctioned might not go down well with key constituencies the Liberals have sought to court with their foreign policy pronouncements. How do you pay for someone from a group you have said you will never talk to, and even sanctioned, to come to a series of secret meetings over time? This difficulty may not play out so much at the official level in Ottawa, though there are some officials in PSOPs who are fiercely devoted to their agenda. As the Cameroon case seems to demonstrate, senior policy-makers no doubt understand that the work of peace is sometimes advanced by being willing to talk to those making war. At the political level, however, it may be difficult to persuade those advising the PM and the Minister to take the risk of being seen to talk to those whom Canada has designated as "terrorists", human rights violators or otherwise. Fears exist that key diaspora communities in Canada, and other constituencies will not be silent if this comes out, and their votes matter.

An alternative would be to support those NGOs and other actors working at the Track 1.5 and Track 2 levels to hold such discussions in unofficial ways. There is a long history of this sort of thing, and it has contributed to many peace talks and agreements (Jones 2015, Chapter 1; Nan et al. 2009; Mapendere 2006). Here there is more scope for creative ambiguity and the web-page of PSOPs does show that Canada has supported international groups known to play this role, such as the HD Centre (PSOPs website, project CA-3-P008777001), InterMediate

(PSOPs website, project CA-3-P007276001) and others. Though a relatively small fraction of PSOPs overall spending, this does seem to show that GAC is open to this sort of involvement. However, based on what is known publicly at least, Canada can hardly be said to be playing a leading role in supporting this kind of dialogue. Moreover, the fact that funding for these projects seems to be, from what can be deduced from the PSOPs website, a small percentage of overall programme spending indicates that this modest level of involvement may be all that the traffic will bear.

In particular, there may be concerns that too obvious a role in supporting such elite-level unofficial dialogues, even at arms-length, could be construed by critics of this kind of dialogue as being counter to PSOPs' mandate and also to Canada's broader inclusion agenda-oriented approach to peacemaking. The champions of the inclusion norm are not known to be quiet if they feel their friends are straying from orthodoxy; difficult questions may be asked by vocal constituencies which the Government claims to be a leading proponent of. Vocal and politically well-organized diaspora groups can also be expected to weigh in. And there is also the fact that arms-length, Track 1.5 dialogues must eventually transition to official talks if deals are to be made. Can a country credibly play a leading role in sponsoring a Track 1.5 or a Track 2 if it is not prepared to eventually take on the responsibility of shepherding the official talks that may result from it? Even if Canada were to increase its support for these kinds of projects, welcome though that might be to the community of those who do this work, it is difficult to argue that this would be the same as Canada itself taking on a role in international mediation unless Canada was ultimately willing to become more involved in actual mediation itself.

The basic problem is how Canada approaches the question of impartiality in mediation. There are two aspects to this question: impartiality as regards the interests of the parties in the dispute; and impartiality as regards the implementation of key norms and standards. In classical terms, a mediator should be able to achieve a degree of impartiality as regards both. This does not mean that they are necessarily without a view; it does mean that they strive, when acting as a mediator, to separate their views from their actions. The imperatives of the inclusion agenda, by contrast, require a stance of advocacy, if not necessarily for any particular side in a dispute, then certainly for action on certain norms. Eileen Babbitt sums up the essential issue thus,

Both human rights and CR (Conflict Resolution) invoke principles of impartiality. However, the concept had completely different meanings for practitioners in each field. To a CR (Conflict Resolution) practitioner, impartiality requires an even-handed treatment of all parties, regardless of their status or resources. For a human rights advocate, impartiality refers to the application of human rights norms, most of which are constructed to protect the weak individual from the abuses of the state or other potentially exploitative authorities. Thus, the human rights result does not appear impartial, but instead looks like (and often is) advocacy for one party over another. This presents a conundrum for the CR practitioner who recognizes that social justice requires creating a more level playing field, but who needs to maintain even-handedness to be credible (Babbitt 2009b: 619).

Elsewhere I have presented this as a matrix of different considerations and suggested that the Canadian governments have put themselves in a place where, though there may be situations where they are not partial to either side in a given conflict, they are always going to be partial as regards the policies and practices of those in conflict (Jones 2022: 196).[1] In practical terms, this tends to mean that current Canadian peacebuilding policy may find it difficult to act as something other than an advocate of such things as the inclusion agenda, in the sense of advocacy as defined by Babbitt. But it is not simply the Liberals who find themselves in this situation. The Conservatives under Stephen Harper were also hard-pressed to accept the idea of impartiality, although their concerns were often over different issues, such as a desire to support one side or the other in a specific conflict (for example, Israel) for ideological and other reasons, including a desire to court certain diaspora groups (Jones 2019).

Of course, the choice need not be a binary one. Other nations who are active mediators on the world stage do not eschew the imperatives of the inclusion agenda. Finland, Norway, Switzerland and others are not silent, or unsupportive of efforts on issues of the inclusion agenda (Finland Foreign Ministry website; Norwegian Foreign Ministry website; Swiss Foreign Ministry website). But they take care to ensure that their support for this agenda does not preclude them from also being able to act as mediators in a more conventional sense. This includes being prepared to talk, both privately and even publicly where necessary, with

---

[1] And, of course, there will be situations where Canada is probably too partial to one side of the conflict to be able to effectively contribute to mediation. The current conflict in Ukraine is likely a case in point.

those violating the norms of the inclusion agenda where they believe the mediation effort requires it. The key is an ability to be impartial where necessary for mediation, while not neutral on the bigger issues, and being prepared to publicly defend, when necessary, this flexible stance in the face of criticism from other norm advocates.

Another key for these countries is that involvement in mediation is, *in itself*, an important foreign policy role, rather than a way to promote a particular set of objectives. It is not entirely clear whether Canada is willing to do the same, under either the Liberals or the Conservatives, or whether its desire to be, and be seen as, an advocate of particular agendas or imperatives trumps other considerations in its approach to peacebuilding policy. In short, if involvement in peacebuilding, and therefore mediation, is framed around or tied to a particular lens, be it a Conservative or a Liberal one, then what happens when that government leaves office and a new government, with a new lens, comes in? Countries which make mediation a foreign policy role overcome this by achieving bipartisan consensus to make mediation *itself* a lens, or framework, for foreign policy activity. Perhaps the role played by Canada in the still unfolding Cameroon case, though it is still not entirely clear, is an indication that some in GAC believe that this approach may be possible.

Conclusion

Given that international mediations can go on for many years, any enhanced efforts to play the role of mediator as an increased aspect of Canada's foreign policy will require long-term, bipartisan support, as it has in countries which make mediation a part of their foreign policy. There is as yet little evidence that this will be possible in Canada under present circumstances, unless, of course, an effort to quietly build such a bipartisan consensus around mediation as a foreign policy role is part of the current effort to explore whether Canada could be a more active mediator. For the most part, Canadian governments seem far more comfortable in the role of champion of certain norms and causes than in the role of a quiet mediator of difficult and morally messy disputes. Indeed, they seem to see such norm advocacy as lying at the heart of their diplomatic efforts and are quick to publicly ban and sanction the very actors that mediators, in the classic sense, accept, however reluctantly, that they must quietly talk to.

The apparent efforts of some officials to find ways whereby Canada might play a greater role in the field of quiet mediation are laudable to those who believe in Canada's ability to play this role. Of course, Canada could attempt, as others do, to have it both ways; to advocate the inclusion norm, while also quietly playing the role of classic mediator, or supporting others who do. In effect, this would involve fusing the two peacebuilding agendas, as others have done. This will require high-level, bipartisan support. At present, loudly denouncing, banning and sanctioning actors in conflict situations for their failures in terms of the inclusion agenda is a key political imperative of the government, as is loudly denouncing those who violate other cherished causes a key imperative of the Conservatives. Neither Party has shown, publicly anyway, much inclination to simultaneously support a policy of long-term efforts to foster quiet, behind-the-scenes exclusive talks involving the very actors they oppose.

The involvement in Cameroon may be indicative that changes are afoot for Canada in the realm of mediation. This would be welcome. Eventually, however, if Canada is to be an active mediator on more than a very occasional basis, there will need to be a deeper discussion of the issues that will arise if Canada is to take on mediation as a broader role of its foreign policy. The prospect of progress on the classic mediation file will always be tenuous unless and until a serious, and ultimately bipartisan consensus can be achieved in Canada over whether or not the roles of norm/cause advocate on the hand and impartial mediator on the other *must* be seen to be mutually exclusive. For Canada, peacebuilding policy has to date been mostly about quietly funding the building of international mediation capacity, and supporting others to do the work, while boisterously advocating certain causes and norms in the midst of conflict situations. Actually, facilitating quiet mediation processes between those who are doing the fighting (and often violating those norms) is a role Canada has been less willing to play. This is not necessarily a criticism; it is just a reality of the position Canada has carved for itself on the peacebuilding file. There is evidence that some in Canada's foreign policy community wish to change this and are taking tentative steps to do so. The next few years may tell whether this is possible.

References

Autesserre, Séverine. 2014. *Peaceland: Conflict Resolution and the Everyday Politics of International Intervention*. Cambridge: Cambridge University Press.

Babbitt, Eileen. 2009a. The Evolution of International Conflict Resolution: From Cold War to Peacebuilding. *Negotiation Journal* 25 (4): 539–549.

Babbitt, Eileen. 2009b. Conflict Resolution and Human Rights: The State of the Art. In *The Sage Handbook of Conflict Resolution*, ed. Jacob Bercovitch, Victor Kremenyuk, and William Zartman, 613–629. Thousand Oaks: Sage.

Boutros-Ghali, Boutros. 1992. *An Agenda for Peace: Preventive Diplomacy, Peacemaking and Peacekeeping*. New York: United Nations.

Dayal, Anjali, and Agathe Christien. 2020. Women's Participation in Informal Peace Processes. *Global Governance: A Review of Multilateralism and International Organisations* 26 (1): 68–98.

Donais, Timothy, and Erin McCandless. 2017. International Peacebuilding and the Emerging Inclusivity Norm. *Third World Quarterly* 38 (2): 291–310.

Enloe, Cynthia. 2013. *Seriously! Investigating Crashes and Crises as if Women Mattered*. Berkeley: University of California Press.

Fazl-E-Haider, Syed. 2022. Oslo Talks Expose the West's Taliban Dilemma. *Lowey Institute Interpreter*, February 2022. Accessed 21 November. https://www.lowyinstitute.org/the-interpreter/oslo-talks-expose-west-s-taliban-dilemma.

Finland, Ministry for Foreign Affairs. 2022. *Peace Mediation as a Stronger Priority in Foreign Policy*. Accessed 9 Dec 2022. https://um.fi/peacemediation.

Fisher, Ronald J. 2002. Historical Mapping of the Field of Inter-active Conflict Resolution. In *Second Track/Citizen's Diplomacy: Concepts and Techniques for Conflict Transformation*, ed. John Davies and Edward Kaufman, 64–75. Lanham, MD: Rowman & Littlefield.

Gamaghelyan, Phillip. 2021. Towards an Inclusive Conception of Best Practices in Peace and Conflict Initiatives: The Case of the South Caucasus. *International Negotiation* 26 (1): 125–150.

Global Affairs Canada. 2023. Statement on Peace Process in Cameroon. 20 January at https://www.canada.ca/en/global-affairs/news/2023/01/statement-on-peace-process-in-cameroon.html.

Hara, Fabienne. 2003. Burundi: A Case of Parallel Diplomacy. In *Herding Cats: Multiparty Mediation in a Complex World*, ed. Chester A. Crocker, Fen O. Hampson, and Pamela Aall, 135–158. Washington: United States Institute of Peace Press.

Hellmuller, Sara, Jamie Pring, and Oliver P. Richmond. 2020. How Norms Matter in Mediation; An Introduction. *Swiss Political Science Review* 26 (4): 345–363.

Hirblinger, Andreas, and Dana D. Landau. 2020. Daring to Differ? Strategies of Inclusion in Peacemaking. *Security Dialogue* 51 (4): 305–322.
Hoffman, Evan. 2013. Interviews with 3 Former Canadian Ambassadors Regarding Their Previous Mediation Efforts. *Canadian Foreign Policy Journal* 19 (1): 96–109.
Hudson, Valerie, Mary Caprioli, Bonnie Ballif-Spanvill, Rose McDermott, and Emmet Chad. 2008–2009. The Heart of the Matter: The Security of Women and the Security of States. *International Security* 33(3): 7–35.
Inclusive Peace. Accessed 24 Nov 2022. https://www.inclusivepeace.org/about-us/.
Inclusive Security. Accessed 24 Nov 2022. https://www.inclusivesecurity.org/.
Institute for Inclusive Security. Accessed 24 Nov 2022. https://issat.dcaf.ch/Share/People-Organisations/Organisations/Institute-for-Inclusive-Security.
Joly, Mélanie. 2022. Canada's National Statement at the General Debate—Opening of the 77th Session of the UN General Assembly. Accessed 21 Nov 2022. https://www.international.gc.ca/world-monde/international_relations-relations_internationales/un-onu/statements-declarations/2022-09-26-unga-agnu.aspx?lang=eng.
Jones, Peter. 2013. Canada and International Conflict Mediation. *International Negotiation* 18: 219–244.
Jones, Peter. 2015. *Track Two Diplomacy: In Theory and Practice*. Stanford: Stanford University Press.
Jones, Peter. 2019. Middle Power Liberal Internationalism and Mediation in Messy Places: The Canadian Dilemma. *International Journal* 74 (1): 119–134.
Jones, Peter. 2022. A Question of Impartiality: Canada and Peacemaking in the Middle East. In *Middle Power in the Middle East: Canada's Foreign and Defence Policies in a Changing Region*, eds. T. Juneau, and B. Momani. Toronto: University of Toronto Press.
Kelman, Herbert C. 2002. Interactive Problem-solving: Informal Mediation by the Scholar Practitioner. In *Studies in International Mediation: Essays in Honor of Jeffrey Z. Rubin*, ed. J. Bercovitch, 167–193. New York: Palgrave MacMillan.
Keyton, David. 2022. Taliban Talks in Norway Raise New Debate About Recognition. Associated Press, January 23. Accessed 21 Nov 2022. https://apnews.com/article/talks-with-taliban-begin-in-norway-281532ba4dc8ba968ed7a6643aa31c71.
Koppell, Carla. 2022. Making the Case: The Opportunity and Need to Address Diversity in Conflict Resolution and Development. In *Untapped Power: Leveraging Diversity and Inclusion for Conflict and Development*, ed. Carla Koppell, 49–84. Oxford: Oxford University Press.

Krause, Jana, Werner Krause, and Bränfors. Piia. 2018. Women's Participation in Peace Negotiations and the Durability of Peace. *International Interactions* 44 (6): 985–1016.

Lederach, John Paul. 2005. *The Moral Imagination: The Art and Soul of Building Peace*. New York: Oxford University Press.

Mapendere, Jeffrey. 2006. Track One and a Half Diplomacy and the Complementarity of Tracks. *Culture of Peace Online Journal* 2 (1): 66–81.

Mendes, Isa. 2020. Inclusion and Political Representation in Peace Negotiations: The Case of the Colombian Victims' Delegations. *Journal of Politics in Latin America* 11 (3): 272–297.

Minister of Global Affairs Mandate Letter. Accessed 18 Nov 2022. https://pm.gc.ca/en/mandate-letters/2015/11/12/archived-minister-foreign-affairs-mandate-letter.

Mitchell, Christopher. 2001. From Controlled Communication to Problem Solving: The Origins of Facilitated Conflict Resolution. *The International Journal of Peace Studies* 6 (1): 62–74.

Nan, Susan Allen, Daniel, and Jana El DruckmanHor. 2009. Unofficial International Conflict Resolution: Is There a Track One and a Half? Are There Best Practices? *Conflict Resolution Quarterly* 27 (1): 65–82.

Norwegian Foreign Ministry. 2020. Women, Peace and Security. Accessed 9 Dec 2020. https://www.regjeringen.no/en/topics/foreign-affairs/the-un/wps/id660488/.

Paffenholtz, Thania, William, and Zartman. 2019. Inclusive Peace Negotiations—From a Neglected Topic to New Hype. *International Negotiation* 24 (1): 1–6.

Palmiano Federer, J. Forthcoming. NGOs Mediatiing Peace: Promoting Inclusion in Myanmar's Ceasefire Negotiations. London: Palgrave Macmillian.

Palmiano Federer, J. 2021. Cowboys or Mavericks? The Normative Agency of NGO Mediators. In *Rethinking Peace Mediation: Challenges of Contemporary Peacemaking Practice*, ed. Catherine Turner and Martin Wählisch, 71–92. Bristol: Bristol University Press.

Papagianni, Katia, and Sarah Federman. 2022. Enabling Inclusive Peace Mediation and Negotiation: Structures and Tactics. In *Untapped Power: Leveraging Diversity and Inclusion for Conflict and Development*, ed. Carla Koppell, 265–287. Oxford: Oxford University Press.

Peace and Stabilization Operations Programme (PSOPS). Accessed 18 Nov 2022. https://www.international.gc.ca/world-monde/issues_development-enjeux_developpement/response_conflict-reponse_conflits/psop.aspx?lang=eng#a2.

PSOPs Website, Project CA-3-P008777001. Accessed 21 Nov 2022. https://w05.international.gc.ca/projectbrowser-banqueprojets/project-projet/details/P008777001.

PSOPs Website, Project CA-3-P007276001. Accessed 21 Nov 2022. https://w05.international.gc.ca/projectbrowser-banqueprojets/vendor-vendeur/index/30486?iatiid=CA-3-P007276001.

Robertson, Dylan. 2023. Foreign Minister Mélanie Joly Says Cameroon Peace Talks 'messy' but Should Continue. *CBC News*, January 24. https://www.cbc.ca/news/politics/joly-cameroon-peace-talks-1.6724847.

Shams, Shamil, and Masood Shaifullah. 2022. Afghanistan: How the Taliban Stand to Benefit from Norway Talks. *Die Welt*, January 25. Accessed 21 Nov 2022. https://www.dw.com/en/afghanistan-how-the-taliban-stand-to-benefit-from-norway-talks/a-60548374.

Switzerland, Federal Department of Foreign Affairs. Women, Peace and Security. Website Accessed 9 Dec 2022. https://www.eda.admin.ch/eda/en/fdfa/foreign-policy/human-rights/peace/women-armed-conflicts.html.

United Nations. 2012. *UN Guidance on Effective Mediation*. New York: United Nations.

Vuković, Siniša. 2021. Norm Diffusion in International Peace Mediation. In *Rethinking Peace Mediation: Challenges of Contemporary Peacemaking Practice*, ed. C. Turner and M. Wählisch, 37–52. Bristol: Bristol University Press.

York, Geoffrey. 2023. Cameroon Denies Canadian Government Announcement of Peace Talks. *Globe and Mail*, 23 January. https://www.theglobeandmail.com/world/article-cameroon-denies-canadian-government-announcement-of-peace-talks/.

York, Geoffrey, and Paul Njie. 2023. After Secret Talks, Canada Becomes Mediator in Cameroon Peace Process. *Globe and Mail*, 22 January. https://www.theglobeandmail.com/world/article-after-secret-talks-canada-becomes-mediator-in-cameroon-peace-process/.

Zahar, Marie-Joëlle. 2012. Norm Transmission in Peace and Statebuilding: Lessons from Democracy Promotion in Sudan and Lebanon. *Global Governance* 18 (1): 73–88.

CHAPTER 11

Canada's Enduring Populism

David Moscrop

Populism is not a new phenomenon in Canada. Each generation produces its own populist politicians, parties, and movements. From the agrarian populists of the early-to-mid twentieth century to the neoliberal or market populists of its latter half and into the twenty-first century, populism endures in Canada. These populist iterations appear nationally, provincially, locally, sometimes crossing jurisdictional boundaries and orders of government. They also exist beyond Canada's borders. Indeed, populists have been popping up around the globe in recent years, on the left and the right, in power and in opposition, extremist and non-extremist. They include Donald Trump in the United States, proponents of Brexit in the United Kingdom, Jair Bolsonaro in Brazil, Giorgia Meloni in Italy, Viktor Orban in Hungary, Syriza in Greece, the Finns Party in Finland, Podemos in Spain, and plenty of others.

At home, populist manifestations tend to be muted at times but, in other years, they are much louder—more vocal, more stringent, and, perhaps, more successful. In recent years, national and provincial populist

D. Moscrop (✉)
University of British Columbia, Vancouver, BC, Canada
e-mail: davidmoscrop@cunet.carleton.ca

© The Author(s), under exclusive license to Springer Nature
Switzerland AG 2023
M. A. Cameron et al. (eds.), *Democracy and Foreign Policy in an Era of Uncertainty*, Canada and International Affairs,
https://doi.org/10.1007/978-3-031-35490-8_11

politics have returned, shaping politics federally and in a handful of provinces. Whether particular outbreaks of populism endure and what sort of outcomes they produce depend upon internal and external factors, from the success or failure of politicians and parties to the state of domestic and global economies, to broader social, political, and economic discourses. Today, they also depend upon the future of the COVID-19 pandemic and the effects of climate change.

Observers ought to be concerned about the rise of particular manifestations of populism, especially nativist and authoritarian versions, which exist in Canada. However, we ought to undertake a contemporary reading of populist politics in historical and present context. That way, we can understand the challenges, opportunities, and imperatives that accompany populist politics, which are typically an expression of popular anger, frustrations, anxieties, and prejudices, some of which are legitimate and some of which are not. Before that undertaking, however, we must understand what we mean when we use the term "populism."

DEFINING POPULISM(S)

Populism is a notoriously difficult phenomenon to define. And yet, a shared definition of the term is necessary, at least for our purposes, given that it will produce borders around the concept. Those borders will determine who and what falls within them, who and what does not, and the criteria for determining which is which. Vague or inconsistent definitions render analysis difficult if not impossible. But there are sufficient approaches to defining populism to make sense of it in different contexts and cases, including our own.

The Oxford Handbook of Populism (Mudde 2017) identifies three approaches: the ideational approach (Mudde), the political-strategic approach (Weyland), and the socio-cultural approach (Ostiguy). This chapter uses the ideational approach, which I explore in greater depth below. The political-strategic approach focuses on "the principal ways and means by which a political act captures the government and makes and enforces authoritative decisions" (Weyland 2017: 55), and treats populism as a strategy device used by political actors, particularly a "personalistic leader," for winning and keeping power (Weyland 2017: 59). The socio-cultural approach employs "a conception of populism that is fundamentally relational, emphasizing a socio-cultural dimension..." (Ostiguy 2017: 73). This approach emphasizes the "flaunting of the low," (Ostiguy

2017: 73) which cuts across ideologies to forge cultural connections at the political and social levels through to "coarse" appeals, nativism, and personalist affinities (Ostiguy 2017: 78–83).

Whilst there is not likely to ever be a universally accepted definition of this essentially contested concept (Panizza 2005), Mudde and Kaltwasser's ideational approach is commonly used. They define populism as "a thin-centred ideology that considers society to be ultimately separated into two homogenous and antagonist camps, 'the pure people' versus 'the corrupt elite,' and which argues that politics should be an expression of the *volonté générale* (general will) of the people" (Mudde and Kaltwasser 2017: 6). To call populism a "thin centred" ideology is to say that it can only exist when attached to or accompanied by "thick" ideologies with comprehensive worldviews and normative programs (Mudde and Kaltwasser 2017). Populism is thus not a standalone program, but a construction of politics based on a distinction of the world into two broad camps that requires a host ideology to give it a thicker, coherent form (Mudde and Kaltwasser 2017: 104). Accordingly, there can be left populisms and right populisms, both of which, for instance, Canada has seen.

The construction of a single, virtuous "people" is essential to populism and varieties of definitions rely on that construction. Like Mudde and Kaltwasser, Canovan (1981: 294) argues wherever it appears, populism, despite not having a stable core, will "without exception involve some kind of exaltation and appeal to 'the people'." Ionescu and Gellner (1969: 4) take it step further, arguing populism "worships the people." Hawkins and Kaltwasser (2018: 3) see populism as casting political conflict "as a Manichean struggle between a reified will of the people and a conspiring elite."

The notion of "the people," however, is a construction with its own borders. For instance, nativist populism will exclude those who do not belong to a pre-determined definition of a local, subnational, national, religious, or ethnic community. Nativist populist thus typically excludes immigrants and those it defines as "the other." The division between insider and outside can manifest in other ways, too. As Brubaker (2017: 363) notes, populism breaks down into "vertical and horizontal oppositions," with "the people" in the vertical dimension "defined in opposition to economic, political, and cultural elites." The people "are represented as morally decent (though not necessarily pure), economically struggling, hard-working, family-oriented, plain-spoken, and endowed with common sense" and stand in contrast to the those at the bottom of the vertical dimension who "may be represented as parasites or spongers, as addicts or deviants, as disorderly or dangerous, as undeserving of benefits and unworthy of respect...".

As mentioned, in this chapter I use the ideational approach to defining populism. I do so because the definition offers the flexibility to assess populist movements and figures in the context of their own time and ideology—or aspects of their ideologies in the case of more complex iterations—whilst identifying discursive, strategic, or relational approaches as elements of their particular brand of populism. Moreover, the definition functions as "a minimal definition" of populism that encompasses the content of the thin ideology. Spruyt et al. (2016: 336) find scholars converging on four central ideas within that minimal definition which produces the logic of populism. Those ideas include "(1) the existence of two homogeneous groups, that is, 'the people' and 'the established elite'; (2) between which an antagonistic relationship exists; (3) whereby 'the people' are portrayed as virtuous, and the elite are denigrated; and (4) the will of the people is considered the ultimate source of legitimacy (popular sovereignty)" (see also Pruysers 2021, 108). Because populism is mixed and matched with other types of politics and because it is a moving target in many cases, which may fail to subsume the entirety of a person, party, or movement's politics, the ideational approach provides the flexibility required to sort populist from non-populist aspects within a given context.

Populism in Canada: Then

The twentieth century saw the rise of several populist movements throughout Canada at the municipal, provincial, and federal levels. Populism existed in Canada pre-confederation, too; its source was disaffected farmers distrustful of the banking system—a recurring populist theme in the country. As Calombiris and Haber (2014: 301–302) write in reference to special charters for branching banks in Canada, "A serious challenge was mounted in 1850, when an agrarian populist movement that favoured unit banking pushed for legislation to create a free-banking system modelled on that of New York State." From the get-go, farmers in Canada tended to be wary of centralization, particularly of the banking system.

The most prominent and lasting populist movements of the twentieth century tended to come from Western Canada. On the right, in the early-to-mid-century, Western populism took the form of the Social Credit movement (Macpherson 1953) and its attendant and eponymous political parties. These parties were particularly successful in governing British Columbia and Alberta for long stretches between the 1930s and 1960s. Populism on the left was also common, predominantly in its prairie form, driven by farmers and particularly pronounced in Saskatchewan (Lipset 1967).

Western populism, then as now, tends to take on the grievance-centred form of "the West wants in" as a response to perceptions that elites in Ontario and Quebec—especially the banks and financial class on Bay Street who control access to credit (Calombiris and Haber 2014; Laycock 2012: 47)—are exploiting prairie and western provinces. The perception, in this case, is that central Canada elites insist they know what is best for the periphery from their perch in the distant core, or, perhaps, do not care as long as they can serve the needs of the country's more populous cities and regions. In the past, those concerns drove calls for participatory democracy in which "the people" could determine for themselves how to live together, a sentiment that would return to the region and the national stage in force through the Reform Party (1987–2000).

As Blake et al. (1991) put it, "In the prairie west, populism had its roots in an agrarian society which, faced with what it took to be economic exploitation of the farming community by the institutions and elites of central Canada, called for greater direct democracy and the decentralization of power to ordinary people as the means to achieve more equitable policies" (see also Laycock 1990). As noted, the left iteration of populism took the form of various iterations of prairie (and Ontario) farmer movements. Those included the United Farmers of Ontario and the United Farmers of Alberta, as well the Commonwealth Co-operative Federation (CCF), which would become the New Democratic Party (NDP) in 1961 when the party merged with the Canadian Labour Congress. Of note, as Finkel (1989: 208) finds, a handful of scholars have concluded that CCF and Social Credit iterations of populism—left and right, respectively—are "similar" but not "indistinguishable," though the debate over that point is robust and trying to settle it is beyond the parameters of this chapter.

In Québec, populism was manifest in the province's own social credit movement and federal and provincial parties. The social credit movement in Québec was driven predominantly by rural Québecois and those outside the City of Montreal (Gagnon 1976). It emerged in the aftermath of the long-reign of the province's Union Nationale, which governed Québec under the premiership of Maurice Duplessis from 1936 to 1939 and 1944 until his death 1959, after which it was soon replaced by the Liberal government of Jean Lesage. Duplessis's government included populist elements, but Boily (2002) refers to it as an "incomplete" form that was mostly adopted for strategic purposes.

In the late 1980s and early 1990s, the Reform Party of Canada emerged in response to Western grievances such as official bilingualism and efforts to amend the constitution and recognize Québec as a distinct society (Sawer and Laycock 2009: 136–137). Indeed, as Sawer and Laycock note (2009: 138), the party's electoral fortunes took to turn for the better in 1993 when it "opposed the 'elite-driven' Charlottetown Accord on constitutional reform, which had been supported by leaders of the three established parties." Reform's populist politics were shaped by the Alberta Social Credit Party and "picked up on the regionalist and anti-statist ideological threads laid out by Social Credit, reigniting regional opposition against federal politicians and bureaucrats" (Budd 2021: 160). As Budd summarizes, the core elements of the Reform agenda included neoliberal market reforms (a commitment that would live on post-Reform and continues today on the right), reducing the social welfare state, curbing if not eliminating the power of "special interests" and replacing that with negative liberty and formal equality, resisting multiculturalism and limiting immigration (though these commitments were strategically tempered as time went on, see Budd 2021: 164) and adopting participatory democratic practices (See also Laycock 1994).

In 2000, the Canadian Alliance replaced the Reform Party ahead of a 2003 merger with the Progressive Conservative Party and the creation of the Conservative Party of Canada. In the years following the merger, federal conservative populism changed but never disappeared. It continued in a subtler manifestation during the government of Conservative Prime Minister Stephen Harper, who was a protegé of the Reform Party's founding leader Preston Manning. After Harper's 2015 election loss to Justin Trudeau and the Liberal Party of Canada, the process of a revival of right-populism, or populisms, began.

POPULISM IN CANADA: NOW

Despite back-to-back federal elections in which the Conservative Party won the highest share of the popular vote, the Liberal Party led by Prime Minister Justin Trudeau held on to government. In October 2019, Conservative leader Andrew Scheer secured over 200,000 more votes than Justin Trudeau's Liberals but lost the election. He was soon under pressure to resign and did so in December 2019. In 2021, the same scenario played out once more, this time with Conservative leader Erin O'Toole, who once again won over 200,000 more votes than the Liberals. His caucus used the Reform Act provisions which it had adopted to internally review O'Toole's leadership. He lost the review with 61 percent of voting members of caucus expressing no confidence.

In the summer of 2022, *the Economist* featured an article billing the leadership ambitions of Conservative Party contender Pierre Poilievre as "a politer kind of populism" (Economist 2022). The magazine cast Poilievre as "Canada's answer to Donald Trump," who "seeks to convert unease into anger." In typical fashion, this was branded "populism with Canadian characteristics," which is to say a populism that eschews the nativism that could undermine a party's electoral ambitions in a culturally and ethnically diverse polity. During the Reform era, conservatives quickly learned that the path to government passed through Canada's many different communities, which is why the Reform Party moderated its positions on multicultural accommodation and immigration (Budd 2021: 164).

In the context of an enduring pandemic, an inflation and affordability crisis, and global instability, Poilievre won the leadership of his party by railing against the Liberal government and claiming it could not solve the problems of the day—indeed, suggesting, they had caused them or at least made them worse. Poilievre won on the first ballot with an extraordinary 68.15 percent. He embraces a libertarian politics reminiscent of the Thatcher-Reagan era, backed by a particular brand of contemporary populism. He is a neoliberal or market populist. His variety of neoliberal populism is typified by a commitment to framing the world through populist discursive categories of "the people" and the "elite," and appending it to a thicker ideological commitment to economic liberalism and individualism (See: Betz 1994; Budd 2021: 156) and arguing for a smaller state characterized by lower taxes and minimal public spending.

Market populism has a history in Canada that dates back to the 1980s. Sawer and Laycock (2009: 133–134) define market populism as "a flexible, originally American variant of populist ideology…" that has been adopted in Canada via the United States. Citing Canovan (2002), Sawer, and Laycock note this flexible variant shares a core similar to other forms of populism insofar as it "presents society as divided between elites and 'ordinary people' and seeks to mobilise the latter against the former." However, market populism differs from other forms of populism by shifting its focus "from business elites to the so-called elites and special interests responsible for maintaining a large welfare state at taxpayers' expense" (Sawer and Laycock 2009: 134).

At the provincial and municipal level, market populism has found champions in recent years in the form of the Ford brothers, Rob and Doug, and "Ford Nation." As mayor of Toronto, the late Rob Ford was a "back-to-basics fiscal conservative" who eschewed "common contemporary right-populist tropes: nativist and anti-immigration sentiment, Christian nationalism, and the moral superiority of the rural 'heartland'." (Silver et al. 2019: 5). Instead, Ford built a broad, multi-ethnic coalition in the market populist tradition, focusing on "a message of 'respect for taxpayers' and criticism of a 'downtown elite' portrayed as out of touch with and insulated from the concerns of suburban communities" (Silver et al. 2019: 5),—not to mention his promise to stop the City Hall "gravy train" (which, it turns out, was not running).

Doug Ford became premier of Ontario in 2018, displacing the provincial Liberal Party, which had governed since 2003. Ford replaced Progressive Conservative leader Patrick Brown who resigned on the eve of the election. Like his brother, Rob, Doug adopted a neoliberal populist program, which he styled "For the People" and which focused on standing up for taxpayers and the middle class against government elites and special interests (Budd 2020: 176–177). This approach is reminiscent of the Mike Harris government in Ontario, which governed during the mid-to-late 1990s. Harris undertook a populist "Common Sense Revolution" marked by deregulation and austerity and which was itself influenced by Preston Manning and the Reform Party (Budd 2020: 174).

Returning to the federal stage, by railing against the Bank of Canada, Elections Canada, the World Economic Forum, and various state "gatekeepers," and arguing for a smaller, leaner state that unburdens taxpayers, Poilievre performs the style that typifies neoliberal or market populism. During his campaign for the leadership of the party, he defined these gatekeepers as "the consulting class, politicians, bureaucrats, or agencies" who "create roadblocks for progress and charge a hefty fee for anyone who would want to build anything" (Bailey 2022a, b). He constructs a manichean world of the people versus elites, even if he declines to embrace participatory democracy as a discursive strategy—an old approach for populist politicians (Canovan 1981; Sawer and Laycock 2009).

Thin, anti-elite populist posturing is not a new approach for the Conservative Party. Whilst former Conservative leader and prime minister Stephen Harper did not adopt the plebiscitarian populism of the Reform Party and his mentor Preston Manning, he did adopt its anti-elitist negative populist form as a way of separating the "virtuous" people from the "insiders" (Budd 2021; Farney 2012), just as the new leader does. Poilievre and Harper share more than one affinity. Market populist attacks on the welfare state are rooted in Hayekian economics (Sawer and Laycock 2009: 140), to which Poilievre subscribes, as does Harper. During the leadership race, Harper went so far as to endorse Poilievre, which was atypical; Canadian Broadcasting Corporation journalist Aaron Wherry framed the move as the former prime minister passing a torch in the former's preferred style of "populist conservatism" (Wherry 2022).

The Conservative Party of Canada is not the only recent federal electoral manifestation of populism. In 2018, former CPC Cabinet minister Maxine Bernier left the party to join the People's Party of Canada (PPC). The party holds no seats in the House of Commons and its two electoral contests saw it win 1.62 percent and 4.94 percent of the popular vote in 2019 and 2021 respectively. In the latter case, that translates to over 840,000 votes—over a quarter of the roughly 3 million votes received by the New Democratic Party.

Budd (2021: 168) argues the PPC "represents a rate case of radical right-wing populist in Canadian federal politics." Historically, Canadian populists who take part in electoral politics have been hesitant to embrace authoritarian and nativist ideological iterations of populism, particularly, as noted earlier, because the country's single member plurality electoral system discourages it. And yet Bernier and the PPC advocates restricting immigration and opposing "radical multiculturalism" (Cheung 2019) alongside typical neoliberal populist priorities of smaller government and fewer regulations for industry and, of course, de rigueur anti-elitist discourse.

The CPC's populist dabbling and occasional foray into boundary-pushing authoritarian populism may be feeding Bernier and the PPC.

As Budd (2021: 169) argues in the context of Harper's 2015 electoral gambit in which he supported the idea of a "barbaric cultural practices" tip line and pursued anti-hijab politics, "Bernier and the PPC sought to capitalize on the ideological niche created by the Harper government's mainstreaming of anti-multicultural and anti-immigrant discourse," particularly in its e-mail communications with supporters (Budd and Small 2022).

Drawing on Stewart Hall's conception of the term, Carlaw (2017: 785) summarizes authoritarian populism as one that "aims to achieve an electoral and social hegemony by mobilizing a law and order narrative involving the manipulation and generation of 'moral panic' and fears of social anarchy." It is a variety of ordered populism. The authoritarian approach is discursive, a style in service of an "ultimate aim," which is "the normalization of the politics and practices of neo-liberalism and neo-conservatism" (Carlaw 2017: 785; Hall 1985: 116). Given that assessment, we can see a trend in Canadian populist expression on the right to mix authoritarian and neoliberal styles of populism. It is of note, as Carlaw points out, that after Harper had been replaced as CPC leader by Andrew Scheer in 2017, the latter maintained a similar populist authoritarian posture, particularly in his opposition to a House of Commons motion to study "Systemic racism and religious discrimination," particularly Islamophobia, (M-103) and his narrow approach to refugee policy (Carlaw 2017: 807–808) and immigration (Wherry 2019).

In the January and February of 2021, a "Freedom Convoy" occupied Ottawa as part of a movement that also led to supporters setting up blockades the Canada–United States border at Coutts, Alberta and along the Ambassador Bridge between Ontario and Michigan. The occupation of Ottawa and blockades were evidence of a toxic populist backlash in Canada, pitting, once more "the people"—as defined by convoy organizers, participants, and supports against "the elite." Ostensibly about "freedom" from mandates related to the COVID-19 vaccination and mitigation efforts but was replete with reactionary white grievance politics (Moscrop 2022) and conspiracy-laden right-wing ideological extremism that goes back years to the Yellow Vest movement and M103 protests (Balgord 2022). Indeed, the convoy and blockades have led to calls to pay greater attention ideologically motivated extremism (Thompson 2022). That the occupation and blockades were not about mandates is evidenced by the fact that mandates were ending as the convoy participants mobilized the movement continued in the same way months after mandates had been lifted, shifting their grievance frame to generalized concerns about "freedom" and opposition to the federal Liberal government. The movement endures still, long after mandates have been abandoned and did not return.

Bernier and the PPC supported the 2022 Freedom Convoy. Poilievre and several Conservative members of Parliament, including then-interim leader Candace Bergen, did, too—though Poilievre qualified his support, limiting it to "peaceful and law-abiding protesters" (Lévesque 2022). In keeping with the core discursive norms of populism, each supported the convoy participants by casting them as an oppressed people up against governments overstepping their boundaries and infringing on civic rights and freedoms.

As neoliberal populism persists in Canada, accompanied by a spike in nativist, authoritarian populism, one might imagine it has subsumed or replaced older forms of Western grievance populism rooted in provincial opposition to a far-flung, out of touch central government. Anyone doubting the persistence of traditional Western populism need not look any further than the fall 2022 return of Danielle Smith to provincial politics in Alberta. In May, 2022 former Harper Cabinet minister and federal MP Jason Kenney announced he would resign as premier after a receiving 51.4 percent support in a leadership review brought about by disaffected members of his caucus. Kenney was no stranger to attacking Ottawa and dabbling in populist politics, but Smith, who replaced him on the sixth ballot of the United Conservative Party leadership contest, quickly took the fight to a new level.

Smith combines a Western, anti-centralist grievance populism with appeals the pandemic populism embodied by the Freedom Convoy. During her first press conference after becoming premier, Smith said unvaccinated individuals were "the most discriminated against group that I've ever witnessed in my lifetime." Wesley (2022) points out Smith's approach is a classic play from the populist playbook in which leaders attempt to "Convince a dominant group they are being marginalized" and that they are "in the 'silent majority'" whilst also trying to "convince the broader public that the group is both a victim and too dominant to challenge."

In late November 2022, Smith unveiled Bill 1 in the legislature, the "Alberta Sovereignty Within a United Canada Act." Smith had campaigned for the leadership on the back of the sovereignty bill, which was derided at the time by her opponents and Premier Kenney. The bill, which was widely panned upon release by critics as a massive and unconstitutional executive overreach, would give Cabinet powers to bypass the legislature as it sought to identify and upend or ignore federal laws it deems harmful to the province or its interest. The bill was eventually passed with amendments clarifying and limiting executive capacity to circumvent the legislature. It also sets up a fight with Ottawa, with Smith acting in the capacity as leader of the aggrieved, regionally alienated "ordinary people" against "elite" Ottawa. La plus ça change.

Populist Hearts and Minds

Populism can be characterized as a top–down or bottom–up phenomenon—or as a function of the interplay between each. This chapter has focused on populism as practiced by political elites, particularly party leaders, but what about the public?

In the midst of the rise of Donald Trump's nativist, authoritarian populism in the United States and similar populist backlashes in Europe, particularly the United Kingdom and the Brexit movement, Adams (2017: 15) asked of Canada "Could it happen here?" What would become of Canada as American and European populists influenced the country? Adams argues that whilst anything is possible, Canadian political culture, values, attitudes, and institutions make that less likely than it may be elsewhere. "*Of course*, it can happen here!" he writes. However, "countries that have managed…to foster social resilience, reduce inequality and provide collective tax-supported government insurance against ill health or unemployment are more likely to be able to withstand the clarion calls from the Trumps of this world." And Canada is one of those countries. Adams seems a moderating force in Canada tilting away from populism, both historically and today. He concludes "We've had our flings with polarizing populists, but when the buzz wears off, we always seem to muddle our way back to the middle."

Is that still true? Nanos (2018: 142) warns "democracy is very much about who shows up." He notes small swings in electoral turnout in particular directions can have outsized impacts on outcomes. He finds that a change in as few as 1 in 20 votes can change electoral outcomes. Like Adams, he finds that populist impulses and the economic (and non-economic) factors that drive them can cross borders, leading to copycat politicians (146). Moreover, he finds this populist moment to be different, noting it is "high velocity, tinged by anger, driven by minority opinion and propped by computational propaganda in the semblance of social media and human interaction" (174)—and particularly successful amongst those disenfranchised from the economy and those with lower levels of education (144–145).

In the years since Nanos wrote those sentences, things in Canada have not improved significantly on the fronts he mentions; indeed, right now, things seem much worse than before as the country stares down economic instability, rising prices, an ongoing pandemic, worsening effects of climate change, and global conflict. Coupled with rising declinism—the perception that things are getting worse generation over generation—those factors produce a terrain on which populists can march freely, particularly if politicians are prepared to lead the march.

Before the pandemic, in the context of the 2019 federal election, Nanos (2019) found "…Canada should not be considered an exception to populist-style politics," particularly since "perceptions of declinism exist in the populace." If populism thrives on disaffection, Canada had reason to be concern. As Nanos concluded, "The 2019 Canadian General Election was similar to elections in other major Western democracies which had outcomes of a weakening political consensus." In 2019, Bernier and Scheer were prepared to lead the populist march at the federal level. The 2021 election seemed to mirror those findings, even if Scheer's replacement, Erin O'Toole, was less inclined to indulge the populist impulses of his predecessors and the Liberal Party was able to once again hang on to a minority government, in no small part thanks to its efficient vote distribution in key regions of the country. Next time around, with Poilievre at the helm, the federal election might play out differently.

Indeed, as Graves finds, the pandemic may be driving a further populist turn. He writes, "Issues of Canada's place in the world have been dramatically reshaped and it appears that the pandemic may produce accelerated social change that would not have been possible without this great disruption. The future is highly uncertain, but most think we are on the cusp of a great transformation" (Graves 2021: 166). He worries in particular about the rise of ordered populism, an authoritarian variety that "emphasizes obedience, order and hostility to outgoups," which is "triggered under certain conditions," and "…produces a search for a strongman and a desire to turn back the clock and pull up the drawbridge" (Graves 2021: 167).

The core issues on which this variety of populism turn include "trade, borders, globalization, and immigration," (Graves 2021: 166). These issues remain live in Canadian politics. So, too, do the key conditions for the rise of ordered populism, which are acute during times of polarization, and include

> (1) declining middle class, wage stagnation, and hyper-concentration of wealth at the very top of the system; (2) major value shifts which see more progressive values displacing traditional social conservative values which, in concert with (1), produce a cultural backlash by those seeing loss of identity and privilege; (3) a growing sense of external threat expressed in both a sharp long-term rise in the belief that the world has become overwhelmingly more dangerous and rising normative threat which sees the country and its public institutions moving in the wrong direction; and (4) declining trust and ideological polarization. (Graves 2021: 167)

The Freedom Convoy reflects much of these conditions. Moreover, popular and political elite support for them indicate a growing populist backlash driven by toxic reactionary grievance politics both in Canada and globally that politicians feel that may be able to capitalize on. Graves finds that Canadians are not generally embracing ordered populism (Graves 2020, 2021); however, the social, political, and economic grounds remain fertile for populism to thrive, especially if populist politicians can find a way to succeed despite, or even because of, Canada's single member plurality electoral system. Over time, these populist sentiments may become normalized and embedded in the country's politics—and policy—at home and abroad.

Populism and Foreign Policy

As we have seen, populism at home affects policy towards states abroad. As Verbeek and Zaslove (2017) put it, in the contemporary world "the distinction between domestic and foreign has become less clear: domestic events spill over into the international context, whilst international events affect domestic affairs." They cite Hugo Chavez's populism as partly an anti-American phenomenon and Polish and Hungarian populist movements as producing a response from the European Union. And, of course, there's Brexit. Global capital, trade, and communications have helped ensure that domestic affairs, including populist movements, are often global affairs. Indeed, as Friedman Lissner and Rapp-Hooper (2018) argue, global populism has the power to shape and re-shape the global order, particularly the liberal international order.

Populism is centred on the creation of ingroups and outgroups, including domestic and foreign groups, with populists tending to prefer to serve the interests of the former over the latter and often exhibiting a commitment to ethnic or civic nationalism. Populists of the ordered variety may also focus on anti-multicultural politics, as Reform did for years, or some iteration of it. In the years of the Stephen Harper government, tinged as it was by populism, Canada focused its limited foreign aid around conservative, "Judaeo-Christian" values and a focus on "religious freedom," going so far as to launch The Office of Religious Freedom—an agency within Global Affairs Canada concerned with religious freedom around the world. The Harper government reshaped immigration in Canada, shifting refugee policy towards private sponsorship during a time of overlapping migrant crises and leaning into immigration policy as a tool for filling labour shortages through temporary work programs—even whilst raising immigration targets.

The exclusionary boundaries that define the "people" within a state may thus set external boundaries, too—and those decisions can have lasting implications for politics and policy.

As Budd (2021: 170) notes,

> We can understand the recent spike of overtly xenophobic and nativist populism on the Canadian right as an evolution in the types of cultural and nationalistic discourses championed by the Harper Conservatives. The push to re-signify Canadian identity around exclusionary historical narratives and values has set the stage or more extremist actors and parties like Bernier and the PPC to put forward their radical right-wing ideologies.

In that sense, populist pressure to focus on domestic priorities, limit foreign aid, and, when engaging in aid, direct it towards goals consistent with a narrow normative conception of acceptable ways of living shapes foreign policy in distinct and substantive ways.

Populist movements may also have foreign policy implications insofar as they may be comprised of actors who network, communicate, plan, and act across borders (Kandel 2021). The 2022 convoy occupation in Ottawa was shaped by, amongst other considerations, vaccine mandates limiting travel between Canada and the United States—and the movement was a cross-border affair, including its participants and financial resources. As Balgord (2022) noted, the far-right populist movement in Canada has been inspired by France's Yellow Vest movement—which was also present in several other countries, including the United Kingdom, Belgium, and Germany—and one can trace a line from those 2019 protests to the current convoy movement.

As noted, populism has effects across borders—and in more than one direction. Canada, for instance, was affected by the United States president Donald Trump's "America First" populist foreign policy. The North American Free Trade Agreement renegotiations took up considerable time and resources and were driven by populist sentiment south of the border. It was framed as "the people" against "elites" and the deal was criticized as requiring a populist corrective (Csehi and Heldt 2021).Whilst President Joe Biden is not a populist in the manner of Trump, soon after taking office he unveiled his own populist "Build Back Better" plan and an industrial strategy premised on "buy American" rules and policy geared towards the return of manufacturing jobs. The same concerns have not shaped Canadian trade policy as of yet. But they could.

Whilst Canada's current Liberal government has largely avoided populist politics that conservative politicians at home have taken up, contemporary pressures and policy from foreign states may cause them to rethink their strategy, particularly as they stare down what may be the waning days of Justin Trudeau's reign. Moreover, should Pierre Poilievre and the Conservative Party form government, the country may return to the foreign policy of the Harper years, reshaping both Canada and, in a small way, the world.

Conclusion: Canada's Unfinished Populist History

Populism in Canada comes in waves, ebbing and flowing over time according to material, discursive, and strategic contexts at home and abroad. Those waves, however, are never far off. Rooted in a fundamental bifurcation of the population into categories, "the people" and "elites," populist ideology is an add-on to thicker ideologies common in Canadian political history, even if its content and manner of presentation varies.

In recent years, left-wing populism in Canada has been muted, even though NDP leader Jagmeet Singh may embrace a populist style (Beauchamp 2021). Meanwhile, right-wing market or neoliberal populism has presented at provincial and federal levels. So too has nativist, authoritarian populism, particularly in recent years with the rise of networked, toxic, grievance-based iterations in the form of the Yellow Vest and Freedom Convoy movements. These movements have found both grassroots and elite political support. So far, however, their electoral effect has been limited, in large part thanks to Canada's single member plurality electoral system and the regional incentives, disincentives, and aggregate structural tendencies it produces (Budd 2021).

As Laycock (2019: 176) writes of populism in the context of "tax revolts" by the Canadian and American right in recent decades, "Riding a populist Trojan horse decorated with representative claims for the people turned out very well for conservative politicians. However, sustaining political momentum for this agenda over the past two decades seems only to have required a populist argument about representational failure." The same might, indeed, be said now as we add the pandemic and global financial woes to the mix alongside war, climate change, reactionary discourses around immigration and social progressive politics, class dealignment, declinism, and significant technological and cultural shifts. Whilst no full-blown populist has won government federally, a handful govern provincially, and discursive populist elements have been a part of federal politics on both the opposition and government sides, shaping rhetoric, elections, and policy outcomes at home and abroad. The domestic terrain is favourable to populists and that may not change any time soon. Moreover, populists from the United States and Europe influence their counterparts in Canada—and vice versa—as the movement has embraced a networked politics online and offline that enhances and strengthens it and has the power to shape the country's social, political, economic, and cultural landscape for many years to come.

When asking of populism in Canada, "Could it happen here?" we can answer that it is happening here and it has been happening here for a long time. Whether it can happen here is therefore a less interesting question than "What does populism produce when it *does* happen here?" The answer, as complex answers often are, may not be wholly satisfactory insofar as it suggests "It depends." Indeed, it depends on which thick ideology elites and mass supporters of populism connect to and how political elites choose to discursively perform their iteration of it. From there, almost anything can happen, even if we expect Canada's institutions to often, though not always, moderate more extreme outcomes. Hoping that history will continue is not a solution to the rise of toxic populism, however. Canada needs a strategy to combat the rise of far-right-driven populist politics that comprises domestic and foreign approaches to assessing and defusing grievances whilst holding extremists to account.

References

Adams, Michael. 2017. *Could It Happen Here? Canada in the Age of Trump and Brexit*. Toronto: Simon and Schuster.

Bailey, Ian. 2022a. Conservatives Say Queen's Death Won't Delay Announcement of New Leader This Weekend. *The Globe and Mail*, September 9. https://www.theglobeandmail.com/politics/article-conservative-leadership-vote-canada.

Balgord, Evan. 2022. Far-Right Populism in Canada: From M103 to the Ottawa Occupation. *Journal of Intelligence, Conflict, and Warfare* 5 (1).

Betz, Hans-Georg. 1994. *Radical Right-Wing Populism in Western Europe*. New York: St. Martin's Press.

Blake, Donald E., R.K. Carty, and Lynda Erickson. 1991. *Grassroots Politicians: Party Activists in British Columbia*. Vancouver: University of British Columbia Press.

Boily, Frederic. 2002. Duplessism or Unachieved Populism. *Politique Et Sociétés* 21 (2): 101–122.

Brubaker, Rogers. 2017. Why Populism? *Theory and Society* 45 (5): 357–385.

Budd, Brian. 2020. The People's Champ: Doug Ford and Neoliberal Right-Wing Populism in the 2018 Ontario Election. *Politics and Governance* 8 (1): 171–181.

Budd, Brian. 2021. Maple Glazed Populism: Political Opportunity Structures and Right-Wing Populist Ideology in Canada. *Journal of Canadian Studies* 55 (1): 152–176.

Budd, Brian, and Tamara A. Small. 2022. 'Many Thanks for Your Support': Email Populism and the People's Party of Canada. In *Electoral Campaigns, Media, and the New World of Digital Politics*, ed. David Taras and Richard Davis, 143–162. Ann Arbor: University of Michigan Press.

Canovan, Margaret. 1981. *Populism*. New York: Harcourt Brace Jovanovich.

Canovan, Margaret. 2002. Making Sense of Populism. In *Democracies and the Populist Challenge*, ed. Yves Mény and Yves Surel, 25–44. Houndmills: Palgrave.

Carlaw, John. 2017. Authoritarian Populism and Canada's Conservative Decade (2006–2015) in Citizenship and Immigration: The Politics and Practices of Kenneyism and Neo-conservative Multiculturalism. *Journal of Canadian Studies* 51 (3): 782–816.

Cheung, Christopher. 2019. Unpacking the People's Party's Fear of 'Radical Multiculturalism'. *The Tyee*, September 23. https://thetyee.ca/Analysis/2019/09/23/Unpacking-People-Party-Fear-Radical-Multiculturalism/

Csehi, Robert, and Eugenia C. Heldt. 2021. Populism as a 'Corrective' to Trade Agreements? 'America First' and the Readjustment of NAFTA. In *International Politics*. https://doi.org/10.1057/s411311-021-00306-3.
Economist. 2022. A Politer Kind of Populism; Canada. *Economist Intelligent Unit*, June 11.
Farney, James H. 2012. *Social Conservatives and Party Politics in Canada and the United States*. Toronto: University of Toronto Press.
Finkel, Alvin. 1989. *The Social Credit Phenomenon in Alberta*. Toronto: University of Toronto Press.
Friedman Lissner, Rebecca, and Mira Rapp-Hooper. 2018. The Day After Trump: American Strategy for a New International Order. *The Washington Quarterly* 41 (1): 7–25.
Gagnon, Gabriel. 1976. Populisme et Progrès: Les Créditises Québécois. *Recherches Sociographiques* 17 (1): 24–34.
Hall, Stuart. 1985. Authoritarian Populism: A Reply. *New Left Review* 251: 115125.
Hawkins, Kirk A., and Cristóbal Rovira Kaltwasser. 2018. The Ideational Approach. In *The Ideational Approach to Populism: Concept, Theory, and Analysis*, ed. Kirk A. Hawkins, Ryan E. Carlin, Levente Littvay, and Cristóbal Rovira Kaltwasser, 1–24. New York: Routledge.
Ionescu, Ghita, and Ernest Gellner. 1969. *Populism: Its Meaning and National Characteristics*. London: Macmillan.
Kandel, Maya. 2021. The Populist Challenge to Foreign Policy. In *The Faces of Contemporary Populism in Western Europe and the US*, ed. Karine Tournier-Sol and Marie Gaye, 239–257. Cham, Switzerland: Palgrave Macmillan.
Laycock, David. 1990. *Populism and Democratic Through in the Canadian Praries, 1910–1945*. Toronto: University of Toronto Press.
Laycock, David. 1994. Reforming Canadian Democracy? Institutions and Ideology in the Reform Party Project. *Canadian Journal of Political Science* 27 (2): 213–247.
Laycock, David. 2012. "Populism and Democracy in Canada's Reform Party." In *Populism in Europe and the Americas: Threat or Corrective for Democracy?*, ed. Cas Mudde and Cristóbal Rovira Kaltwasser, 46–67. Cambridge: Cambridge University Press.
Laycock, David. 2019. Tax Revolts, Direct Democracy and Representation: Populist Politics in the US and Canada. *Journal of Political Ideologies* 24 (2): 158–181.
Lévesque, Catherine. 2022. Poilievre Says Inquiry Has Not Changed His Support for 'Peaceful and Law-Abiding' Freedom Convoy Protesters. *The National Post*, November 9. https://nationalpost.com/news/poilievre-fre edom-convoy-protesters.

Lipset, Seymour Martin. 1967. *Agrarian Socialism: The Cooperative Commonwealth Federation in Saskatchewan*. Berkeley: University of California Press.

Macpherson, C.B. 1953. *Democracy in Alberta: Social Credit and the Party System*. Toronto: University of Toronto Press.

Moscrop, David. 2022. Canada Must Confront the Toxic 'Freedom Convoy' Head-On. *The Washington Post*, January 28. https://www.washingtonpost.com/opinions/2022/01/28/canada-must-confront-toxic-protest-freedom-convoy/.

Mudde, Cas. 2017. Populism: An Ideational Approach. In *The Oxford Handbook of Populism*, ed. Cristóbal Rovira Kaltwasser, Paul Taggart, Paulina Ochoa Espejo, and Pierre Ostiguy, 27–47. Oxford: Oxford University Press.

Mudde, Cas, and Cristóbal Rovira. Kaltwasser. 2017. *Populism: A Very Short Introduction*. Oxford: Oxford University Press.

Ostiguy, Pierre. 2017. Populism: A Socio-Cultural Approach. In *The Oxford Handbook of Populism*, ed. Cristóbal Rovira Kaltwasser, Paul Taggart, Paulina Ochoa Espejo, and Pierre Ostiguy, 73–97. Oxford: Oxford University Press.

Panizza, Francisco. 2005. *Populism and the Mirror of Democracy*. New York: Verso.

Pruysers, Scott. 2021. A Psychological Predisposition Towards Populism? Evidence from Canada. *Contemporary Politics* 27 (1): 105–124.

Sawer, Marian, and David Laycock. 2009. Down with Elites and Up with Inequality: Market Populism in Australia and Canada. *Commonwealth & Comparative Politics* 47 (2): 133–150.

Spruyt, Bram, Gil Keppens, and Filip Van Droogenbroeck. 2006. Who Supports Populism and What Attracts People to It? *Political Research Quarterly* 69 (2): 335–346.

Thompson, Elizabeth. 2022. Federal Government Already Preparing for What Organizers Call 'Freedom Convoy 2.0. *Canadian Broadcasting Corporation*, December 1. https://www.cbc.ca/news/politics/freedom-convoy-protest-2023-1.6671784.

Verbeek, Bertjan, and Andrej Zaslove. 2017. In *The Oxford Handbook of Populism*, ed. Cristóbal Rovira Kaltwasser, Paul Taggart, Paulina Ochoa Espejo, and Pierre Ostiguy, 27–47. Oxford: Oxford University Press.

Wesley, Jared. 2022. Danielle Smith's Populist Playbook: Make the Dominant Feel Marginalized. *Canadian Broadcasting Corporation*, October 16. https://www.cbc.ca/news/canada/calgary/opinion-danielle-smith-populism-playbook-1.6617059.

Weyland, Kurt. 2017. Populism and Foreign Policy. In *The Oxford Handbook of Populism*, ed. Cristóbal Rovira Kaltwasser, Paul Taggart, Paulina Ochoa Espejo, and Pierre Ostiguy, 384–401. Oxford: Oxford University Press.

Wherry, Aaron. 2022. Harper Passes the Populist-Conservative Torch to Poilievre." *Canadian Broadcasting Corporation*, July 28. https://www.cbc.ca/news/politics/harper-poilievre-conservative-leadership-1.6534017.

Wherry, Aaron. 2019. On Immigration, Scheer Is Trying to Place Two Different Audiences at Once. *Canadian Broadcasting Corporation*, May 30. https://www.cbc.ca/news/politics/andrew-scheer-immigration-trudeau-1.5153952.

CHAPTER 12

The Opportunities and Challenges of Courting India

Sanjay Ruparelia

In 2022, the Trudeau government unveiled its long-awaited Indo-Pacific strategy for Canada. It had five broad objectives: to promote peace, resilience and security; to expand trade, investment and diverse supply chains; to forge people-to-people connections between Canada and the region; to build a sustainable future; and to strengthen whole-of-society partnerships. The launch of the new strategy, given the shifting center of gravity in the global political economy to the Pacific, was overdue. Yet the key political motivation driving its timing was clear: to contain the rise of China, described as "an increasingly disruptive global power", whose values and interests "increasingly depart from ours" (Global Affairs Canada 2022: 7).

Canada's Indo-Pacific strategy perceives India to be a "critical partner" in the region given its strategic, economic and demographic weight.

S. Ruparelia (✉)
Toronto Metropolitan University, Toronto, ON, Canada
e-mail: ruparelia@torontomu.ca

© The Author(s), under exclusive license to Springer Nature Switzerland AG 2023
M. A. Cameron et al. (eds.), *Democracy and Foreign Policy in an Era of Uncertainty*, Canada and International Affairs, https://doi.org/10.1007/978-3-031-35490-8_12

241

Several presumptions inform this view: "a shared tradition of democracy and pluralism, a common commitment to a rules-based international system and multilateralism, mutual interest in expanding our commercial relationship and extensive and growing people-to-people connections" (Global Affairs Canada 2022: 9).

India and Canada share important commonalities as well as convergent interests along each of these dimensions. Since establishing a federal democratic republic in 1950, India has represented an alternative model of political modernity in Asia vis-a-vis the communist party-state of the People's Republic of China, which is approaching its 75th anniversary. Indeed, the constitution of the world's largest democracy codifies a deeper separation of powers and series of checks and balances than found in Canada's political regime. Second, successive governments in New Delhi have upheld key aspects of the post-1945 international order, most importantly the United Nations and principles of national sovereignty and territorial integrity. The growing willingness of China to press its claims along the contested Line of Actual Control (LaC) over the last few years, and assert its dominance in Asia more widely, has tested Sino-Indian relations. Since the millennium, the United States has buttressed ties with India along multiple dimensions, from trade and investment to security and defense, actively supporting India's rise to balance China's rising power. Third, the size and trajectory of India's economy, projected to be the third largest in the world by 2030, offers Canada opportunities to expand trade and investment in manufacturing and services in the digital era, to construct new supply chains with greater resilience, and to advance cutting-edge technologies and policy innovations to improve global public health and achieve a net-zero global economy. Finally, Indo-Canadian relations have improved considerably over the last two decades, driven by efforts to expand commercial opportunities, while the size and influence of various diaspora communities grows significantly in many realms.

Yet courting India poses genuine challenges. First, like many democracies around the world, India has witnessed significant backsliding since the Hindu nationalist Bharatiya Janata Party (BJP) captured power in 2014. The routine emphasis on democracy and pluralism that Canada routinely touts to distinguish its closest allies and to criticize traditional autocratic regimes invites charges of selective morality and political hypocrisy. Second, a variety of factors limit opportunities for ramping up trade and investment between India and Canada, from the structure and interests of their respective political economies and self-perceived vulnerabilities and red lines to asymmetric bargaining positions. Third, despite its growing defense and security ties with the United States and other western allies, India continues to prioritize strategic autonomy in international affairs. It relies on arms from Russia and energy from the Persian Gulf, while seeking to bolster trade with Britain, Australia and the EU, as well as Brazil, South Africa and China. India seeks to craft a multipolar post-Western international order, not a return to superpower bipolarity in a new Cold War, and thus will likely continue to hedge and balance its interests in the Indo-Pacific region and beyond. Finally, notwithstanding deepening ties between India and Canada, conflicting interests and divergent views on important matters persist. Indeed, as India grows more powerful and confident, they are likely to grow in multiple realms, from differences over how to advance trade liberalization and mitigate climate change, to how to address diaspora politics and reform power asymmetries in key multilateral institutions.

As a result, Canada's aim to pursue its purported democratic values and strategic interests in the Indo-Pacific in a coherent manner will prove to be a tough balancing act.

DEMOCRACY UNDER DURESS[1]

Post-independent India's soft power rests significantly on its status, against unprecedented odds, as the world's largest democracy. Electoral competition remains vibrant at multiple levels. The 2019 general election, which returned the BJP to power with a larger parliamentary majority than it won in 2014, saw the highest turnout since independence. Over 67 percent of the electorate, comprising almost 880 million citizens, cast their ballots. Women and men comprised roughly equal shares among registered voters. Urban residents, who unlike their western counterparts traditionally vote less, turned out in greater numbers than ever before. Voting among Adivasi communities in Scheduled Tribe constituencies reached almost 75 percent (Verniers 2019).

Despite the national political dominance of the BJP under Prime Minister Narendra Modi, opposition parties have ousted the ruling party and its allies in various state-level elections in India's sprawling federal

---

[1] Parts of this section draw from an earlier report I wrote (Ruparelia 2021b).

parliamentary democracy. The BJP lost several regional bastions between 2016 and 2019 as well as important contests in 2021. Today, it governs sixteen of the 30 states and union territories that have legislative assemblies.[2] The party commands a seat majority in ten of these states, compelling it to share power through multi-party coalitions in the other six, which together represent half of the population of India (Poddar 2023).[3]

In addition, opposition parties have stymied attempts by the ruling party to push controversial legislation in New Delhi at various points, ranging from land acquisition and agricultural marketing to labor laws (Ninan 2022). The former can veto the latter given its minority status in the upper house of parliament. And social protests and mass demonstrations can force the Modi government to reconsider contentious policies. The passage of three bills in the fall of 2021 to deregulate the agricultural sector, without consulting state governments and trade unions, inspired hundreds of thousands of farmers to encircle the main road arteries of the national capital for a year. The most powerful social movement India has witnessed since the 1980s forced the government to retreat (Ruparelia 2021a).

Nevertheless, India has experienced significant democratic backsliding in recent years, thanks to the autocratic majoritarian character of the new ruling dispensation. New legislation, executive action and political discourse have eroded civil liberties, institutional autonomy and minority rights, challenging the secular foundations of its democratic constitution and the complex pluralism of its everyday social fabric.

Since capturing power in 2014, Prime Minister Modi has concentrated executive power to an extent last seen in the 1970s under his Congress predecessor, Indira Gandhi. Few members of the Council of Ministers exercise genuine independence. Modi rarely grants opposition members the opportunity to scrutinize him in parliament. A classic populist, the prime minister generally avoids press conferences, directly communicating with his tens of millions of followers through social media and digital apps, to create a powerful cult of personality and presidential style of rule.

---

[2] The remaining six union territories, ruled directly by New Delhi, do not have legislative assemblies.

[3] Based on 2011 Census figures.

In addition, opposition parties confront an increasingly skewed electoral field. Campaign finance laws in India, ill-designed and poorly enforced, have allowed money to disproportionately shape politics for many years. But the introduction of so-called electoral bonds in 2017, which concealed the identity of donors to the public but not to the government, made campaign finance even more opaque. The BJP accrues a staggering share of such donations. After returning to power in 2020, its declared assets of $655 million exceeded the cumulative total of the next 51 parties, reflecting an increase of roughly 440 percent since 2015 (*The Economist* 2022a). More broadly, supporters of and politicians from the BJP frequently question the legitimacy of opposition parties, depicting partisan rivals as anti-national forces that undermine sound governance and national unity.

Perhaps the most disturbing change over the last decade is the increasing militancy of Hindu nationalist forces. The political dominance of the BJP encourages party hardliners and associated social organizations to pursue their long-standing desire to transform India into a Hindu nation. State governments run by the party have introduced, or amended, cow protection laws with harsher penalties. Legislation against religious conversion and interfaith marriages stipulate onerous conditions that undermine individual liberty and the right to equality (Mehta 2022). Public displays of Hindu religious identity are increasing and expected (Jayal 2019). Indeed, militant activists and vigilante groups have sought to enforce these laws through harassment, intimidation and violence, leading to a rising number of deadly incidents and mob lynchings that principally target Muslims (Varshney 2019). The failure of the police to intervene in time, or their complicity, allows the perpetrators to act with growing impunity in many cases.

The campaign for the 2019 general election displayed an unprecedented level of religious polarization (Varshney 2019). The return to power of the BJP rallied its hardliners to advance a militant agenda. The government annulled Article 370 of the constitution, which conferred special rights to the contested Muslim-majority state of Jammu and Kashmir, transforming its constituent regions into union territories directly ruled by the Centre. The official rationale for the move was to bolster domestic security and economic development. But foreign journalists and diplomats were barred from entering the territory. The presence of 500,000 troops, house arrest of opposition party leaders and sweeping communications lock down in the region, which lasted six months, underscored its autocratic character (Schultz and Yasir 2020). Internet connection remains extremely poor and many journalists cannot travel abroad (Dhawan 2022). In addition, the Modi government passed the Citizenship Amendment Act (CAA), allowing illegal migrants fleeing religious persecution in Afghanistan, Pakistan and Bangladesh to gain citizenship more quickly, but exempted Muslims. Its intent was clear: to legalize the idea that India was a natural homeland for Hindus. The act violated the secular foundation of Indian citizenship.

Members of India's vibrant civil society have condemned these events and broader developments. Historically, freedom of speech, assembly and association have faced restrictions. But the space for criticism and dissent in the public sphere is narrower today. The professional risks—sometimes personal—are greater too. Traditional newspapers, legacy media and intrepid journalists that criticize the new ruling establishment can suffer bureaucratic harassment, political interference and unemployment. Self-censorship and selective reporting are rising; corporate advertising is declining. Similarly, academic freedom and freedom of speech in university campuses and artistic centers face growing constraints (Jayal 2019). In extreme cases, students, writers and activists criticizing official government policy and human rights violations have been charged with attempting to "incite [religious] hatred" and "hurt religious feelings". A tweet by the Swedish climate activist Greta Thunberg, supporting the farmers' protest, compelled the ruling party to warn of a "conspiracy to wage economic, social, cultural and regional war against India", charge an associated Indian activist with sedition, and force Twitter and Facebook to suspend hundreds of accounts in the name of national security (Ellis-Petersen 2021). It later introduced new Internet rules, enabling the state to remove material, hold social media companies' executives liable for violations and create systems to identify the author of "offensive" posts (PRS Legislative Research 2021). Finally, NGOs and independent research institutes that cross the party can find themselves accused of tax violations and lose their licenses to receive funding from abroad, jeopardizing the activities and sometimes even the viability of organizations, ranging from national affiliates of Oxfam, Amnesty and Greenpeace to internationally renowned think tanks such as the Centre for Policy Research. Media organizations are subject to similar measures too. The ruling party invoked emergency laws to block YouTube and Twitter sharing a BBC documentary that revisited the failure of the prime minister to prevent an anti-Muslim pogrom in Gujarat under his watch in 2002, calling it "hostile propaganda and anti-India garbage", with a "colonial mind-set" (*New York Times* 2023). Tax agents subsequently raided two BBC offices. India currently ranks 150 out of 180 in the World Press Freedom Index (Reed 2022).

The Supreme Court of India, constitutionally one of the most powerful in the world, checked executive overreach at the start. In 2015, the Court struck down a new judicial appointments commission designed to favor the executive. A landmark ruling in 2017 declared privacy to be a fundamental constitutional right. But the Modi government countered, reportedly transferring justices perceived to be hostile to the BJP, blocking the elevation of others and allegedly even conspiring to fix the composition of benches in sensitive judicial cases. And the apex judiciary abdicated its constitutional responsibilities on several momentous issues. In Kashmir, the Court delayed hearing cases invoking habeas corpus, denied bail to opposition leaders and failed to investigate mass detentions in the region. In Uttar Pradesh, it noted that Hindu nationalists' destruction of the Babri mosque in Ayodhya in 1992 violated the rule of law, but still ruled that the Hindu plaintiffs could build a temple on the contested site.

The repression of civil liberties and institutional autonomy in India, alongside the growing crackdown on minority rights, significantly lowered its ranking in leading global surveys of democracy. In 2021, Freedom House and the Varieties of Democracy research institute classified the world's largest democracy as "partly free" (Freedom House 2021) and an "electoral autocracy" (V-Dem Institute 2022: 15), respectively. The BJP external affairs minister, S. Jaishankar, dismissed both reports: "It is hypocrisy. Because you have a set of self-appointed custodians of the world who find it very difficult to stomach that somebody in India is not looking for their approval, is not willing to play the game they want to play. So they invent their rules, their parameters, pass their judgments and make it look as if it is some kind of global exercise" (Roy 2021). Similarly, when his counterpart Anthony Blinken remarked that the US was "monitoring some recent concerning developments in India, including a rise in human rights abuses by some government, police and prison officials", Jaishankar retorted: "I would tell you that we also take our views on other people's human rights situation, including that of the United States" (Mashal 2022).

Such exchanges underscore a complex predicament. On the one hand, the conspicuous silence of many western leaders at recent G7 summits regarding developments in India reflects prudence, given their focus on China. But it mocks their professed commitments to "freedom of expression", the "independence of civil society", and other democratic values, institutions and practices (Mashal 2022). On the other hand, western democracies are ill-placed to pass quick moral judgments. Persistent colonial legacies, and their expedient support during the Cold War and since its end for autocratic regimes when it serves perceived interests, inform popular consciousness in many Southern polities. Moreover, many western democracies themselves suffer from serious backsliding, from persistent Republican attempts to doubt the credibility of the 2020 US presidential election and disenfranchise Black voters, to the surge of anti-immigrant right-wing nationalist parties with fascist roots in Germany, France, Italy, Denmark and Sweden. They must be willing to face a critical external gaze to lessen the understandable cynicism of many postcolonial societies.

Trajectories and Challenges of Development

Since 1980, India has achieved rapid economic growth, lessened absolute poverty and improved outcomes in public health and basic education. By 2014, India was the tenth largest economy in the world. Current projections estimate that it will be the third largest by 2030, following China and the US (Pasricha 2022).

Several factors drive these projections. First, India now has the largest population in the world, with a median age of 28 (Rizwan 2022). Compared to China, which risks becoming old before getting rich due to the legacy of its one-child policy, India enjoys a demographic dividend of young workers.

Second, the country possesses a dynamic entrepreneurial culture and leading business conglomerates. Its world-renowned information technology and outsourcing industry, led by Infosys and Tata Consultancy Services, doubled in size over the past decade to US$230bn in annual revenues, making India the world's fifth-biggest exporter of services. A global shortage of software engineers is likely to fuel its growth (*The Economist* 2022b). Big national firms in automobiles, such as Bajaj, and pharmaceutical companies, most notably Cipla and Syngene, are joining the ranks of significant global players in other sectors (Flood 2022). The number of unicorns in India (start-ups worth greater than US$1bn), which range across education, finance, digital payments, tourism, entertainment and cloud computing, puts it third in the world (*The Economist* 2022b). The returns of its stock market, the fourth largest, have doubled the global average since 1990. Indeed, over the last decade, 150 stocks rose more than 500 percent, representing almost 40 percent of India's $1bn+ stocks, the highest concentration among emerging markets. Two-thirds of its billionaires, whose number increased from 55 to 140, made their fortunes in technology and manufacturing (Sharma 2022).

Third, a range of policies and initiatives have integrated the national economy. The passage of the goods and services tax in 2017 reduced inter-state trade barriers. The rapid expansion of infrastructural capacities has furthered the prospects for growth and development. Since 2014, the national highway network and number of domestic air passengers has doubled, while mobile-phone base stations have tripled, supporting almost 800 million users today (*The Economist* 2022b). Government provision has greatly expanded the number of households with access to electricity, sanitation and bank accounts (Subramanian and Felman 2022).

Finally, the country enjoys massive potential for greater structural transformation. The share of formal sector employment and manufacturing in the economy remains extremely low compared to East and South-East Asia. India failed to embrace labor intensive industrialization and the opportunities created by the expansion of global value chains, which transformed the Pacific rim (Batra 2022). The BJP came to power vowing to modernize the economy. The Make in India programme set a target of creating 100 million new jobs in manufacturing and increasing the share of the latter to GDP to 25 percent by 2022. In 2020, the Modi government launched a new industrial policy, Aatmanirbhar Bharat, allocating $26bn in subsidies over the next five years to incentivize domestic and foreign firms to reach specified production targets in 13 sectors (Subramanian and Felman 2022). The disruption to global supply chains during the pandemic, and efforts by the US and other western countries to de-couple from China, has created new economic opportunities. Reports that Apple may produce half of its iPhones in India by 2027—compared to projections of 25 percent by 2025 just two years ago (*Times of India* 2023)—buoy expectations of similar trends in electronics, chemicals, textiles, pharmaceuticals and industrial machinery (Jain et al. 2022).

Yet these bullish market sentiments must contend with policy mistakes and disconcerting trends over the last decade that continue to unfold.

The decision to demonetize the economy in 2016, when New Delhi removed 86 percent of all currency from circulation in an alleged bid to flush out corrupt black money, followed by severe lockdowns during the pandemic, caused a deep economic shock to small- and medium-sized firms that employ the bulk of workers and rely on cash payments in vast informal markets. As a result, many critical measures of the economy have regressed, from economic growth, investment and exports to agriculture, employment and social sector spending (Inamdar and Alluri 2021). On the one hand, manufacturing employment nearly halved from 51 million in 2016–2017 to 27 million in 2020–2021. Millions of young workers exited the labor force, signaling mounting distress (Bhardwaj 2022). The Modi government delayed or suppressed economic surveys of politically sensitive indicators, which showed rising poverty, declining consumption and falling employment. On the other hand, corporate profits are becoming more concentrated. Today, the top 20 listed firms capture two-thirds of the total (Ninan 2022).

In addition, after decades of gradual external liberalization, New Delhi has reversed tack. Since 2014, tariffs have increased 3200 times, affecting roughly 70 percent of total exports, to an average rate to 18 percent (Subramanian and Felman 2022). Moreover, after signing almost a dozen preferential trade agreements between 2004 and 2014, India refused to join the Regional Comprehensive Economic Partnership (RCEP) in 2019. Reportedly, the negotiations failed to offer enough new opportunities for its globally competitive IT firms to offset domestic industrialists' fears of foreign competition (*The Economist* 2019) and persistent anxieties about food security. The stance was rational in the short run—supporting liberalization where it enjoyed comparative global advantages, protecting sectors where it had strategic vulnerabilities (Hopewell 2018)—and reflected the unusual divergence of its rich–poor economy. But these decisions make it more expensive for firms to import high-quality inputs required to realize India's manufacturing ambitions, and to export to Asia's most comprehensive trade zone, in the long run (Subramanian and Felman 2022). The dilemma of high corporate profits amid a narrow domestic market, and premature deindustrialization (Rodrik 2015) amid a rapidly growing workforce, risks becoming acute.

The Desire to Maintain Strategic Autonomy

The dramatic rise of China raises significant questions for every country. The willingness of Beijing to increase domestic repression, and to pursue its perceived core interests abroad more forcefully, challenges several norms, rules and practices of the contemporary international order. Hence the growing alarm and shifting attitudes, elite and popular, in many Western democracies.

New Delhi shares many of these concerns. Modi and Xi met almost 20 times between 2014 and 2019, signaling the importance of the bilateral relationship. Deadly clashes erupted in the Galwan valley in 2020 when Chinese troops occupied Indian territory, however, following several years of escalation along the LaC. The Modi government retaliated by imposing a stiffer review process on Chinese investments, restrictions on bids for government procurement and 5G technology, and bans on several apps. Why Beijing provoked these clashes generates debate: from demonstrating its greater power to signaling its displeasure at the truncation of Kashmir and growing Indo-US ties (Menon 2022). The stand-off, and new status quo, prevails. Sino-Indian relations are at their lowest point since the 1962 war.

Strategic, economic and defense ties between India and the United States, whose relations were fraught during the Cold War, deepened remarkably over the last two decades. The Indo-US civil-nuclear deal, signed by Manmohan Singh and George W. Bush, recognized India's legitimacy as a nuclear power. Barack Obama visited India twice during his tenure, announcing a "pivot to Asia". The Trump administration, which initiated the 2 + 2 Dialogue, announced major US investments in renewables and defense, and agreed a significant accord enabling Washington to share high-level intelligence with New Delhi (Kugelman 2022). It also embraced the concept, formulated by Japanese Prime Minister Shinzo Abe, of a "free and open Indo-Pacific", identifying India as "the most consequential partner [in the region] … in this century" (Outlook Web Desk 2020b).

Joe Biden criticized India during his presidential campaign for abrogating Kashmir's constitutional powers (Outlook Web Desk 2020a). Yet he had played a key role in securing the civil nuclear deal. Since assuming office, the Biden administration has made the Indo-Pacific region a focal point of its national strategic framework, appointing a coordinator in the National Security Council (Press Trust of India 2023). The first leaders' summit, in March 2021, elevated the status and scope of the Quadrilateral Security Dialogue (Quad) to encompass cybersecurity and critical and emerging technologies as well as climate change and global public health. The alliance also designated the Indian ocean, where China's military footprint is growing, as part of its ambit (Kugelman 2022). And the US unveiled the Indo-Pacific Economic Framework (IPEF). Encompassing twelve countries in the region, and designed in response to the Trans-Pacific Partnership (TPP) and RCEP, the IPEF seeks to establish standards and create incentives to boost digital trade and clean energy, improve supply chain resilience and combat tax evasion (Banyan 2022). For the US, "India is a like-minded partner and leader in South Asia and the Indian Ocean, active in and connected to Southeast Asia, a driving force of the Quad and other regional fora, and an engine for regional growth and development" (Mohan 2022a). The most recent steps include the Initiative on Critical and Emerging Technologies, to boost cooperation on quantum computing, artificial intelligence, 5G wireless networks and semiconductors, and a mechanism to facilitate joint weapons production. India is "the key" to US ambitions in the Indo-Pacific (Sevastopulo and Reed 2023).

However, despite the rise of voices in New Delhi that advocate deeper Indo-US ties against the old Nehruvian reflex toward non-alignment (Bajpai 2011), successive national governments continue to prioritize strategic autonomy. The desire for recognition, a seat at the high table where rules are made and the capacity to mediate disputes, conflicts and differences as a "rising bridge power", rather than accommodation or alliance with the west, are key elements of this ambition (Sinha 2016: 228). According to former national security advisor Shivshankar Menon, India should "work simultaneously with multifarious partners, such as Russia and the US and Iran and Japan ... [through] issue-based coalitions of the willing ... a variable geometry" (Menon 2022).

Neoliberals counter that India must strengthen its tilt to the US given congruent interests in many realms, growing American support for India's great power ambitions and mounting tensions with China. Notably, Modi was the first Indian prime minister since 1979 to skip the annual summit of the Non-Aligned Movement (NAM), signaling a shift. Since 2017, however, India has voted alongside the US in the UN General Assembly 28 percent of the time, only slightly more than China and slightly less than Russia. The tally for traditional US allies, in contrast, was more than 50 percent (*The Economist* 2022a). India remains averse to the idea of the "global west" (see Rachman 2022), bringing Australia, New Zealand, Japan and South Korea into the orbit of NATO. To describe the Quad as an "Asian NATO", contends the BJP's external affairs minister, is "completely misleading" (Press Trust of India 2022b). Rather, its establishment reflects a new multipolar era where multilateralism is working poorly and reforming too slowly (Australian National University 2021). Tellingly, he stated: "We have to put the Cold War behind us, only those who are stuck in the Cold War can't understand the Quad" (Bagchi 2021). The target of his riposte was China, which decried the US Indo-Pacific strategy in such terms. Yet it could equally apply to NATO. New Delhi prefers overlapping mini-lateral coalitions (Mohan 2021).

Similarly, India is unlikely to join growing western efforts to construe international conflicts through the prism of democracy versus autocracy. India played a key role in crafting the UN Declaration of Human Rights and exposing western efforts to protect South African apartheid from scrutiny (Mehta 2011: 100). Since independence, however, successive governments prioritized the principles of national sovereignty and domestic non-intervention championed by the NAM and G77, and generally eschewed promoting democracy abroad. India was a founding member of the Community of Democracies, spearheaded by the Clinton administration in 2000, and supported the creation of the UN Democracy Fund (UNDEF) in 2006, rivaling the financial contributions made by the subsequent Bush administration. Yet New Delhi declined Washington's invitation to lead the UN Democracy Caucus (Mohan 2007: 103–107). The disastrous US intervention in Iraq in the name of freedom reinforced long-standing skepticism among Indian policymakers of the motives and capacity of western powers instigating regime change. Rather, they favored "democracy assistance": targeted support under the auspices of the UNDEF, at the request of host governments, offering technical knowledge, training sessions and financial support to local organizations. The Modi government has significantly reduced support for the UNDEF, however (Hall 2017: 87–92).

Few issues illustrate the complex balancing act India seeks to maintain, its "cautious prudence" (Mehta 2011: 108), better than its contemporary relations vis-a-vis Russia and China and the US.

India refused to condemn the Russian invasion of Ukraine, abstained in successive UN votes and failed to join western sanctions at the start. Several factors drove its stance. India is the third biggest military spender in the world after the US and China. Its defense budget increased 50 percent over the last decade. Yet China's military expenditure is still four times bigger, and its air and naval forces are far superior (Reed and Cornish 2022). Moreover, India's arms imports, which comprise 84 per cent of total procurement, make it the second largest importer in the world (*The Indian Express* 2022). In recent years, India has increased military supplies from France, Israel and especially the US. But Russia supplies roughly 60 percent of its arms, its only aircraft carrier and nuclear-powered submarine, and most of its tanks and jets (Patel 2022). The tense standoff between India and China along the LaC makes the former dependent on parts and maintenance and wary of driving Russia closer to the latter. Viewing a possible mediating role, New Delhi also believed its abstentions at the UN kept diplomacy open. And many remember the EU advocating peaceful resolution when violent clashes erupted along the LaC in 2020.

As the war in Ukraine intensified, however, New Delhi emphasized "its respect for international law, territorial integrity and political sovereignty … its disapproval of the use of force to resolve disputes and of unilateral changes of the status quo … the shelling of nuclear facilities … and distanced itself from China's more supportive position vis-à-vis Russia" (Madan 2022). At a joint press conference with President Vladimir Putin at the Shanghai Cooperation Organization (SCO) summit in September 2022, Prime Minister Modi declared: "I know that today's era is not the time of war" (Bilefsky and Mashal 2022). Many western commentators interpreted his remarks favorably. Yet India's imports of discounted Russian crude have soared since the war began, rising from less than one percent before the invasion to 17 percent. New Delhi highlighted its precarious financial position and continued European purchases (Schmall and Reed 2022)—a justification top EU officials accept while maintaining that supporting Ukraine is a vital western interest (Laskar 2023).

The meetings of the G20 finance and foreign ministers in Bengaluru in February 2023, under India's presidency, failed to produce a joint communique. Russia and China refused to condemn the war and reject the use of nuclear weapons. Thus India released a "chair's summary and outcome document", backed by 17 of its 20 members, which "deplored [the war] in the strongest possible terms" for its "immense human suffering and exacerbating existing fragilities in the global economy", demanded "complete and unconditional" withdrawal from Ukraine territory, and declared "the use or threat of use of nuclear weapons is inadmissible" (Wheatley 2023). But its diplomatic representatives refused to say whether India, which abstained from UNGA vote condemning the war preceding the G20 meetings, was among the 17 members.

The dilemmas facing Sino-Indian relations are clear too. The size of their respective national economies and average incomes were roughly equal at the end of the Cold War. India's GDP has grown tenfold to $3.2 trillion, and its average per capita income fivefold to $2200, over the last three decades. But China is now five times bigger and richer (Sharma 2022). Moreover, the terms of trade weigh heavily against India with roughly $70 billion in deficit, provoking complaints from its IT and pharmaceutical firms of restricted access to the Chinese market (Press Trust of India 2022a). Hence calls for decoupling following the border clashes and invasion of Ukraine have grown in some quarters (see Mohan 2022b).

Yet the value of trade between India and China, on the one hand, and India and the United States, on the other, is similar. China is a key foreign investor in several economic sectors in India, from IT and electronics to start-ups and autos, totaling roughly $6 billion (Mondal 2020). And leading diplomatic figures in New Delhi doubt the US can reverse the long-term decline of western power (Saran 2022). Hence they counsel that India should rebalance the terms of trade vis-a-vis China and join regional pacts in Asia, rather than decouple, as many in the west now advocate (Menon 2022). India's relations with the US and China, while a triangle, have their own bilateral dynamics (see Madan 2020).

Arguably, the ideal strategic vision for many foreign policymakers in New Delhi remains a robust multipolar order in a post-Atlanticist world. Acknowledging the United States is a "natural ally", they nonetheless caution:

> "Governments in the Indo-Pacific want to avoid geopolitical games: they have lives to improve, economies to develop, borders to secure, infrastructure to build and dreams to fulfil. ... America's competition with China must not chart a course for the future of the region in a way that causes irrevocable fault lines. Simplifications like "my enemy's enemy is my friend" or picking sides do not apply in South-East Asia in particular. ... Hedging and balancing are in their political DNA ... Countries in the region would prefer that America's hub-and-spoke approach to security (where countries are connected to it but not to each other) be replaced by a regional order built on "multiple stilts of different sizes and functions..."" (Rao 2021)

Many leaders in the broader region, beyond Japan and South Korea, express similar views. They desire reliable US security guarantees vis-a-vis

China. Yet their closer neighbor remains a vital source of trade and investment. Formally, Washington has encouraged partnerships among many allies in the Indo-Pacific, to create a "more networked regional architecture": "finding new opportunities to link our defense industrial bases, integrating our defense supply chains, and co-producing key technologies that will shore up our collective military advantages" (Mohan 2022a). But the growing confrontational rhetoric in Washington, and its explicit desire to contain China's technological rise, alarms them (*The Economist* 2022c).

Many similar tensions infuse the G20. Historically, the G7 has set its agenda, pushing the interests of advanced industrial economies. Hence the desire among emerging powers to reorient its priorities. It is hard to imagine any of them describing the G7 as the "steering committee of the free world". For the first time since its establishment, the G20 presidency will pass successively between four Southern heavyweights: Indonesia (2022), India (2023), Brazil (2024) and South Africa (2025). New Delhi has expressed a "steadfast commitment to South-South Cooperation" during its term. Key concerns include how to restore economic growth and food and energy security, combat climate change and the global debt crisis equitably and reform the governance of key multilateral institutions (Subramanian 2022). The global inequities exposed by the pandemic and the war in Ukraine exacerbate these problems. Emerging powers from the South are more likely to believe that a new cold war, forcing countries to align with China or the United States, would make them harder to address.

THE IMPLICATIONS FOR INDO-CANADIAN RELATIONS

Indo-Canadian relations have improved considerably over the last two decades, driven by efforts to expand commercial opportunities and the growing influence of diaspora communities in many realms. The prospects for strengthening a range of ties and connections are considerable.

First, both countries share mounting security concerns about China. Compared to the deadly clashes along the LaC, the decision by Beijing to engage in arbitrary hostage diplomacy and impose retaliatory trade bans following the arrest of Meng Wanzhou, and now mounting evidence of alleged Chinese interference in the last two federal elections, do not threaten the territorial integrity of Canada. But such measures violate key aspects of national sovereignty and international law, which New Delhi traditionally champions. Calls for Canada to join the Quad would bolster a shared commitment to maintain an open Indo-Pacific. Second, flows of trade and investment between Canada and India are relatively insignificant compared to other partners. Trade in goods and services in 2021 totaled less than Cdn$15 billion (Global Affairs Canada 2022: 10). The scope for improvement, especially in manufacturing, energy transition and digital innovation, is thus large (Nachiappan 2023). The recent signing of bilateral trade deals between New Delhi vis-a-vis Canberra and Dubai, and fast-track negotiations with London and Brussels, raises the prospects of a pact with Ottawa. Finally, members of the Indian diaspora play a significant role in many realms of Canada, from academia, journalism and civil society to business, public service and government. Indeed, Indian nationals now comprise roughly one-fifth of all new immigrants, the largest ratio among sending countries and double the percentage coming from China (Smith 2022). Unlike previous waves, they are more likely to settle outside the major cities of Toronto, Montreal and Vancouver (Bascaramurty 2022), diversifying their presence across the country. Bolstering our capacity to process visas, and expanding academic, education and cultural exchanges, will deepen these important ties.

Yet conflicting interests and divergent views on significant matters persist.

First, recent events have deepened Canada's long-standing commitment to its traditional post-1945 alliances, from the Five Eyes and G7 to NATO. Comprehensive western sanctions against Russia, and the recent call by Foreign Minister Chrystia Freeland for democracies to pursue "friend-shoring" with each other (McCarten 2022), underscore this North Atlantic worldview. In contrast, India will continue to pursue its various diplomatic, economic and security interests by partnering with states and regimes that Canada increasingly seeks to isolate, from Russia and China to Iran. Similarly, despite its growing strategic partnership with the US and presence in ventures such as the Quad, New Delhi will maintain its membership in a diversity of forums that seek to promote the interests and views of the postcolonial South, such as the NAM and G77, its rising powers, from the BRICS and IBSA to the G20, and various regional groupings, including ASEAN, SAARC and the SCO. Canada's self-understanding as an Indo-Pacific nation, sensitive to the views, interests and concerns of potential Asian partners, has a long way to go (Woo 2022).

Second, attempts by Ottawa and New Delhi to boost trade and investment face long-standing obstacles. Canada successfully attracts students and workers from India, many of whom possess or acquire highly valued skills that serve critical needs. But our administrative capacity to process applications for permanent residency in a timely manner is wanting. Thus many students and workers presently return to India once their work permits expire (Subramaniam 2022). In addition, efforts to strike a trade deal remain protracted. Asymmetries in the size and structure of the two economies, and hence their bargaining positions, frustrate easy progress. Despite six rounds of bilateral negotiations, attempts to secure an Early Progress Trade Agreement are behind schedule, let alone a Comprehensive Economic Partnership Agreement. Ottawa wants New Delhi to liberalize the agricultural sector and uphold labor protocols to a greater extent; New Delhi wants greater access for Indian firms in services. Disagreements on rules of origin, and dispute settlement mechanisms regarding foreign investment, persist (Moss 2023). The dualistic character of the Indian economy—"developing" in agriculture and manufacturing but "advanced" in many services—will shape prospects of cooperation regarding the transition to a net-zero economy too. India has ramped up renewable energy supplies over the last decade, creating many opportunities for bilateral investment in clean tech, especially with France. Yet it remains a lower-middle income economy whose per capita carbon footprint remains a fraction of western industrial democracies, not least Canada, which has one of the highest in the world. Consequently, New Delhi will likely continue to demand the burden of adjustment falls on the developed west and the right of developing countries to consume a greater share of the global carbon budget, and to expect richer countries to finally meet and scale up failed promises of climate finance while opposing measures such as imposing carbon border tariffs vis-a-vis developing economies.

Finally, the rise of militant Hindu nationalism and India's democratic regression accentuates traditional diplomatic challenges. Officially, Ottawa maintains that "Canada will continue to engage with India on issues related to security, democracy, pluralism and human rights" (Xing 2023). In general, however, western governments demonstrate conspicuous silence regarding these developments. Various factors are at play: lip service to purported values, diplomatic prudence, reasons of state. It may also reflect belated recognition in many western democracies of their own democratic challenges, making it hard to criticize others without subjecting themselves to similar censure. Such reticence will stoke political cynicism, however.

The rise of the BJP in recent years makes the politics of the Indian diaspora more difficult to handle too. On the one hand, the willingness of politicians in Canada to support the political demands of diasporic communities will always remain a diplomatic flashpoint. Facing pressure from local Sikh organizations to support the farmers' protest movement in India in 2020, Prime Minister Trudeau stated: "…Canada will always be there to defend the rights of peaceful protesters. We believe in the process of dialogue. We've reached out through multiple means to the Indian authorities to highlight our concerns…" (Roy 2022). His comments provoked an official rebuke from New Delhi: "We have seen some ill-informed comments by Canadian leaders relating to farmers in India. Such comments are unwarranted, especially when pertaining to the internal affairs of a democratic country…". If such "unacceptable interference" continued, it would have a "seriously damaging" impact on bilateral ties (Roy 2022).

Diasporic efforts to support long-distance separatism naturally provoke a stronger reaction. The decision by Sikhs for Justice to host an unofficial referendum in Toronto in 2022, to create a Khalistan homeland, compelled the Indian High Commissioner to ask the Trudeau government to suppress the event, saying it was illegally raising funds and promoting secession. Global Affairs responded by saying Ottawa did not support the referenda or bid to secede, but protected freedom of expression (Fife and Chase 2022). Irked, New Delhi subsequently issued a travel advisory, following the desecration of a local Hindu temple in Toronto by Khalistani sympathizers. It warned Indian nationals of "a sharp increase in incidents of hate crimes, sectarian violence and anti-India activities in Canada… [since] these perpetrators have not been brought to justice so far… [Indian nationals] are advised to exercise due caution and remain vigilant" (Woods 2022). Regardless of the government in office, New Delhi perceives such overtures as infringing on its domestic affairs and violating the principle of non-interference, using language similar to Beijing.

On the other hand, though, many supporters of Hindu nationalism are seeking to curtail academic freedom and freedom of expression in Canada. Speakers, events and publications deemed too critical of the current BJP government, either its politics or policies, increasingly suffer harassment, intimidation and calls to cancel events (Xing 2023). Writers and scholars that belong either to lower caste groups or religious minorities confront greater risks. The frequent denunciation of opposition toward Hindu nationalist excesses as "anti-Hindu" and "Hinduphobic" parallels attempts to conflate criticisms of Israeli government policy as anti-Semitism. Given the rising number of new immigrants from India, the doubling of the number of self-identified Muslims, Hindus and Sikhs since 2001 (Smith 2022) and growing communal tensions in India, such conflicts are likely to grow.

Concluding Remarks

India occupies a pivotal role in Canada's new Indo-Pacific strategy for many good reasons. Its developmental trajectory, and twin status as the most populous country and largest democracy in the world, draws the attention of many countries. The size and influence of the Indian diaspora in Canada, and opportunities to expand diplomatic, economic and strategic ties, are significant and growing. Hence there exist many incentives for political leaders and public servants, and academics, business actors and civic organizations, to pursue cooperation and explore prospects at various levels in multiple realms. Courting India through a whole-of-society approach makes sense.

Yet the framework of Canada's Indo-Pacific strategy, which champions democracy and pluralism and the norms and rules of existing international order, poses two major challenges.

The first concerns the commitment to pluralism and democracy. Elections remain competitive in India. A national coalition of opposition parties might unseat the BJP and form a new government in New Delhi in the 2024 general election. Nonetheless, the severe erosion of civil liberties, institutional autonomy and minority rights in India over the last decade generates serious questions about its status as the world's largest democracy. The recent disqualification of the Congress leader Rahul Gandhi from parliament, following a controversial judicial order from the home state of Prime Minister Modi (Vishwanath 2023), suggests the BJP perceives a threat to its rule. Altering the electoral playing field, by preventing opposition politicians from contesting and casting doubt on the integrity of polls, is a key aspect of democratic backsliding. The unwillingness of the Modi government to readily accept potential electoral defeat in 2024, echoing recent events in Brazil and the United States, thus cannot be ruled out.

Hence efforts by Ottawa to proclaim that a commitment to democracy and pluralism distinguishes Canada and its partners in the Indo-Pacific vis-a-vis China face obvious risks. Recent calls by the United States for mutual learning and frank talk (Blinken 2021) are a salutary belated corrective to previous efforts of "democracy promotion" by the west on the 20th anniversary of the invasion of Iraq. Moreover, many western democracies exhibit serious backsliding, making it hard to scrutinize others without subjecting ourselves to similar criticism. But such political exchanges will likely occur through quiet diplomacy. A minimal conception of democracy, placing the greatest value on parties competing for power through competitive elections, will likely become the litmus test for international recognition and club membership. The participation of many autocratic leaders at the 2023 Summit of Democracies, hosted by the United States despite its own deficits, underscores this selective morality and political hypocrisy. Civil liberties, minority rights and the rule of law face growing threats around the world. But realpolitik rules.

The second challenge in courting India, distinct but related, concerns the existing international order. Ottawa and New Delhi share growing concern over China's willingness to forcefully assert its economic, military and strategic power. Despite its desire to embrace new partners in the Indo-Pacific, however, Canada appears far more committed to maintaining the post-1945 international order shaped by the interests of western industrial democracies of the North Atlantic. Indeed, the Russian invasion of Ukraine and increasingly aggressive posture by China has reinforced its Atlanticist self-image and traditional alliances. In contrast, despite growing strategic ties with the US, India seems committed to enhancing its strategic autonomy vis-a-vis great powers and fashioning a multipolar international order whose norms, institutions and practices no longer favor the interests of the west. Governments in New Delhi, regardless of the political ideologies, are unlikely to fully embrace a policy of "friend-shoring" in trade, investment and developmental aid, join formal security alliances or frame international conflicts simply through a simple prism that pits democracy versus autocracy. Whether the pursuit of strategic autonomy is sustainable given the growing clash between China and the US remains an open question. But India and other rising powers from the South are more likely to believe that a new cold war would make it harder to address the severe challenges posed by global poverty, late development and climate change equitably.

References

Australian National University. 2021. Quad to Take Central Role on Global Stage. September 7. https://www.anu.edu.au/news/all-news/quad-to-take-central-role-on-global-stage.

Bagchi, Indrani. 2021. Through the Covid Crisis, Quad Finds a Home. *The Times of India*, June 8. https://timesofindia.indiatimes.com/blogs/Globespotting/through-the-covid-crisis-quad-finds-a-home/.

Bajpai, Kanti. 2011. India and the World. In *The Oxford Companion to Politics in India*, ed. Niraja Gopal Jayal and Pratap Bhanu Mehta, 521–541. New Delhi: Oxford University Press.

Banyan. 2022. What Is the Point of the Indo-Pacific Economic Framework? *The Economist*, June 9. https://www.economist.com/asia/2022/06/09/what-is-the-point-of-the-indo-pacific-economic-framework.

Bascaramurty, Dakshana. 2022. Smaller Cities, Atlantic Provinces Attracting Immigrants, According to 2021 Census Data. *The Globe and Mail*, October 27. https://www.theglobeandmail.com/canada/article-immigrants-canadian-population-2021-census/.

Batra, Amita. 2022. *India's Trade Policy in the 21st Century*. New Delhi: Routledge.

Bhardwaj, Ankur. 2022. Unemployed Youth's Frustration Points to Wounded Economy, Social Pain Ahead. *The India Cable*, March 1. https://www.theindiacable.com/.

Bilefsky, Dan, and Mujib Mashal. 2022. Amid Russia's Growing International Isolation, India's Leader Tells Putin That Today Is No Time for War. *New York Times*, September 16. https://www.nytimes.com/2022/09/16/world/europe/modi-putin-ukraine-russia.html.

Blinken, Anthony J. 2021. Opening Remarks at a Civil Society Roundtable. US Department of State, July 28. https://www.state.gov/opening-remarks-at-a-civil-society-roundtable/#.YQEjdFQTDdI.twitter.

Dhawan, Sonali. 2022. 'An Open-Air Prison': Kashmiri Journalists on How Travel Bans Undermine Press Freedom. Committee to Protect Journalists, September 19. https://cpj.org/2022/09/an-open-air-prison-kashmiri-journalists-on-how-travel-bans-undermine-press-freedom/.

Ellis-Petersen, Hannah. 2021. India: Activist Arrested Over Protest 'Toolkit' Shared by Greta Thunberg. *The Guardian*, February 15. https://www.theguardian.com/world/2021/feb/15/india-activist-arrested-over-protest-toolkit-shared-by-greta-thunberg.

Fife, Robert, and Steve Chase. 2022. Ottawa Says It Takes Seriously India's Allegations of Illegal Funding of Khalistan Movement. *The Globe and Mail*, December 1. https://www.theglobeandmail.com/politics/article-ottawa-says-it-takes-seriously-indias-allegations-of-illegal-funding/.

Flood, Chris. 2022. Indian Equities Hit Record Highs as Investors Look Beyond China. *Financial Times*, December 6. https://www.ft.com/content/f65249ee-243a-485a-8b79-a1c4534f460f.

Freedom House. 2021. Freedom in the World: India. https://freedomhouse.org/country/india/freedom-world/2021.

Global Affairs Canada. 2022. *Canada's Indo-Pacific Strategy*. Government of Canada.

Hall, Ian. 2017. Not Promoting, Not Exporting: India's Democracy Assistance. *Rising Powers Quarterly* 2 (3): 81–97.

Hopewell, Kristen. 2018. Recalcitrant Spoiler? Contesting Dominant Accounts of India's Role in Global Trade Governance. *Third World Quarterly* 39 (3): 577–593. https://doi.org/10.1080/01436597.2017.1369033.

Inamdar, Nikhil, and Aparna Alluri. 2021. India Economy: Seven Years of Modi in Seven Charts. BBC, June 22. https://www.bbc.com/news/world-asia-india-57437944.

Jain, Deepak, Sushil Pasricha, and Sambit Patra. 2022. The Trillion-Dollar Manufacturing Exports Opportunity for India. Bain & Company, January 13. https://www.bain.com/insights/the-trillion-dollar-manufacturing-exports-opportunity-for-india/.

Jayal, Niraja Gopal. 2019. Introduction: The Re-forming of India. In *Re-forming India: The Nation Today*, ed. Niraja Gopal Jayal, xi–xxxix. New Delhi: Penguin Viking.

Kugelman, Michael. 2022. The Quad Looks West. *Foreign Policy*, May 26. https://foreignpolicy.com/2022/05/26/quad-tokyo-south-asia-indian-ocean-region/.

Laskar, Rezaul H. 2023. 'Has Russia Been Invaded': Top EU Official Rebuts Sergey Lavrov on Ukraine War. *Hindustan Times*, March 4. https://www.hindustantimes.com/india-news/incredible-someone-could-lie-like-this-top-eu-official-pans-russia-s-lavrov-101677859377596.html.

Madan, Tanvi. 2020. *Fateful Triangle: How China Shaped US-India Relations During the Cold War*. New York: Penguin.

Madan, Tanvi. 2022. Russia and Ukraine. *The Economist*, May 7. https://www.economist.com/by-invitation/2022/05/07/tanvi-madan-explains-why-india-is-not-in-russias-camp.

Mashal, Mujib. 2022. The New India: Aiding Democracy Abroad, Straining It at Home. *New York Times*, September 24. https://www.nytimes.com/2022/09/24/world/asia/india-democracy.html.

McCarten, James. 2022. Let's Get Serious about a Putin-Era Strategy for Energy, Economy, Climate, Freeland Says. *The Globe and Mail*, October 12. https://www.theglobeandmail.com/canada/article-lets-get-serious-about-a-putin-era-strategy-for-energy-economy-climate/.

Menon, Shivshankar. 2022. The Crisis in India-China Relations. *Seminar #749*, January. https://www.india-seminar.com/semframe.html.
Mehta, Pratap Bhanu. 2011. Do New Democracies Support Democracy? Reluctant India. *Journal of Democracy* 22 (4): 97–109.
Mehta, Pratap Bhanu. 2022. Hindu Nationalism: From Ethnic Identity to Authoritarian Repression. *Studies in Indian Politics* 10 (1): 31–47.
Mohan, C. Raja. 2007. Balancing Interests and Values: India's Struggle with Democracy Promotion. *The Washington Quarterly* 30 (3): 99–115.
Mohan, C. Raja. 2021. India Welcomes AUKUS Pact as China Deterrent. *Foreign Policy*, September 16. https://foreignpolicy.com/2021/09/16/aukus-india-australia-uk-us-submarines/?utm_source=PostUp&utm_medium=email&utm_campaign=36450&utm_term=South%20Asia%20Brief%20OC&tpcc=36450.
Mohan, C. Raja. 2022a. The Significance of the Indo-Pacific for India. *The Indian Express*, February 16. https://indianexpress.com/article/opinion/columns/the-significance-of-the-indo-pacific-for-india-7774066/?utm_source=newzmate&utm_medium=email&utm_campaign=opinion&pnespid=Wq0nr0sD5ylMxAie8cHUFFtHpAop3a8qtloQE6UYb8zKMOINuLLmYGSaYwHCpJ_6kXyou5w.
Mohan, C. Raja. 2022b. India, Europe and the Russian Complication. *The Indian Express*, April 26. https://indianexpress.com/article/opinion/columns/india-europe-and-the-russian-emmanuel-macron-france-7887278/?utm_source=newzmate&utm_medium=email&utm_campaign=opinion&pnespid=H7MnpUVT7noRiVGU5szXTRFIpQ0kxahwrAYTH6xeI5fKm0CMB7b.Xi.Vjk0Gas550h2YjK0T.
Mondal, Dibyendu. 2020. Chinese Investments Are Deep-Rooted in India. *The Sunday Guardian*, June 20. https://www.sundayguardianlive.com/news/chinese-investments-deep-rooted-india.
Moss, Neil. 2023. Progress Lags in Canada-India Trade Talks. *The Hill Times*, February 22. https://www.hilltimes.com/story/2023/02/22/progress-lags-in-canada-india-trade-talks/379167/?utm_source=Subscriber+-++Hill+Times+Publishing&utm_campaign=623b61439f-Foreign-Policy-Subscribers&utm_medium=email&utm_term=0_8edecd9364-623b61439f-%5BLIST_EMAIL_ID%5D&mc_cid=623b61439f&mc_eid=65deceb4a6.
Nachiappan, Karthik. 2023. Canada, India Should Change Script and Become Real Partners. *The Toronto Sun*, March 7. https://torontosun.com/opinion/columnists/nachiappan-canada-india-should-change-script-and-become-real-partners.
Ninan, T.N. 2022. "India under Modi." *Seminar #749*, January. https://www.india-seminar.com/semframe.html.
Outlook Web Desk. 2020a. US Presidential Nominee Biden Seeks Restoration of Rights in Kashmir; Disappointed with NRC, CAA. *Outlook India*, June

26. https://www.outlookindia.com/website/story/world-news-us-president
ial-nominee-biden-seeks-restoration-of-rights-in-kashmir-disappointed-with-
nrc-caa/355446.

Outlook Web Desk. 2020b. Mike Pompeo, US Defence Secretary Esper to Visit India for 2+2 Talks. *Outlook India*, October 21. https://www.outlookindia.com/website/story/world-news-mike-pompeo-us-defence-secretary-esper-to-visit-india-next-week-for-22-talks/362620.

Pasricha, Anjana. 2022. Forecasts Show India May Become World's Third Largest Economy by 2030. Voice of America News, December 14. https://www.voanews.com/a/forecasts-show-india-may-become-world-s-third-largest-economy-by-2030/6875735.html.

Patel, Aakar. 2022. Vote to Abstain at UN Will Hurt India as It Fails to Live Up to Ideals. *Deccan Chronicle*, March 1. https://www.deccanchronicle.com/opinion/columnists/010322/aakar-patel-vote-to-abstain-at-un-will-hurt-india-as-it-fails-to-liv.html.

Poddar, Umang. 2023. The BJP Is Hegemonic at the National Level–but Weak in the States. *Scroll.in*, December 22. https://scroll.in/article/1039337/election-results-the-bjp-is-hegemonic-at-the-national-level-but-weak-in-the-states.

PRS Legislative Research. 2021. The Information Technology (Intermediary Guidelines and Digital Media Ethics Code) Rules, 2021. https://prsindia.org/billtrack/the-information-technology-intermediary-guidelines-and-digital-media-ethics-code-rules-2021.

Press Trust of India. 2022a. India-China Trade Grows to Record $125 billion in 2021 amid Tension. *Outlook India*, January 14. https://www.outlookindia.com/website/story/business-news-india-china-trade-grows-to-record-125-billion-in-2021-amid-tension/409719?utm_source=related_story.

Press Trust of India. 2022b. 'State of Border Will Determine State of Relationship with China': S. Jaishankar at Munich Security Conference. *Outlook India*, February 20. https://www.outlookindia.com/international/-state-of-border-will-determine-state-of-relationship-with-china-s-jaishankar-at-munich-security-conference-news-183248.

Press Trust of India. 2023. US: Biden Proposes USD1.8 Billion for Indo-Pacific strategy, USD400 Million More to Deal with China. *Outlook India*, March 29. https://www.outlookindia.com/international/us-biden-proposes-usd-1-8-billion-for-indo-pacific-strategy-usd-400-million-more-to-deal-with-china-news-188991.

Rachman, Gideon. 2022. Xi's China and the Rise of the 'Global West'. *Financial Times*, October 25. https://www.ft.com/content/d885aecf-4202-41cd-ad3f-476ffb19631e.

Rao, Nirupama. 2021. America's Need for Wisdom and Allies in Asia. *The Economist*, September 27. https://www.economist.com/by-invitation/2021/09/27/nirupama-rao-on-americas-need-for-wisdom-and-allies-in-asia.

Reed, John. 2022. Crackdowns, Lawsuits and Intimidation: The Threat to Freedom of Expression in India. *Financial Times*, October 10. https://www.ft.com/content/c6d19165-079f-442c-8a2c-47eb91ad9c72.

Reed, John, and Chloe Cornish. 2022. Can India Build a Military Strong Enough to Deter China? *Financial Times*, December 12. https://www.ft.com/content/333aa07e-93ff-4e97-95c4-548bdccb5661.

Rizwan, Hera. 2022. Explained: Where Does India Stand in the UN Population Report? *India Times*, November 20. https://www.indiatimes.com/explainers/news/explained-where-does-india-stand-in-the-un-population-report-585031.html.

Rodrik, Dani. 2015. Premature Industrialization. National Bureau of Economic Research Working Paper No. 20935. https://www.nber.org/papers/w20935.

Roy, Shubhajit. 2021. Jaishankar on Global Democracy Downgrade: 'Custodians Can't Stomach We Don't Want Their Approval'. *The Indian Express*, March 15. https://indianexpress.com/article/india/global-democarcy-downgrade-custodians-cant-stomach-we-dont-want-their-approval-7228422/.

Roy, Shubhajit. 2022. Explained: In India's Response to Foreign Criticism, Claimed Assertion and Perceived Touchiness. *The Indian Express*, February 19. https://indianexpress.com/article/explained/india-response-foreign-criticism-claimed-assertion-perceived-touchiness-7780444/?utm_source=newzmate&utm_medium=email&utm_campaign=opinion&pnespid=Hbcy6kgC5z1Jm1ub9crTT0NPrhxmwKpp_hsRQvsFa5rKkvdRrwEyLa5fdYpUvKwVchYwoq9C.

Ruparelia, Sanjay. 2021a. India's Farmers Are Right to Protest Against Agricultural Reforms. *The Conversation*, January 24. https://theconversation.com/indias-farmers-are-right-to-protest-against-agricultural-reforms-152726.

Ruparelia, Sanjay. 2021b. Pandemic Failure, Democratic Backslide. *Open Canada*, July 15. https://opencanada.org/pandemic-failure-democratic-backslide/.

Saran, Shyam. 2022. *How China Sees India and the World*. New Delhi: Juggernaut.

Schmall, Emily, and Stanley Reed. 2022. India Finds Russian Oil an Irresistible Deal, No Matter the Diplomatic Pressure. *New York Times*, May 4. https://www.nytimes.com/2022/05/04/world/asia/india-russia-oil.html.

Schultz, Kai, and Sameer Yasir. 2020. India Restores Some Internet Access in Kashmir after Long Shutdown. *New York Times*, January

26. https://www.nytimes.com/2020/01/26/world/asia/kashmir-internet-shutdown-india.html.
Sevastopulo, Demetri, and John Reed. 2023. US and India Launch Ambitious Tech and Defence Initiatives. *Financial Times*, January 31. https://www.ft.com/content/0fad1ae7-07f8-44cc-9df6-c8e2e03d404f.
Sharma, Ruchir. 2022. At 75, India Is Finally Ready to Join the Global Party. *Financial Times*, August 15. https://www.ft.com/content/dec674c5-9009-4da1-a857-c2e68473c9ae.
Sinha, Aseema. 2016. Partial Accommodation Without Conflict: India as a Rising Link Power. In *Accommodating Rising Powers: Past, Present and Future*, ed. T.V. Paul, 222–245. Cambridge: Cambridge University Press.
Smith, Alanna. 2022. Religious Affiliation, Big City Draw on the Decline, Statistics Canada Census Finds. *The Globe and Mail*, October 26. https://www.theglobeandmail.com/canada/article-religious-affiliation-big-city-draw-on-the-decline-statistics-canada/.
Subramaniam, Vanmala. 2022. Canada's Permanent Resident Application Backlog Is Forcing Thousands of Skilled Workers to Quit and Return Home. *The Globe and Mail*, October 12. https://www.theglobeandmail.com/business/article-canada-permanent-residence-application-backlog/.
Subramanian, Arvind, and Josh Felman. 2022. Is India Back? The Race Between Hardware and Software. *Seminar #749*, January. https://www.india-seminar.com/semframe.html.
Subramanian, Nirupama. 2022. Road to G20, Delhi 2023. *The Indian Express*, November 19. https://indianexpress.com/article/explained/g20-presidency-india-agenda-themes-global-south8275035/?utm_source=newzmate&utm_medium=email&utm_campaign=explained&utm_content=6386461&pnespid=WbYr.VwL7z8XkQmI8svLTxBV.Akiw6t18wFKBrgFbZDK2Fsq7awJQ_A8tDzWpxN3yaJB0yyn
The Economist. 2019. Spare Wheel. November 7. https://www.economist.com/asia/2019/11/07/asias-trade-negotiators-decide-they-can-no-longer-wait-for-india.
The Economist. 2022a. The Ailing Body Politic. February 12. https://www.economist.com/asia/2022/02/12/the-organs-of-indias-democracy-are-decaying.
The Economist. 2022b. A New Formula. May 14. https://www.economist.com/briefing/2022/05/14/india-is-likely-to-be-the-worlds-fastest-growing-big-economy-this-year.
The Economist. 2022c. Elephants in the Long Grass. November 17. https://www.economist.com/asia/2022/11/17/how-the-rivalry-between-america-and-china-worries-south-east-asia.

The Indian Express. 2022. Aatmanirbhar in Defence Production: Where India Stands among Indo-Pacific Nations. October 8. https://indianexpress.com/article/explained/india-defence-production-exports-imports-capabilities-exp lained-8196801/?utm_source=newzmate&utm_medium=email&utm_cam paign=explained&utm_content=6386461&pnespid=ALgm81ML6n4ImFjJ4c qKBkEQvQknmKdpsVkSB7waboHKjoAnYjfDlfgPd7n7WBhD6SYOWd_e.

The New York Times. 2023. India's Proud Tradition of a Free Press Is at Risk. February 12. https://www.nytimes.com/2023/02/12/opinion/modi-bbc-documentary-india.html.

The Times of India. 2023. 50% of All iPhones Could Be Produced in India by 2027: Report. January 17. https://timesofindia.indiatimes.com/gadgets-news/50-of-all-iphones-could-be-produced-in-india-by-2027-report/articl eshow/97050815.cms.

Varshney, Ashutosh. 2019. The Emergence of Right-Wing Populism in India. In *Re-forming India: The Nation Today*, ed. Niraja Gopal Jayal, 327–345. New Delhi: Penguin Viking.

V-Dem Institute. 2022. *Democracy Report 2022: Autocratization Changing Nature?* University of Gothenburg, March. https://v-dem.net/media/pub lications/dr_2022.pdf.

Verniers, Gilles. 2019. Verdict 2019 in charts and maps. *Scroll.in*, May 28. https://scroll.in/article/924965/verdict-2019-in-charts-and-maps-more-voters-turned-out-than-ever-beforemore-parties-contested.

Vishwanath, Apurva. 2023. Rahul Gandhi Disqualified as Lok Sabha MP after Conviction. *The Indian Express*, March 26. https://indianexpress.com/art icle/explained/explained-law/rahul-gandhi-can-avert-disqualification-as-mp-if-conviction-stayed-8515487/.

Wheatley, Jonathan. 2023. G20 Finance Ministers Split over Ukraine. *Financial Times*, February 27.

Xing, Lisa. 2023. Movement Out of India That 'Disseminates Hate' Victimizes Religious Minority Groups, Report Says. CBC News, March 1. https://www.cbc.ca/news/canada/rss-hindutva-india-report-1.6764114.

Woo, Senator Yuen Pau. 2022. Opening Remarks at HardTalk: Canada and the Asia Pacific. *iAffairs*, November 7. https://iaffairscanada.com/2022/ope ning-remarks-at-hardtalk-canada-and-the-asia-pacific/.

Woods, Alan. 2022. Why India's Canadian Travel Advisory Was Really a Diplomatic Shot Across the Bow. *Toronto Star*, September 23. https://www.thestar.com/news/canada/2022/09/23/india-is-warning-its-citizens-about-canadian-hate-crimes-sectarian-violence.html.

PART III

Conclusion

CHAPTER 13

Conclusion

Maxwell A. Cameron, David Gillies, and David Carment

Drawing on issues and insights emerging from individual chapters, this concluding chapter addresses some of the broader themes about the state of democracy worldwide and in Canada as they are being shaped by recent events. These include the Ukraine crisis and its trajectory, growing signs of polarization in established democracies, the shrinking of civic space and alleged foreign interference in Canada's electoral system and politics.

M. A. Cameron (✉)
Department of Political Science, School of Public Policy and Global Affairs, University of British Columbia, Vancouver, BC, Canada
e-mail: Max.Cameron@ubc.ca

D. Carment
School of Indigenous and Canadian Studies, Carleton University, Ottawa, ON, Canada
e-mail: david.carment@carleton.ca

D. Gillies
Research Fellow, Centre for the Study of Democracy and Diversity, Queen's University, Kingston, ON, Canada

© The Author(s), under exclusive license to Springer Nature Switzerland AG 2023
M. A. Cameron et al. (eds.), *Democracy and Foreign Policy in an Era of Uncertainty*, Canada and International Affairs, https://doi.org/10.1007/978-3-031-35490-8_13

DEMOCRACY IN HARD TIMES

That democracy has fallen on hard times is not in dispute. It is enough to read the titles of recent books on the subject—*Democracy in Retreat* (Kurlantzick 2013); *Democracy in Decline?* (Diamond and Plattner 2015); *How Democracies Die* (Levitsky and Ziblatt 2018); *Twilight of Democracy* (Applebaum 2020); and most ominously, *Surviving Autocracy* (Gessen 2020), to name just a few—to appreciate the dismal mood among analysts. Many of the chapters in this volume share the pessimism. David Carment and Marshall Palmer review the literature on the "global decline" of democracy. Jeremy Kinsman offers a practitioner's perspective on the way that "1989's confidence that democratization would be the prevailing global outcome" gave way to the disappointments of the past decade or more.

It is not just that the outside world seems more menacing; domestic politics has also become more rancorous. Partisanship has intensified and so has polarization—including affective polarization and negative partisanship (Klein 2020). Although by no means on the scale or intensity of politics in the United States, Canada is not immune to the trend away from moderate partisanship and towards the kind of polarization that has nefarious consequences for democratic politics (Ekos 2023). In this volume, David Moscrop advises observers to be "concerned about the rise of particular manifestations of populism, especially nativist and authoritarian versions, which exist in Canada."

Matters could be worse. The United States has experienced a significant erosion due to the radicalization of the Republican Party and the election of Trump in 2016, but it survived an attempted self-coup. Most of Latin America is far more democratic than it was three decades ago, with the exception of Cuba, Venezuela and Nicaragua, and Bolsonaro's supporters were unable to prevent President Lula from returning to office in Brazil. One reason for the gloom among analysts is disappointment with the Arab Spring. The fizzling of the Arab Spring was disappointing, but in retrospect the optimism of over a decade ago was clearly misplaced. The failure of Russia to democratize after 1990 is, likewise, disappointing, but hardly surprising. The picture is mixed in Africa and Asia. India has experienced "significant democratic backsliding" as Sanjay Ruparelia notes in his chapter, and is now governed by an "autocratic, majoritarian, and populist" leader. Likewise, South Africa has experienced backsliding, but remains a democracy. In other cases, erosion has occurred in countries that never democratized, as in Afghanistan, which fell back under the control of the Taliban immediately after the US withdrawal in 2020. In short, although there are good reasons for concern that democracy is not advancing, nor is it about to vanish from the face of the earth.

Indeed, in many countries, the challenges to democracy are either due to the poor quality of governance, because institutions have not kept pace with social change, or because of conflicts that, while often ugly and destructive, reflect deeper processes of change that demand political expression. For example, political inclusion can generate a backlash among those who fear the loss of status and power. The rise of the radical right in the United States, Europe and Latin America is in many ways a reaction to the growing power of women, immigrants, sexual minorities and other historically marginalized groups. Moreover, political polarization is not always pernicious, nor is it necessarily anti-democratic; it becomes pernicious when it undermines the functioning of democratic institutions (McCoy and Somer 2019).

It is also the case that fears of the assertiveness of authoritarian regimes may reflect the fact that leaders of the world's democracies have less confidence—some might say hubris—about their superiority and the historic inevitability of the spread of democracy. The rise of China, India, Brazil and Russia (once called the BRICs and embraced as "emerging markets") reflects real shifts in the global distribution of power and wealth. This intensifies perceived vulnerability of foreign meddling in democratic elections, as most strikingly illustrated by contentious claims of interference by Russia in the US presidential election in 2016. And yet, here, again, it is critical to acknowledge that it is not entirely unusual for countries to seek to influence the outcome of elections in other countries, that much of this can be done quite legally, and that democratic countries have a long history of seeking to influence the outcome of election in other countries.

The point is that, as David Gillies notes, the discussion of democracy and foreign policy now occurs under difficult conditions: "Renewed policy activity today is driven by democratic backsliding and growing authoritarianism abroad and some impetus for democratic renewal at home to address external interference in our politics and electoral system, converging governance challenges, and signs of polarization." This is why the foreign policy agenda has shifted from an offensive to a defensive stance. In the heady days following the end of the Cold War, it seemed possible that a more cooperative world would supersede old animosities and give way to a new sense of common purpose. Today, democratic nations are more concerned to protect their domestic institutions and practices, and support one another, than they are to advance democracy globally.

Kate Hecht notes that the democratic club is shrinking and the appeal of membership is declining. She argues for a return to inclusive multilateralism. "Contestation against exclusive approaches by democratic and non-democratic states alike," she argues, has "called attention to the salience of additional values, unintended security consequences of isolation, and widespread interest in active participation in less stratified multilateral processes." Similarly, in the context of the Western Hemisphere, Kendra Carrion Vivar and Tom Legler argue that Canada's approach to democracy support seems to be shifting to the support of civil society, vulnerable groups, "friendshoring" and new forms of influence. Another element of this defensive and indirect approach is Canada's feminist foreign policy. Such a policy is democratic insofar as "strengthening women's political participation and protecting gender equality" is an excellent way to support democracy and resist authoritarianism, as Gabrielle Bardall argues, because it contributing to a more intersectional understanding of what equality and justice demands.

We conclude by reflecting on the implication of the shift from offence to defence in the support for democracy, which we take to be a matter of convenience not principle. By this we mean to capture the shift from the promotion of democracy where it is missing to the defence of democracy where it is threatened—which increasingly includes established democracies. In making these distinctions, we note that democratic regimes take diverse forms, but they share common attributes. Solidarity is contingent not upon a particular set of institutions alone, but on the core principle of alternation between government and opposition by means of fair and institutionalized elections. This is the principle that, combined with the separation of powers and the rule of law, makes it possible to think of popular sovereignty in the context of modern states. Democratic regimes as expressions of public will have every right to give preference to other democracies—i.e. systems that likewise meet the condition of being self-governing. Although disagreement over what counts as democratic is to some extent inescapable, there is considerable clarity with respect to the boundary between democratic and non-democratic regimes. Few analysts would accept claims by Putin and Xi that Russia and China are "real" democracies for the simple reason that alternation between government and opposition does not occur in these systems. They cannot claim to rest their legitimacy on popular sovereignty expressed by means of electoral competition.

Contestation within democratic regimes concerning the proper functioning of democratic institutions is pervasive, and indeed, it is constitutive of democracy. There can be no democracy—no self-governing polity—unless the people can decide not only who shall govern but also by means of what institutions such matters are to be settled. Political leaders responsible for democratic backsliding often defend their actions by appealing to alternative understandings of democracy. Their demagoguery is transparent to anyone who has worked out the proper functioning of a democratic system, but such knowledge is not spread evenly throughout the political community. This makes it imperative to clarify the minimal conditions that need to be met by a democratic political regime and to educate the public in this respect.

Beyond the defence of democracy as a system in which, minimally, government and opposition alternate, democratic states show solidarity with one another by recognizing the necessity of creating the conditions under which the minimal attributes of democracy are secure. These involve, in addition elections with integrity and credibility, the provision of basic rights and freedoms associated with citizenship, including freedom of speech, assembly and press, as well as the right to organize parties and vote and run for office. These rights and freedoms are only as secure as the constitutional and legal guarantees that uphold them.

So much for the defensive agenda. On what basis do states affirm the necessity of democracy as a foundation of international sovereignty—and seek to promote that conditions that support it? There is, as Immanuel Kant recognized in *Perpetual Peace*, an intimate connection between the constitution of republican rule based on just domestic institutions and the possibility of the rule of law among nations. The sovereignty of the state is not (or should not be) a *carte blanche* to be cashed out by any despot who can concentrate enough power to exclude potential adversaries. It must be grounded in *popular* sovereignty. Just as every citizen in a democracy has an investment in the character and judgement of all other citizens, every democracy in the international system has an investment in the democratic character of every other state. A dramatic example of this interest arises in the context of the interference of non-democracies in the internal affairs of democratic nations.

Electoral Interference: The State of Play

As we go to press, the issue of electoral interference has assumed unprecedented salience in Canadian politics, and the way this debate has unfolded has potentially significant implications for democracy. Here we reflect on these implications, in particular for civil society. Irrespective of political systems or culture, in virtually all countries, civil society organizations and the non-profit sector are key for social cohesion, economic development, and as sources of innovation and citizen voice that are essential for good governance. In sub-Saharan Africa, for example, trade unions, student organizations and church-based groups played a large role in the waves of political liberalization and democratization from the 1990s and beyond. But "civic space" has been shrinking in many countries in the last decade, in some cases even longer.

Western democracies have not always responded effectively to restrictions on human rights and democracy advocacy groups in backsliding democracies, hybrid regimes and countries facing conflict and instability. As Saskia Brechenmacher and Tom Carothers explain: "closing civic space [is] just one part of a much broader pattern of democratic recession and authoritarian resurgence. The international response seems stuck: some useful efforts have been undertaken, but they appear too limited, loosely focused, and reactive."

Growing restrictions on civil society are evident across all continents: from Nicaragua and Venezuela to Georgia and Pakistan, India and Israel. Repressive regimes and backsliding democracies can draw on a variety of regulatory and technological tools to monitor, restrict or shut down civic institutions critical of ruling elites. Seizing records, closing offices, bureaucratic delays and new regulations and foreign agent laws are some of the ways governments are cracking down against rights and democracy advocates or other groups critical of the state. Constraints on Western support for local struggle are multiple. The hardening of geopolitical alliances coupled with the impact of the pandemic on supply chains is prompting more economic self-reliance less commitment to globalization and emerging signs of regional trading among like-minded democratic and more autocratic political systems. In a multi-polar or post-hegemonic world in which culture not ideology is a key organizing principle, local actors and 'civilizational states' are doing more in the 'near-abroad' to manage their own economic and security affairs. Consider the recent agreement between Iran and Saudi Arabia to normalize relations as good example of this new form of multipolarity and self-sufficiency.

FROM DEFENCE BACK TO OFFENCE—OR DOUBLING DOWN ON DEFENCE?

Canada's credibility in supporting democracy abroad is inseparable from its democratic performance at home. Canada is one of the world's oldest and most successful liberal democracies. But public confidence in our public institutions has been rudely shaken not only by the Trucker Convoy protests but also by renewed allegations of malign external actors in our politics and elections. The evidence that is publicly available suggests that foreign 'interference' in Canada's democratic institutions is orchestrated, far reaching and has been sustained over many years. It can be difficult in practice to effectively demarcate legitimate public diplomacy and influence from illegal foreign interference, including in our electoral processes and particularly in the pre-election environment. These activities exist in a definitional grey zone which is influenced by all the vagaries of intelligence gathering: its timeliness, reliability and quality.[1] Nevertheless, intelligence experts have for years been calling for a whole-of-government approach to address alleged interference that would go well beyond a core group of agencies, notably CSIS and CSEC and on occasion Global Affairs Canada and the Department of National Defence.

Allegations of Chinese interference in Canada's democracy have periodically surfaced since at least the 2010 when then CSIS Director, Richard Fadden, spoke publicly of ethnic minority "agents of influence," two cabinet ministers from unnamed provinces reportedly under the control of foreign powers, and the role of Confucius Institutes in organizing demonstrations on Taiwan and Falun Gong in Canada.

Why did the Prime Minister not go public about Chinese efforts to influence and allegedly interfere with federal elections in 2019 and 2021?

---

[1] In March 2023 expert testimony before the Parliamentary Standing Committee on Procedure and House Affairs, David Morrison, Deputy Minister of Foreign Affairs, underlined that intelligence reports are 'not truth' and 'rarely paint a full or concrete or actionable picture.' In obliquely disparaging media reliance on unnamed and uncorroborated sources as little more than rumour, Morrison's testimony also cast a very poor light on the quality and veracity of intelligence available to high-level Canadian national security officials.

The motivations remain unclear. Plausibly, tense bilateral relations, during the protracted Meng Wanzhou extradition proceedings and the potential added risk in the arbitrary detention of Michael Spavor and Michael Kovrig, may have made private representations a preferred option. Whatever the motivations, once intelligence assessments were illegally shared with the media by a whistleblower, the Liberal government faced a storm of public protest regarding alleged Chinese meddling in Canada's democratic institutions.

The Conservatives, the New Democrats and prominent public figures from Jean-Pierre Kingsley, formerly head of Elections Canada, to Richard Fadden, former CSIS Director, have called for a public inquiry. Jody Thomas, Canada's national security adviser, told the Procedures and House Affairs parliamentary committee that China was the greatest "foreign interference threat to Canada," but cautioned that "a public inquiry will have the same limitations that this committee does, in that we cannot talk about national security information in a public forum."

Prime Minister Trudeau's initial response was to insist that recent federal elections were not impacted by alleged interference. He refused to agree to a public inquiry and voiced "total confidence that the outcomes of the 2019 and 2021 elections were determined by Canadians, and Canadians alone, at the voting booth."

Following the 2019 federal election, the government established the Critical Election Incident Public Protocol, a mechanism for public servants to inform Canadians about incidents that threaten election integrity, and the Security and Intelligence Threats to Elections (SITE) Task Force, whose job is to provide intelligence on hostile state activities to the government and Elections Canada. On February 28, the government issued a report indicating that national security agencies believed the attempts at foreign interference had not "met the threshold of impacting electoral integrity." But there is no real clarity on what that threshold constitutes, a point conceded by Michael Rosenberg, a former Deputy Minister, who penned the report. The report, and assurances that all the key mechanisms to investigate the allegations were in play, did not diminish public outcry and debate. As CSIS has advised, public transparency is crucial in situations of alleged foreign interference. After downplaying the issue, the Prime Minister eventually agreed to nominate an 'eminent Canadian' as independent 'special rapporteur' with a wide mandate to investigate alleged interference and make public recommendations. Citing privacy and security risks, Canada also banned the use of TikTok, the Chinese-owned social media app, on government-issued devices. Still to be determined is whether the government would include the creation of a foreign agent registry, already on the books in Australia and the United States, which would require the public disclosure of those working for foreign interests. One aspect of the debate over Chinese interference is the way that hyperbole can undermine confidence in the integrity of elections—which is later exploited by claims of fraud. Max Cameron briefly discusses the evolution of the rhetoric on democracy coming from the Liberals since 2015, noting both their growing concern with interference and their declining interest in democratic reform.

Trust is the bedrock of open societies. The issue of alleged foreign interference underscores the need to pay careful attention to the functioning of our democratic institutions, our politicians and our electoral systems. In addressing these issues, Prime Minister Trudeau has raised concern about the need to avoid reinforcing well-documented anti-Asian racism in Canada. That appropriate concern should not, however, prevent public debate and scrutiny of alleged interference in our elections and other democratic institutions. Notwithstanding the oblique criticism of the media coverage, the willingness of whistleblowers to risk sanction, the persistence of investigative journalism and an engaged public suggests that when comes to defending our democracy, Canadians are prepared to ask difficult questions and not simply defer to political elites or remote mandarins.

A crucial point is that failures by Canada to engage China diplomatically have resulted in increased mobilization of non-state actors—e.g. diasporas—to pursue and maintain connections with the homeland. Today, decisions to withdraw from or scale back diplomatic connections weaken Canadian influence in crucial places, such as China, Russia and Iran (decisions which themselves are the result of diaspora lobbying). The current foreign agent registry is a good example of a policy instrument that is likely to become deeply politicized if, for example, it does not consider the impact that dual citizen lobbying has on foreign policy. Responding to public pressure, the Liberal government has launched public consultations to "guide the creation of a Foreign Influence Transparency Registry." And in the March 2023 federal budget, the government has allocated $49 million to strengthen RCMP investigation into interference and $13.5 million for a new National Counterintelligence Office at Public Safety. It is hard to predict what difference these new measures will make to an already quite robust set of high-level intelligence and national security coordination and deliberation bodies. Although the several new announcements signal government efforts to be responsive to growing public concern, the public debate and policy process around external interference risk becoming deeply politicized, divisive and potentially even counterproductive.[2] The unintended consequences of poorly considered public policy may be to create conditions in which states can become the enemy of their own open societies. How governments deal with the issue of alleged foreign interference will resonate for years to come and say much about the quality and resilience of Canada's democratic system.

Canada can only grow and prosper if politicians understand that diaspora is not an instrument for their own personal or political gains. Diaspora politics has become a useful political football. Parties carefully select those diaspora targets that fit nicely with its own foreign policy priorities. There are many MPs whose actions indicate they have loyalties to their homelands whether that be India, Israel or Ukraine, to name a few.

War in the Ukraine

The war in the Ukraine represents a rare moment of unity and collective response among all MPs within Canada's major political parties. However, as the war grinds on into its second year the lofty principles once invoked by Justin Trudeau, Melanie Joly and Chrystia Freeland to secure a world in which democracies thrive rank well behind Russia's defeat on the battlefield. Geopolitics and democracy are once again closely intertwined as politicians and media fall back on binary descriptions of the forces and issues at stake. The Ukraine crisis and the recognition that democracy is fragile, closely linked to Canada's security and may need to be defended has galvanized a modest increase in defence spending. But is the appeal to binary choices more than a cover for a global geopolitical struggle?

---

[2] Allegations, which can lead to infringements of democratic rights and personal safety, have been made against members of the Canadian Chinese community, including a respected Chinese Canadian senator (from Singapore) and a newly elected mayor accused of being agents of the Chinese government. Unfounded accusations tarnished the reputations of Maher Arar, John Holmes, Paul Lin and Herbert Norman. See "Open Letter: Discussions of foreign interference and national security can quickly become toxic." *Canadian Dimension.* March 25, 2023.

As an ally of Ukraine, Canada has been supporting Kyiv diplomatically as well as through the supply of war materiel and training. Canada has two overarching objectives: helping Ukraine in developing an inclusive and open democratic society that is tolerant of all minorities and political parties. The second is to find a way to wean Ukraine away from its dependence on an informal economy. These two goals are intertwined and go to the heart of Ukraine's structural problems. Since Russia's invasion of Ukraine in February 2022, Canada has focused on ensuring Ukraine's simple survival as a nation providing loans to service Kiev's sizeable debt, hosting a sizeable number of displaced people, keeping the lights on and supporting the public sector. Working against these objectives there is Canada's support for long-term protracted war. Protracted conflict frequently marginalizes moderate factions when governance vacuums created by delegitimized politicians are filled by radical leaders.

In opening the March 2023 Second Summit for Democracy, President Joe Biden took solace from signs of democracy's resilience. "Today, we can say, with pride, democracies of the world are getting stronger, not weaker," Biden said. "Autocracies of the world are getting weaker, not stronger. That's a direct result of all of us." Against this confident projection of democratic progress, Xu Xueyuan, the charge d'affaires of China's embassy in Washington, found the summit "at odds with the spirit of democracy. The U.S. draws an ideological line between countries, and through its narrative of 'democracy versus authoritarianism,' it has formed factions and caused divisions in the international community," she said. Both views may contain elements of the truth.

A (But Not *The*) Final Word

Democracy is an unfinished project and remains a work in progress everywhere. As Prime Minister Trudeau remarked at the March 2023 Second Summit for Democracy: "strong democracies do not happen by accident, and they do not continue without effort." In navigating powerful geopolitical currents pulling in different directions, Canada will likely deepen engagement with its traditional security and values alliances enabling both continued reliance on multilateralism and participation in newer ad hoc fora with like-minded democracies. These deepening linkages may come at the cost of inextricably linking and potentially subordinating the promotion of democratic values to security interests. At home, governments and citizens alike must address the deep-seated forces that weaken democratic institutions, notably polarization and its perfidious messengers: misinformation and disinformation. Abroad, recognizing that the future of democracy worldwide is more than just the future of the 'West,' Canada can also seize opportunities for mutual learning and democratic cooperation with non-traditional partners from India and Japan to Indonesia and South Korea in the Indo-Pacific and with Brazil and Mexico in the Americas. When it comes to shoring up democracy both at home and abroad, our level of ambition and any success will be influenced by the scope and clarity of our long-term vision, by the wise deployment of our scarce resources and by the sustained engagement and partnerships that we choose to build and maintain.

References

Applebaum, Anne. 2020. *Twilight of Democracy*. New York: Doubleday.
Brechenmacher, Saskia, and Tom Carothers. 2019. *Defending Civic Space: Is the International Community Stuck?*, October 22, 2019. Washington, DC: Carnegie Endowment for International Peace.
Diamond, Larry, and Marc F. Plattner, eds. 2015. *Democracy in Decline?* Baltimore: Johns Hopkins University Press.
Ekos, 2023. *Polarization, Populism, and Evolving Public Outlook on Canada and the World*. https://www.ekospolitics.com/index.php/2023/01/polarization-populism-and-evolving-public-outlook-on-canada-and-the-world/.
Gessen, Masha. 2020. *Surviving Autocracy*. New York: Riverhead.
Kant, Immanuel. 2016 [1795]. *Perpetual Peace*. Project Gutenberg. https://www.gutenberg.org/files/50922/50922-h/50922-h.htm.
Klein, Ezra. 2020. *Why We're Polarized*. New York: Avid Reader Press.
Kurlantzick, Joshua. 2013. *Democracy in Retreat*. New Haven: Yale University Press.
Levitsky, Steven, and Daniel Ziblatt. 2018. *How Democracies Die*. New York: Crown.
McCoy, Jennifer, and Murat Somer. 2019. Toward a Theory of Pernicious Polarization and How It Harms Democracies: Comparative Evidence and Possible Remedies. *The ANNALS of the American Academy of Political and Social Science* 681 (1): 234–271. https://doi.org/10.1177/0002716218818782.

Printed in the United States
by Baker & Taylor Publisher Services